Photoshop® for Right-Brainers

The Art of Photo Manipulation

Al Ward

SYBEX®

Associate Publisher: Dan Brodnitz
Acquisitions Editor: Bonnie Bills
Developmental Editor: James A. Compton
Production Editor: Mae Lum
Copyeditor: Suzanne Goraj
Technical Editor: Colin Smith
Cover, Text Design, and Composition: Mark Ong,
    Susan Riley, Side By Side Studios
CD Coordinator: Dan Mummert
CD Technician: Kevin Ly
Proofreaders: Laurie O'Connell, Amy Rasmussen,
    Nancy Riddiough
Indexer: Ted Laux
Cover Designer: Richard Miller, Calyx Design
Cover Photography: Photos.com
Cover Illustration: Al Ward

Software License Agreement: Terms and Conditions

Foreword

Every time we turn around it seems that another Photoshop book appears on the scene—there are so many Photoshop books that sometimes it's hard to tell them apart. In fact, when I recently tried to come up with a possible title for a new book I was planning, the only name that came to mind was *Yet Another Photoshop Book*. So when Al Ward called to tell me he was writing a new book, I thought, I hope he doesn't steal my title! Well, I've got two pieces of great news for you: he didn't steal my idea for a title and more importantly, this is not just another Photoshop book.

The challenge for any Photoshop author is to create something that's different from all the other books while still providing practical, real-world information. Before I had even seen *Photoshop for Right-Brainers*, I was confident that it would be just that: different and practical. Why? For the last few years, I have enjoyed reading Al's tutorials on the members' website of the National Association of Photoshop Professionals (NAPP). Every week or so, Al has managed to come up with innovative, unusual, and amusing uses for Photoshop—oh, and did I mention that his tutorials are filled with techniques you can use every day? To me, there are several important aspects of a good tutorial: it should be creative, interesting, and practical, and it should get your artistic juices flowing with all kinds of possibilities. Al's web tutorials fit this mold, and so does this book.

Follow along with the step-by-step instructions, have fun with them, and be ready (and willing) to experiment. One of the best ways to learn Photoshop is to be curious—don't be satisfied with simply doing what the author says. Take things a step further and look beyond the book's examples to see what else you can do with a tool, a blending mode, or a layer mask. Although you may never have the need to change someone's lip color to blue, I know you'll have other situations where that basic technique can be adapted and will be the ideal solution. Al has given you some great, practical techniques and encouraged you to experiment. Now it's up to you to put them into practice, using that Right Brain of yours!

© Dave Cross

Dave Cross
Senior Developer, Education & Curriculum
National Association of Photoshop Professionals

Acknowledgements

For some reason, the Acknowledgements page is always the hardest in the book to write. Someone who absolutely deserved to be mentioned is inevitably left out, so if you are one of those who wished you had seen your name here and do not, I apologize upfront.

First off, I not only have to thank my wife and kids, but I really want to. Tonia, Noah, and Ali are the collective force that share my life and more often than not are the reasons I get out of bed every morning. They see (and tolerate) all sides of me, both bad and good; I can't think of any other three people I would rather share my life with.

Thanks to Bonnie, Jim, Mae, and Sen at Sybex. They have made this project a joy to work on, put me back on track when I became hopelessly lost, and made sure my family did not starve in the process. I look forward to working with you all again.

The production team that Sybex put together for this book also deserves special thanks: copyeditor Suzanne Goraj; compositors Mark Ong and Susan Riley; proofreaders Laurie O'Connell, Amy Rasmussen, and Nancy Riddiough; and indexer Ted Laux.

Thanks to my good friend and occasional writing partner Colin Smith. No matter how often my wife tries to get him married off, he still keeps accepting our calls and coming to visit. Now that's friendship!

I can't thank Colin without also mentioning his website (http://www.photoshopcafe.com) and all the people who find solace in the forum there. The Photoshop Café has developed into a great source of inspiration and friendship where Photoshop users of all stripes can find acceptance. The coffee is always hot and fresh; I'll see you there.

I've got to thank my friends at NAPP (National Association of Photoshop Professionals). Scott Kelby gave me my start in this business, and I'm forever in his debt. Jeff, Stacey, Chris, Jim, Dave, etc. etc. etc.… without a doubt, you sincerely ROCK.

To Richard Lynch, a good friend and trusted sounding board when I need him most. Thanks, buddy!

To the people who know my work and keep coming back anyway; those who both visit and join my website (http://Actionfx.com).

To my good friend Wade, a hopeless left-brainer, but a marvel at PHP. I feel another website revision coming on…

To Mom, Dad, Ole, Linda, and my extended family (I'm from Montana, so there are thousands of people who qualify for this): I love you all, in spite of the restraining order. (Just kidding…I had it lifted so you can visit again.) To Uncle Ed: Thanks for the bandwidth!

Special thanks to everyone in the MLMBC (you know who you are). We share the same road, and I'm honored to be traveling it with you.

The greatest thanks and highest praise go to my God and Savior, without whom none of this would be possible or worthwhile. He saw fit to allow this Montana boy to realize his dream.

Again, if I forgot anyone who really needed to be here, please forgive me and consider yourselves included. To all my readers and friends far and wide, my deepest regards and a hearty thank you from the bottom of my heart.

Contents

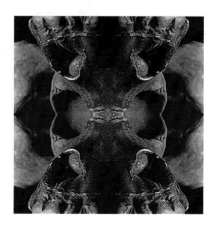

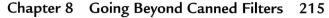

Introduction

Photoshop for Right-Brainers is a guide to using the software's toolkit to unlock your own creativity, as I've used it to unlock mine. The Pause button on my brain evidently ceased working from overuse during my Navy days, and now there is no stopping the cartoons, dramas, and horror movies broadcasting in my head. I'll wake on occasion with some incredible insight and be overcome with an urge to share this unrefined gem of intellectual acrobatics with my wife. She can barely contain her joy; you can see it in the way she smiles, nods, and says "Would you like bacon for breakfast?" or "Stop jumping around and talking nonsense or you'll scare the kids!"

For me, Photoshop has opened pathways for creativity that I had always known were in my head but had no way to translate to the real world. What originally attracted me to the program was not the ability to correct photographs, but the power to warp photographs into something else. This journey started as an experiment in creating something from nothing (I think the first effect that I tried to master was creating fire from thin air), and developed into a career based on corrections, distortions, and manipulations. Photoshop gives me the ability to take the critters in my head and make them a visual reality. Teaching the program and writing about those discoveries was an unexpected, but extremely appreciated, bonus. It's sort of like writing a great (or even mediocre) novel; the novelist doesn't simply shelve the reams of paper to read to himself from time to time, but rather tries to put the book into print so others can appreciate the story. Photoshop is my typewriter, and the entities and scenes that form on my screen are the novel. I share it in hopes that someone out there in the big old world will appreciate it. More often than not people do; occasionally I'll get an e-mail asking me if I want bacon for breakfast. Some folks are just odd.

Why I Wrote This Book

When I approached this project, I wanted to do something a bit different from what I've written in the past. I certainly did not want to write another "These are the basics of Adobe Photoshop" book; there are many authors out there who have tackled that subject and done an excellent job in the process. I also did not want to simply create a recipe book of canned effects. I've done that before, and while recipe books have their place, I wanted this book to be a bit more personal. Don't get me wrong—this book is full of effects that you can follow along and perform. What I want the reader to see, aside from the step-by-step process, is how ideas for projects are developed by this author. Where do the concepts for the various effects come from? When an idea is pieced together in the imagination, what does it look like? And lastly, what tools in Adobe Photoshop CS can be used to make those scenes or creatures take on new life on the computer?

Right Brain? Left Brain?

About 30 years ago, the artist and educator Betty Edwards wrote a book that has become a classic and that is indirectly an inspiration for this one: *Drawing on the Right Side of the*

Brain. At that time, it wasn't widely understood by the general public that the right and left hemispheres of the brain function differently and control different kinds of intelligence, so Edwards devoted a chapter to explaining her premise: The left side is logical, analytical, sequential, verbal, and tends to break things down into parts rather than looking at wholes. The right side is intuitive, synthesizing, spatial, and holistic. It is, in short, the source of visual imagination and creativity. Today, that understanding is much more widespread, to the point where "right-brained" and "left-brained" have become a kind of shorthand for different ways of looking at the world.

This book, although targeted at right-brained designers and photographers, is not simply for them. I suspect that more than a few left-brained people (affectionately referred to as "lefties" in the text) are really closet right-brained people, waiting for someone to lead the way past their math, science, and politics and into the realm of artistic expression. My aim is not that this book will appeal to only the right-brained crowd. Rather, I hope that the book may also serve in some small way as a beacon guiding lefties through the dismal smog of facts and figures and into the Technicolor world that righties have lived in and appreciated for generations. Even a lefty can be a right-brainer; the world could use a few creative politicians, after all.

What Should You Know Already?

Photoshop users are generally lumped into three main categories (not my doing): Beginner, Intermediate, and Advanced. This tends to paint Photoshop users with an extremely broad brush, not taking into account how many genres of digital manipulation that Photoshop is used for. For instance, a person can be exceptional at special effects, but not have the slightest clue about how images are prepared for print.

In general terms, a person hoping to get the most from this book should at least be intermediate in their understanding and experience with the software. By intermediate, I simply mean you should have used the tools, should already be familiar with the interface, have a concept of how layers work, and so forth. The reader should also be familiar with following tutorial-style instruction. If you have just purchased the software and have absolutely no clue what a pixel is, then you should probably pass on this book for now, and come back to it after trying something a bit more introductory. If you have some experience with the program and have a keen desire to try things in new and interesting ways, then this is the book for you.

How the Book Is Organized

The book has two main parts. Part 1, "Tools and Techniques of the Trade," deals with quick effects and concepts, and takes a focused look at techniques applied in later chapters. These chapters are intended to give you a workout on processes that you'll use time and again in the latter half of the book, so that I don't have to bore you by repeating the detailed instructions there.

Chapter 1, "Tools for Building Your Masterpiece" focuses on the most important tools and concepts underlying the techniques you'll explore throughout the book: blending modes, opacity and fills, layer masks, the High Pass filter, channels, extractions, and displacement maps.

Chapter 2, "Techniques for Embellishing Portraits" presents basic cosmetic corrections and enhancements that portrait subjects may often request, such as deepening (or completely changing) eye color, covering up old acne scars, and the like.

Chapter 3, "Advanced Techniques for Embellishing Portraits" goes further into cosmetic corrections, with techniques for more dramatic changes, such as "digital liposuction," facelifts, and—just for fun—things like adding or removing tattoos, and even swapping faces.

Chapter 4, "Techniques for Artistic Effects" stays with human subjects but moves beyond cosmetic correction and embellishment into more creative transformations, such as adding colors and textures.

Whereas Part 1 focuses on examples designed to demonstrate specific techniques, Part 2, "Digital Intensive: Photography as Art," presents a series of complete projects, each of which typically employs many techniques to create a finished image.

Chapter 5, "Landscapes and Nature" leads you through transforming natural and man-made forms. You'll mirror rock formations, create neon reflections on rainy streets, and turn sunny landscapes into nightmare scenes.

Chapter 6, "Animals" continues the theme of transformations as you add human features to animals and vice versa, drape a snake over a model, and more.

Chapter 7, "Objects" shows how to create photo-realistic effects like chrome or the distortion of an image seen through melting ice in a drinking glass, and how to bring out the texture of surfaces such as rusted or pitted steel, among other projects.

Chapter 8, "Going Beyond Canned Filters" works with a Photoshop feature that is often misused. The projects here show that applying a filter should be a starting point, not a finished product. For example, you'll "age" a new photograph for a retro effect, turn photographs into line drawings, and turn a posed photograph into a "vector art" anime cartoon.

Chapter 9, "People as Art—Digital Manipulation" treats the human body as a canvas. You will color it, texture it, melt it and mold it, painting a checkered flag onto a swimsuit model and turning my children into an alien boy and a vampire girl (or at least a very precocious goth-rocker).

Chapter 10, "Displaying Your Work" tackles Photoshop's tools for displaying your photos after the editing is done; you'll create web photo galleries, PDF documents, contact sheets, picture packages, and panoramas.

Concept, Visualize, Realize

Although every project creates a finished image, none of them should be considered "recipes" for you to reproduce by rote. Instead, they demonstrate the process of artistic creation along with the methods for achieving specific effects. At the broadest level, the process has three stages: conceptualizing, visualizing, and realizing. While the text and art in this book necessarily focus on the details of realizing a project, in your own work you won't get to that stage without first creating an idea and then visualizing what it will look like. (And you'll also find that the process isn't entirely sequential; as in many of this book's projects, you'll often be inspired with further ideas as you work and incorporate them into the final product.)

To emphasize the importance of all three stages (and let you know where some of my inspirations have come from), each of these projects is introduced with a "Concept, Visualize, Realize" sidebar such as this one:

Concept Using elements from a photograph, create a photo-realistic object completely unrelated to the original photo.

Visualize Through past experience, I realize the power that Photoshop has for generating realistic spheres and orbs of all types, simply working with the existing filters. Spheres are easily generated from scratch, but can a photograph with reflective elements such as chrome be turned into a sphere using the same metallic color variations and reflections as the photo? You bet.

Realize To realize this project, a photo using an object that is highly reflective should give the desired reflective sphere effect. As an added touch, an additional reflection of a photographer will be added to the face of the final image. Your key Photoshop tools will be the Polar Coordinates filter and the Transform menu, along with some Layer Masking.

As you can see, "Concept" states the general idea; "Visualize" expands the concept by describing concrete imagery; and "Realize" suggests how you will marry the concept and vision in Photoshop.

Using the CD Files

The images used in this book are also provided for your use on the accompanying CD. Some were taken by the author, but the majority are provided by Photos.com. Please note that these photos are for your use with this book only; they are not in the public domain and may not be redistributed in any way, shape, or form.

At each point where you need to use a file from the CD in order to work through an exercise, you'll see a symbol in the margin like the one shown here, and the text will refer to the specific filename. That way, you'll use the same images as I did when completing an exercise. Also, some exercises use specific tools created by the author (gradient, layer style, or other saved preset). These will be on the CD as well, and the text will direct you to load them at the appropriate time.

About the Author

Al Ward is a prominent figure in the Photoshop community. His website, **actionfx.com**, supplies Photoshop actions and information to users. He has authored and contributed to numerous Photoshop books, including *Photoshop Most Wanted*, *Photoshop Elements 2 Special Effects*, and *Photoshop 7 Effects Magic*. He has written for Planet Photoshop, Photoshop Café, and *Photoshop User Magazine*, and he is the official actions guru for the National Association of Photoshop Professionals (NAPP).

Feedback

Both the author and the publisher encourage you to offer feedback on this text. Was it useful to you? What did you learn that you did not know previously? You may leave your comments with the publisher at **www.sybex.com**, or send the author a note through his website at http://actionfx.com.

one

PART

Tools and Techniques
of the Trade

Let me tell you something at the outset: I cannot turn you into an artist. No book can do that. There is no pill, college degree, or self-help video that can tap into the creative side of your brain and give you the ability to "make art."

The following four chapters discuss techniques and tools that are used throughout the book, as well as some that are just plain good to know. I can't teach you to be an artist, but I certainly can show you some of the tools I use that you might find helpful in your own work.

one

Tools for Building Your Masterpiece

Right-brainers are *typically artistic in some fashion and this book is for people who, like me, enjoy the journey. Although right-brainers are constantly chiding left-brained people to think outside of the proverbial box, a right-brainer who works with a piece of software such as Adobe Photoshop CS needs to spend some time in the box, getting to know the tools and techniques that will eventually lead to masterpieces at some future date. This chapter focuses on a few of the most important tools and concepts underlying the techniques that you'll explore throughout the book: blending modes, opacity and fills, layer masks, the High Pass filter, channels, extractions, and displacement maps. Behind all of these is a still more fundamental concept: layers.*

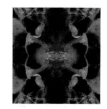

The Photoshop Learning Curve

When a student enters college for a specific degree, they are led through a series of courses that gradually increase their knowledge base in the chosen field. Each course is designed to be a bit more difficult than the last, yet builds on the foundation of information that they learned before. Eventually, students reach a point where they have mastered their course requirements, earned a degree, and entered the work force, where they may then advance what is known about their field.

Learning Photoshop CS follows this pattern. To get the most out of this book, you should already be partly along the learning curve; *Photoshop for Right-Brainers* is not intended to be your first exposure to the software. You should have enough basic familiarity with the Photoshop interface and tools that you are ready to explore the art of photo manipulation.

Having said that, however, let me add that some of the concepts and techniques that are crucial to the work you'll do with this book can also be frustratingly elusive to many users; those concepts are what this chapter is about.

Understanding Layers

Almost every technique and project in this book involves working with layers in some way, so it's essential that you know your way around the Layers palette and the related tools for creating and manipulating layers in a Photoshop image before you begin. But even after you have that hands-on familiarity, the concept of what a layer is can still be hard to grasp.

A very left-brained definition might be that a layer is a "user-defined subset of the information in an image." In other words, it's an element of the image that you've isolated for the purpose of working with it in some way in order to affect the whole image.

Many people find it helpful to compare layers in Photoshop to transparent sheets that can be laid on top of each other, like the pages in old anatomy books that separately show muscles, the circulatory system, and so on. That's useful but incomplete. Layers in Photoshop can indeed contain separate images that you are adding together, but they can also contain different kinds of information from the same image, such as displacement maps, luminosity, or the separate red, green, and blue channels. Changes you make to individual layers, or the top-to-bottom order you assign to them, can create radically different results in the final image—or they can create very subtle but crucial differences.

If you've worked with Photoshop enough to be interested in its possibilities as a tool for artistic expression, then you probably already know how to use layers in making basic corrections. The techniques and tools presented next are those that I've found most useful when thinking creatively about images, and that you'll use in many of the projects and exercises throughout this book.

Using Blending Modes

Blending modes for layers simply tell Photoshop how the pixels in one layer will interact with the pixels in the layers beneath. You knew that already, though, right? Sure you did; at least, you would if you have spent any time with Photoshop in the past. As you work through the next few chapters, you'll use various blending modes. For each new mode that's introduced, you'll find a short definition of the mode.

For right-brainers, blending modes open entirely new doors that perhaps hadn't been considered before, and that is what I hope to point out here. Instead of rambling on about how you *should* use them, I'll show a few examples of how you *can* use them to your advantage.

From this book's CD, open the images film.jpg and director.jpg (see Figure 1.1). Here we have two images of similar tone and theme. The designer might consider what these two photos would look like merged. To check that out, one photo could serve as the foundation image and the other photo pasted into a new layer in that document (see Figure 1.2).

Different blending modes, when applied to the Director layer, are going to give varied results. One might think that the Overlay mode would give a good mix between the two images, so check it out! Figure 1.3 shows the image with the Director layer set to Overlay.

The result here, while both images are visible, looks harsh, and the man is little more than a shadow...not really a good blend for this example. That is just a bit of personal

Figure 1.1:
Choose images to
blend together.

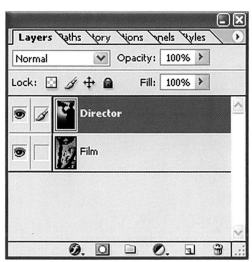

Figure 1.2: Place both images into the same document for merging.

Figure 1.3: Director layer set to Overlay

taste…if you like it, then go with it! Try another test, this time selecting Darken for the blending mode of the Director layer (see Figure 1.4). This is actually a very good melding of the two images. The outline of the man is clearly defined, with the reels nicely back-dropped. The only thing that strikes me as being wrong with this version, other than being a couple of shades too dark, is the area where the film strip overlays the megaphone. As that portion is darker in the Film layer than the Director layer, the dark strip dominates. Think about it: the Director layer is in Darken mode, so those areas darker than the layer beneath will be darkened. Those lighter will not. The megaphone is slightly lighter, so it loses in the battle with the film strip.

There has to be a way to get these photos to work together, so I'll give it another shot. Follow along and see what you come up with. Change the blending mode for the Director layer to Pin Light (see Figure 1.5). That is actually a very good mix for definition between the two photos. The colors are still harsh, but the blending mode works.

Pin Light

This blending mode takes a look at the blend color and replaces colors in relation to that standard. If the light source, or blend color, is lighter than 50% gray, pixels darker than the blend color are replaced while those lighter do not change. If the blend color is darker than 50% gray, the inverse is true. This blending mode is useful for adding special effects to an image.

Figure 1.4: Director layer in Darken blending mode

Figure 1.5: Another version using Pin Light blending mode

When you find a blending mode that does basically what you want to accomplish, as I've done with this example, you may want to keep the blending mode and finish the corrections with other Photoshop features. No one tool or technique is a fix-all: it usually takes a combination of tools and commands working together to get what you are looking for.

Notice the red ring surrounding the yellow spotlight area. This can be reduced in a couple of ways to help maintain the original mood and tone of the two images. One of the quickest ways to isolate and replace the red ring without altering the rest of the images is to use a Replace Color adjustment on the Director layer (see Figure 1.6). Use the eye dropper to select the reddest pixel you can find (such as along the edge of the megaphone) and rather than change the color, just lower the Saturation until the red ring dissipates (see Figure 1.7).

As you work through the book, blending modes are going to become second nature. What I want you to take away from this brief example, in particular for merging layers, is that your choice of blending mode is going to dictate whether a piece fails or succeeds. You have many to choose from but usually one or two come close. You want to get to the point where you intuitively know what additional tools in conjunction with the blending mode will give you the results you are looking for. Photoshop isn't out to get you: it is only as smart and creative as you allow it to be. Photoshop is the tool; you are the craftsman.

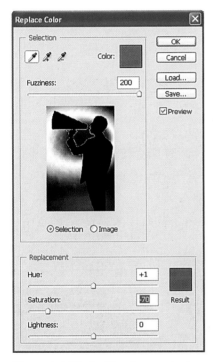

Figure 1.6: Find a blending mode that comes closest to what you envision, then perform the final corrections with other adjustments.

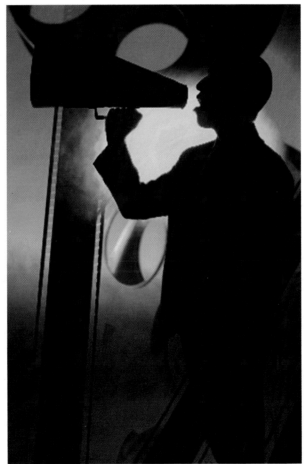

Figure 1.7: Final blended image using original colors

Opacity and Fill: What's the Difference?

Residing at the top of the Layers palette, along with your choice of blending modes for your layers, are two sliders: Opacity and Fill. Each has a percentage, by default 100%. Both control the visibility of pixels in a layer; reducing the percentage of each will gradually allow you to see the pixels beneath as the pixels in the layer that you have selected become more transparent.

The primary difference between these two sliders is this: the Opacity slider affects everything attached to the layer being adjusted, including the blending mode and any layer styles that may be applied to it. The Fill adjustment slider affects only the actual layer pixels, but leaves the blending mode and layer styles attached to the layer untouched.

Opacity and Fill adjustments cannot be performed on the Background layer. The Background layer must first be turned into a standard layer. Double-click the Background layer, give it a new name, and click OK to change it to a standard layer. The Opacity and Fill sliders will now be available.

A quick example will demonstrate the difference. From this book's CD, open the image `weights.jpg` (see Figure 1.8). I'm adding some plain white text in a new layer with the Type tool; nothing special, just plain old text (see Figure 1.9). Try lowering the opacity using first

Figure 1.8: Chrome weights

Figure 1.9: Plain white text added to a new text layer

Figure 1.10: Simple Plastic Chrome layer style

Figure 1.11: The drop in Opacity makes the style transparent.

the Opacity and then the Fill slider; you'll see that the results look identical. Now, when a layer style is applied (such as the Plastic Chrome layer style seen in Figure 1.10, which can be found on this book's CD), the type takes on the attributes saved in the style. Decrease the Opacity for the type layer to 40%. The text, style included, becomes increasingly transparent (see Figure 1.11).

Increase the Opacity back to 100%. Now decrease the Fill Opacity to 0% (see Figure 1.12). The white pixels that make up the type disappear, but the layer style—including bevel, highlights, drop shadow, and so forth—are retained, allowing you to see the image beneath as though through plastic (see Figure 1.13). Keep in mind that this will only work if all the fill elements in the style, such as Color and Gradient, are set to a blending mode that allows them to be seen through, or their opacity is lowered within the style much as you have done with the layer. I won't be going into depth on layer styles in this book, but you can read more about them on my website (http://actionfx.com).

Figure 1.12: Fill Opacity slider

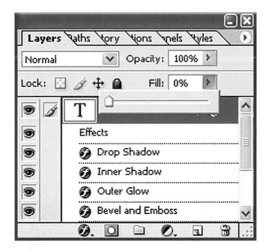

Figure 1.13: White type becomes transparent, but the style effects remain.

Working with Masks

As you delve into all the nifty things Photoshop allows you to do to your images, eventually you will get to Layer masks. Layer masks, at their most basic, are simple bitmaps attached to a layer. The black in the bitmap, or mask, hides the pixels of the standard layer, and white reveals those pixels.

I'll get to some examples of what I'm talking about in a moment. First, some possible uses. What benefit do you see from being able to hide portions of a layer? Here's one practical application using two layers with the same pixel information: you could correct the top layer or do some fancy special effect to it and then mask away portions of the layer so the correction or effect seems to occur only on certain portions of the image. Layer masks are also excellent for merging photos, either gradually or starkly, so collages are a breeze. Masks even go so far as to allow a savvy right-brainer to turn any photograph into a seamless pattern or even a floor tile.

I could list benefits of layer masks all day, but that would bore us both to tears. Let me demonstrate what I've been talking about.

Altering Background Color

Open the image `laptopCH1.jpg` from this book's CD (see Figure 1.14). Say you want to add more color to the backdrop on this photo, but don't want to deal with extractions (those are covered later in this chapter).

Is there a way to do it that will allow you to keep your sanity? Sure thing, if you use a mask. Duplicate the Background layer (see Figure 1.15).

Do a quick Hue/Saturation adjustment (choose Image → Adjustments → Hue/Saturation) and increase the Hue to –180. This changes the colors resident in the layer to those colors opposite on the color wheel (see Figure 1.16). Where the background was orange, now blue resides. In turn, the green ivy has taken on a purple tint (see Figure 1.17).

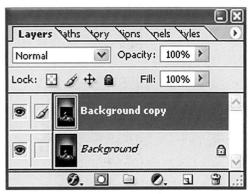

Figure 1.15: Duplicate the Background layer.

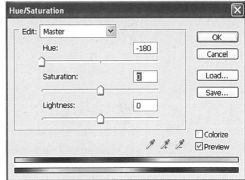

Figure 1.16: Changing color with Hue/Saturation

Figure 1.14: One way to handle problems with your computer

Figure 1.17: *Add A Layer mask*

Figure 1.18: *White in the mask reveals the layer, or retains its visibility.*

At the bottom of the Layers palette, second icon from the left, is the Add A Layer Mask icon. With the Background Copy layer selected and active in the palette, click the Add A Layer Mask icon. A bitmap file will link itself to the layer. As there was no selection active, by default the mask is filled with white (see Figure 1.18).

If you were to select the mask and fill it with black at 100% opacity, the layer would be totally blotted out and the layer beneath entirely visible. Where's the fun in that? Instead, select the mask and then click the Gradient tool. You will have black in the foreground and white in the background, or vice versa. The point is that, with the gradient, you can gradually reveal some areas of the layer while hiding others, giving the impression of a merge with the layer beneath. Set the Gradient tool options to Foreground To Background, and select the Linear Gradient style. Start at the top left of the image and draw the gradient all the way down to the lower-right corner. Your image should look like Figure 1.19; if the orange and blue are reversed, then the gradient was set from white to black and not black to white. That's OK: an easy fix. Simply select the mask and choose Image → Adjustments → Invert, swapping the black and white pixels in the mask. The Layers palette will look something like Figure 1.20.

You need not be stuck with purple leaves, either. You can simply set black as the foreground color, grab the Paintbrush tool, and paint in the mask over the area where the plant resides. This covers, or hides, the purple plant and reveals the green leaves beneath (see Figure 1.21).

Figure 1.19:
Two-toned
background

Figure 1.20:
Layers palette
with mask in
operation

Figure 1.21: Leaves
returned to their original
color

More Fun with Masks

The ivy example was a fairly basic correction/alteration; you can get pretty crazy with masks. As you will see in this section, masks can be used for drastic physical alterations on people. Open the image `face-close.jpg` from this book's CD (see Figure 1.22).

Duplicate the Background layer and flip the new layer (choose Edit → Transform → Flip Horizontal). Now add a layer mask. Select the Gradient tool as before, but this time click directly on the gradient in the Options bar to open the Gradient Editor. In the Gradient field in the lower portion of the Gradient Editor, you will find two arrows pointing up toward the bar on either side (see Figure 1.23). These are called Color Stops. The closer you move these together, the sharper the transition between the colors of the gradient will be. For the stop on the left, set the location to 48%, and for the one on the right, 52% (see Figure 1.24). You can save it as a new gradient if you like, or just click OK. Now draw the gradient from the left to the right, and take a look at your image (see Figure 1.25). How's that for symmetry?

Let's recap what just occurred. By moving the Color Stops closer together in the gradient, you narrowed the transition area between the black and the white. When the gradient was then applied to the mask, rather than a gradual blending of the two layers (the result when the shift from black to white covers 100% of the gradient, producing a wide range of grays), the transition is seen only in the center 4% of the photo. By having one whole side of the mask mostly white and the other mostly black, the white side is mostly revealed and the black mostly hidden, showing the face beneath and resulting in the mirror effect.

Figure 1.22: Extreme close-up

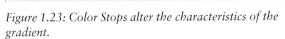

Figure 1.23: Color Stops alter the characteristics of the gradient.

Figure 1.24: Reposition the stops for a harsher transition between colors.

Figure 1.25: Facial reflection

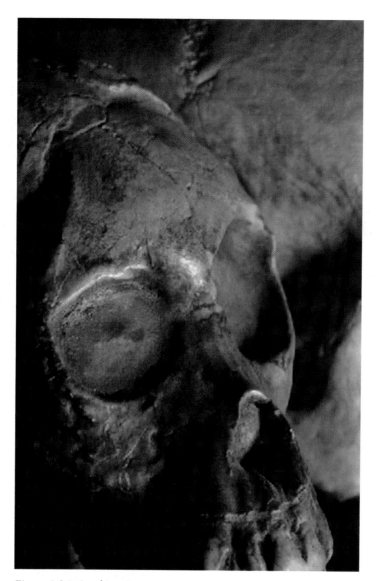

Figure 1.26: Aged cranium

How far can you take the flipping/mirroring process? As far as you like, actually. To demonstrate, I'm going to lay out this next example in a step-by-step format: I encourage you to follow along.

1. Open the image `oldskull.jpg` from this book's CD (see Figure 1.26).
2. Choose Image → Image Size. Uncheck Constrain Proportions, and enter a width value of 400 pixels and a height value of 400 pixels.

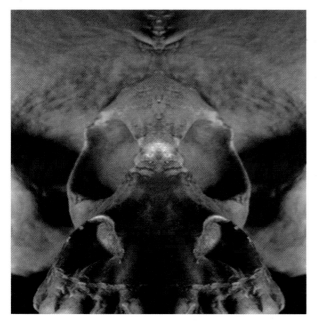

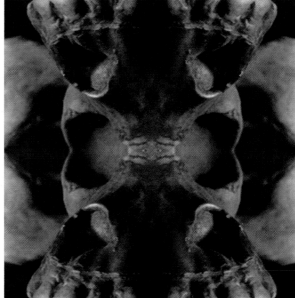

Figure 1.27: First pass of the gradient in the mask   *Figure 1.28: Pillar of bone*

3. Duplicate the Background layer.
4. Choose Edit → Transform → Flip Horizontal.
5. Add a layer mask. Using the same gradient as used on the face in the previous technique, draw the gradient from the right side of the image to the left, from side to side as horizontal as you can (see Figure 1.27).
6. With the masked layer selected, hit Command/Control+E to merge the layer with the background.
7. Duplicate the Background layer again.
8. Flip the new layer vertically, add the mask again, and draw the gradient through the mask. This time draw the gradient from the bottom edge to the top, as straight as you can. If you hold down the Shift key at the same time, Photoshop will ensure that the line drawn for the gradient to follow will be straight if you are working either vertically or horizontally (see Figure 1.28). Merge the layers together.

The image is seamless now, so if you were to lay several of these side by side or stack them, they should fit together like blocks (see Figure 1.29).

I use masks extensively in my work, so it is natural that masks will be a large factor in this book as well. I've just scratched the surface here, but I want to make clear that if you plan to dress up your photos in ways similar to those presented in this text, then masks are going to be your best friends.

Figure 1.29:
Skull pattern as a
background

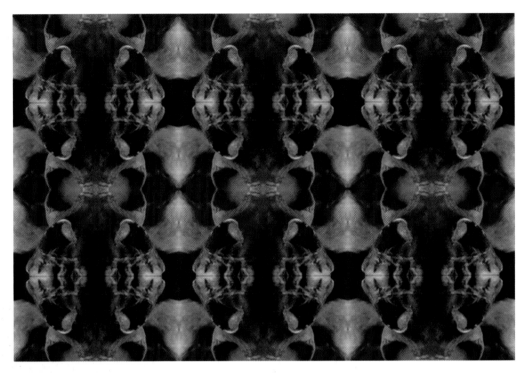

Sharpening Your Image: The High Pass Filter Trick

One benefit to this career I'm following is the interesting people I've met along the way and the friendships that develop. The Photoshop community is like a club, really, where people from all walks of life and of all ages can discuss their passion not only as peers, but as friends.

One relationship I've developed is with Mike Kubiesy. Heard of him? If you don't know him by name but watch television, then you are most likely familiar with his work. He is one of those in-demand photographers in Hollywood, specializing in forensic and crime scene photography for many popular television shows today. You can check out his website at http://www.digitography.tv.

The reason that I bring up Mike is that he clued me in to a sharpening technique I've not seen around much, so I thought I'd share it with you. This technique doesn't use the standard Sharpen filters, but rather another filter called High Pass. It is found under the Filters menu in the least attractive filter group: Other Filters. Sounds like they just threw that group together as a grab bag of things that couldn't find a home anywhere else. This filter deserves respect, as you will soon see.

High Pass Filter

This filter attempts to retain edge details where harsh transitions between colors occur. It grays out, or suppresses, the rest of the image or layer. You set a radius value, and the details are enhanced in that specified radius from the edges being defined. The effect is nearly opposite from that of Gaussian Blur.

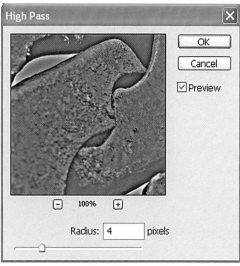

Figure 1.30: Old tools left to the elements

Figure 1.31: High Pass filter dialog box

Allow me to demonstrate the sharpening power of this filter. Open the image `jumpers.jpg` from this book's CD (see Figure 1.30).

Duplicate the Background layer and set the blending mode of the new layer to Overlay. Then choose Filter → Other → High Pass. The High Pass dialog box is seen in Figure 1.31. Set the Radius to 4 and click OK.

Take a look at the areas on the tools in the photo where the rust stands out. Compare the new image (see Figure 1.32) to the original (see Figure 1.30). You can enhance the image further by duplicating the High Pass layer a few more times, but I recommend changing the

Figure 1.32: New life given to old rust

Figure 1.33: Multiple High Pass layers

blending mode for any further copies of the layer to Soft Light (see Figure 1.33). This will help reduce the contrast, yet allow for sharp features (see Figure 1.34).

What would happen if you took this process to extremes? Just how sharp can you get a photo? It occurs to me, after trying a number of variations on this trick, that with the High Pass filter you could probably lift a fingerprint so detailed it would stand up in court.

Would it *really* stand up in court? I'm not a lawyer, folks, so that is simply speculation on my part. As of this writing, there is an excellent discussion on the subject of digital photographs as legal evidence at http://www.seanet.com/~rod/digiphot.html. I encourage you to read this at your leisure.

Figure 1.34: Sharpening intensified

For all the scoffers out there, take a look at this cool variation that shocked even me while I was developing it. You are aware that Photoshop is an excellent tool for softening photos, correcting blemishes, removing scars, and so forth. Did you realize that you can reverse the process? This technique will show how to enhance the blemishes, pores, and scars once again.

I'm going to be working fast, so pay close attention!

1. Open the image `soft portrait.jpg` from this book's CD (see Figure 1.35).
2. Duplicate the Background layer and change the blending mode to Overlay. Duplicate it again and run the High Pass filter as before (with Radius set to 4).

Figure 1.35: Soft portrait photo

3. Duplicate the High Pass layer three times, so that you have four copies of it (see Figure 1.36).

   The photo at this point (see Figure 1.37) looks washed out and highly contrasted, right? No worries; watch this.

4. Create a Levels Adjustment layer. Tweak the red, green, and blue channels by moving the center slider to the far right. Figure 1.38 shows the red channel levels adjustment; repeat the same setting for both the green and blue channels. Click OK.

5. Next, create a Hue/Saturation Adjustment layer. The red is extremely overpowering, so decrease the saturation to −50 and click OK.

6. To brighten the image a bit, create a Curves adjustment and slightly increase the brightness of the darker areas (see Figure 1.39).

7. Lastly, select the Background Copy layer. Choose Image → Adjustments → Shadow/Highlight and enter the settings seen in Figure 1.40.

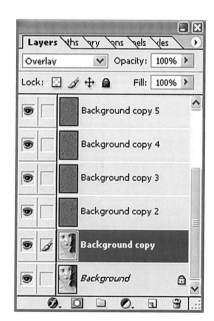

Figure 1.36: Four copies of the High Pass layer

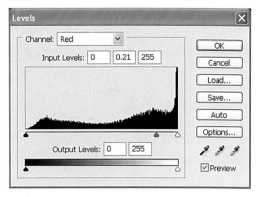

Figure 1.38: Levels adjustments enhance sharpening.

Figure 1.37: Way too much contrast, and little definition. That is about to change…

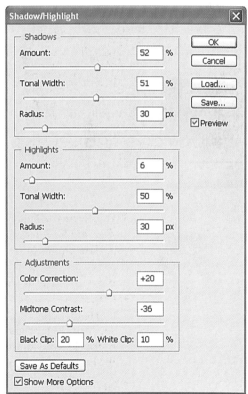

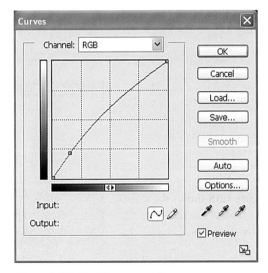

Figure 1.39: Quick curves adjustment

Figure 1.40: Tweak the shadows/highlights of the Background Copy layer.

Figure 1.41: Makeup!

Take a look at the image now (see Figure 1.41), and compare it to the original. In the original shot, some care was taken to present the model at her most glamorous, with soft lens and filtering to wipe away the pores and blemishes. In the final shot, all of those unflattering characteristics of the skin are brought back in shocking detail. The color and contrast are exaggerated, to be certain. The point here is the ability to magnify the fine details that either appear not to exist or are faint at best. For advanced sharpening, I'll take the High Pass filter over any other in the toolbox without question.

Figure 1.42: Dice image

Color Changing Using Channels

Suppose you want to add pure red, green, or blue to replace the color in some part of an image. The red, green, and blue channels that Photoshop stores for every RGB image offer a quick way to do this. I frequently use this trick and thought that you may want to experiment with it.

1. Open image `dice.jpg` from this book's CD (see Figure 1.42).
2. Open the Channels palette and select the Red channel (see Figure 1.43).
3. Set the foreground color to White (press **D** and then **X**).
4. Select the Paintbrush tool and paint over the black spots on the white dice faces. The black becomes bright red. Keep an eye on the Dice image to ensure that you don't apply so much paint that the reflections in the recesses are wiped out (see Figure 1.44).

Figure 1.43: Selecting the red channel

I've retouched only the white faces here simply to keep the demonstration quick and easy. In areas with any black information, such as the shadowed faces of the dice, the red would be picked up on the face if you

Figure 1.44: Retouching the dice by painting the red channel

stepped outside the boundaries of the black. If you think that it makes better visual sense to add red to the spots on the shadowed faces, you can experiment on your own by reducing the size of the brush. To see another example of this trick, check out the Wicked Child project in Chapter 9.

Extractions

I belong to several Photoshop-related forums and lists online (a personal favorite hangout of mine is the Photoshop Café at http://www.photoshopcafe.com), and it amazes me how many posts start with the heading "How do I extract an image from a background?" It boggles the mind, really, considering that there is a perfect tool resident in Photoshop for just this situation.

If the background is a solid color, you can of course use the Background Eraser tool with fair results, but the Extract command is far more powerful. It is tricky to master, however. That may be the primary reason so many ask about it. In a lot of cases, a more complete and honest question might be "How do I extract without using the Extract filter?" Certainly, if there ever was a tool in Photoshop that required patience on the part of the user, this is it. Nonetheless, with patience and care, it's possible to make excellent extractions with the Extract filter.

Throughout the book, I'll be asking you to perform extractions at various stages, so let's get some practice with this tool right out of chute. Open the image moose.jpg from this book's CD (see Figure 1.45).

Figure 1.45: Anyone seen a flying squirrel around these parts?

Let's pull this guy off his background and give him a new home. Duplicate the Background layer. Create a new layer between the two moose layers and fill it with white. Rename the Background Copy layer **Extract** (see Figure 1.46).

Choose Filter → Extract to open the Extract dialog box. It takes up the entire screen, but most of the space is devoted to the preview window. Along the upper left are the tools you will be using, and on the right are the options for those tools.

First, zoom way in with the Magnifying Glass, or hit Command/Control+(+). To get as clean an extraction as possible (in other words, to get the cleanest, most accurate edge), it is best to use the smallest Highlighter you can, while still picking up the fine hairs that may be present. Select the Highlighter tool.

Hold down the spacebar. Notice that the Move cursor appears. This is a cool shortcut that allows you to work without switching back and forth between tools while working close up on the image. Hold down the spacebar and position the image so that you can see where the moose enters the picture. Set the size of the Highlighter to 8 and begin tracing along the back of the animal. You want as little of the animal as possible beneath the

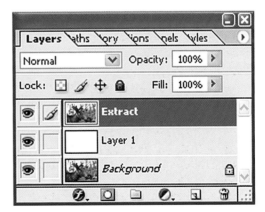

Figure 1.46: Set up the Layer palette for extracting.

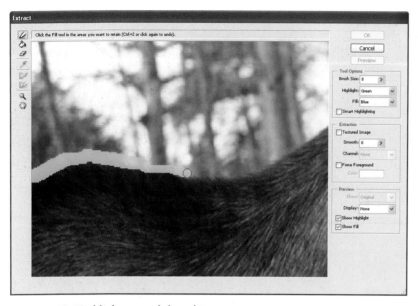

Figure 1.47: Highlight around the subject.

pen, so cut it as close as you can, but ensure that the small hairs sticking up are completely covered by the pen (see Figure 1.47).

Work your way around the entire animal, antlers and all. When you get to tufts of hair (see Figure 1.48), increase the brush size to cover the strands but still maintain your close edge around the moose (see Figure 1.49).

Once you have an outline around the entire moose, go back in between the horns and highlight those edges also. Every place where background can be seen needs to be removed if at all possible (see Figure 1.50).

Once you think you have the entire creature outlined, select the Bucket from the right and click within the selected area. This tells Photoshop what you want to remain; everything outside of this area (not colored) will be removed (see Figure 1.51).

When you are ready, click Preview to view the extracted moose (see Figure 1.52). Don't click OK, because you are not done yet. The Edge Cleanup tools are inside this dialog box as well, so you need to check all the edges first and correct accordingly. Figure 1.53 shows areas where portions of the background made it through the extraction. The Photoshop Extract dialog box has two tools that are made for cleaning up the edges. The first of these is the Cleanup tool (see Figure 1.54), found on the left-side Toolbar. When in normal mode, it acts as an eraser. Again, keep the brush size small, and run the Cleanup tool around the entire extraction. Some areas may not need it, but get the stuff that you can see. If you accidentally erase portions of the moose that you want to keep, hold down the Alt/Option key and pass over that area with the Cleanup tool. This will replace the pixels that were taken away (see Figure 1.55).

Figure 1.48: Hair is always tricky when extracting.

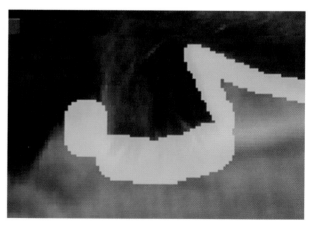

Figure 1.49: Increase the brush size to get the fine hairs.

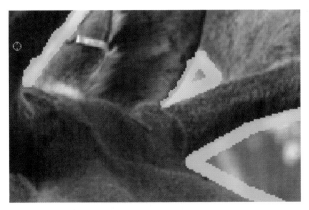

Figure 1.50: Don't forget the spaces between the antlers.

Figure 1.51: Fill the outlined area with the Bucket.

Figure 1.52: Moose, sans background

Figure 1.53: Oops...still some background pixels remaining.

Figure 1.54: The Cleanup tool will fix that problem.

Figure 1.55: Clean up those edges.

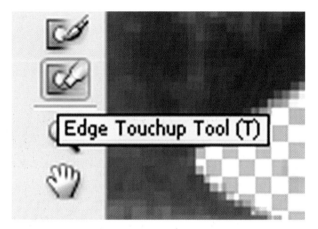

Figure 1.56: Edge Touchup tool

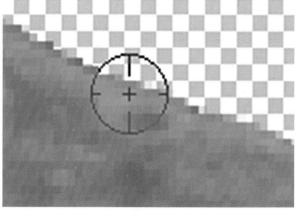

Figure 1.57: Edge Touchup helps define and sharpen the edge.

The second tool to help with the edges is the Edge Touchup tool, found just beneath the Cleanup tool (see Figure 1.56). This tool is a bit different than Cleanup. Again, a small brush size will serve best, but when using this tool the information, or pixels, that you want to keep need to be kept under the crosshair, with the circle of the brush extending beyond the extraction (see Figure 1.57). This tool helps darken and define the edge, wiping away anything that appears not to match what is beneath the crosshair.

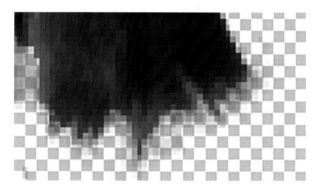

Figure 1.58: Some of the stray hairs retained

Take special care working around the hair. Take away as much background as you can without deleting the fine hairs extending into that backdrop (see Figure 1.58).

When you think you have the extraction down perfect, click OK to see a preview (see Figure 1.59). Against the white layer that you created before, if you zoom in, you'll notice pieces of the background that were left behind and escaped the eye (see Figure 1.60).

Figure 1.59: After the extraction

Figure 1.60: *Still some background left: Clean up with the Eraser tool.*

Figure 1.61: *The moose in a new home*

What to do now? You guessed it; time to make yet one more pass around the moose, this time with the Eraser tool. Clean up all those stray pixels. Again, the key word with this process is patience.

Once all that is done, you can find the moose a new home. Open the image `country road.jpg` from this book's CD, copy the moose, and paste him into the country road image. Position him with the Move tool so that he appears to be walking into the scene (see Figure 1.61).

That's it for extractions, but I can't leave this unfinished. The color of the moose doesn't really match the tone of the background that you have placed him in. Select the Moose layer and, using the settings seen in Figure 1.62, give him a quick makeover with the Match Color feature. Click OK.

Figure 1.63 shows the moose in his new home. Is that the ocean in the background? This must be a Maine moose...

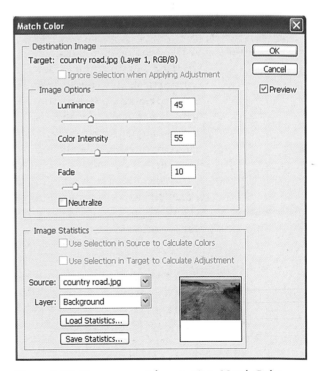

Figure 1.62: *One more quick correction: Match Color*

Figure 1.63: The moose with an ocean view

Distortions and Transformations

One aspect of Photoshop that I find particularly cool, and designers find extremely useful, is the variety of ways that Photoshop can be used to distort a layer or photo and conform it to another surface or shape. The software offers the ability to create wrinkled paper from scratch or the ability to take a flat logo and apply it to a curved surface such as a bottle—or you can simply change a layer's perspective to place it at a different angle.

The filters and commands to achieve various manipulations are located throughout the program, but those that I use most often are found in two areas: the Transform tools, found under Edit → Transform, and the Displace filter, found under Filters → Distort. You will be using both Transform and Distort later in this book, so for those of you who may not be too well versed in their operation, a quick warm-up will get you on the right path.

Displace Filter

This filter uses a second image (displacement map) to determine how a layer or selection will be distorted.

To begin, open the image `television.jpg` from this book's CD (see Figure 1.64). The aim of this little exercise is to take a copy of this image and place it on the screen, conforming it to the shape of the curved glass.

First things first: knowing that the image will eventually fit the curve on the television, a displacement map needs to be created to use with the Distort filter. Select the Channels

Figure 1.64: Perspective shot of a television and chair

Figure 1.65: Duplicate the channel with highest contrast to use as the displacement map.

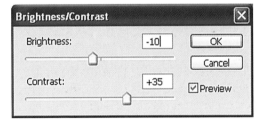

Figure 1.66: Decrease the brightness and increase the contrast even further.

palette. Select each channel one at a time. Specifically, you are looking for the channel (red, green, or blue) that shows the highest amount of contrast. The Distort filter is going to use the whites, blacks, and grays in between to determine how the layer will be distorted. After viewing each channel, you'll notice that the red channel seems to give the highest amount of contrast, so that is the one you want to duplicate (see Figure 1.65).

Although the red channel has the best contrast, you will want to increase that even further, distinguishing even more the areas of light and dark. Choose Image → Adjustments → Brightness/Contrast and decrease the brightness of the red copy channel to −10 and give the Contrast a value of +35 (see Figure 1.66). Click OK.

Figure 1.67: Help the map by painting dark areas around the screen.

Figure 1.68: This should just about do it.

The map is beginning to look good, but I think the contrast can be helped even more by applying a little paint. Press **D** to set black as the foreground color. Select the Paintbrush tool and set the attributes for the brush in the Options Toolbar as follows:

Brush	80, Round, Feathered
Mode	Normal
Opacity	50%
Flow	45%

Paint around the edges of the screen, but be careful to make the change from black to stark white seem gradual (see Figures 1.67 and 1.68).

The next step is to blur the channel. This prevents jagged areas of distortion when the Displace filter is applied. If the map itself has gradual, or blurred, transitions from white to black, then the distortions will be gradual and not stark or sharp. Choose Filter → Blur → Gaussian Blur, set the blur radius to 8 pixels (see Figure 1.69), and click OK.

Let's tweak that contrast one more time. Select Image → Adjustments → Brightness/Contrast again, but leave the Brightness alone this time and increase the Contrast to +25 (see Figure 1.70). Click OK.

The map seems to be working out rather well, so now comes the time to save it. In order for it to be used as a displacement map, it needs to be saved as a separate file somewhere on your computer where you can easily find it. First, right-click the channel. Two menu items appear: Duplicate Channel and Delete Channel. You don't want to delete the channel after all that hard work, so select Duplicate Channel.

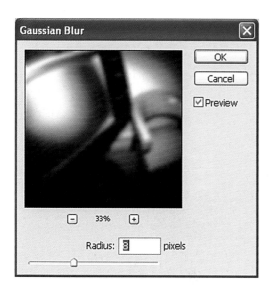

Figure 1.69: Gaussian Blur settings

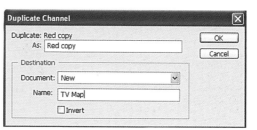

Figure 1.70: Increase the contrast one more time.

Figure 1.71: Name the new displacement map.

In the Duplicate Channel dialog box, set the Destination of the Document to New, and name the new document something descriptive. In this case, I've named mine TV Map (see Figure 1.71). Once you've named it, click OK. The Save As dialog box will open; save this file somewhere you can easily find it and as a PSD file (see Figure 1.72), because you will be using it again in a few minutes. You may close the new channel and return to the original image.

Now that you have the displacement map created and saved, you really do not need the red copy channel. You can simply delete it from the Channels palette, or just shut it off by clicking the small eye to the left. Select the RGB channel (see Figure 1.73).

Now you can set up the Layers palette for the next operation: transforming a copy of the photo to fit on the television screen. Duplicate the Background layer twice. Rename the first copy (the one just above the Background layer) **TV Room**, and the second copy, at the top of the layer stack, **Screen Image** (see Figure 1.74).

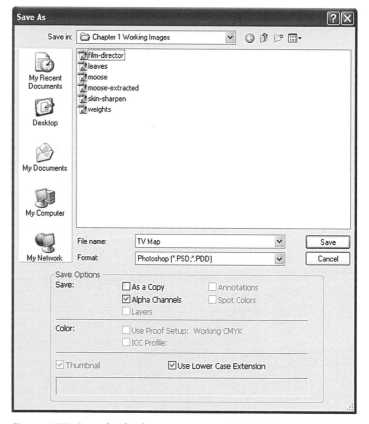

Figure 1.72: Save the displacement map to the hard drive.

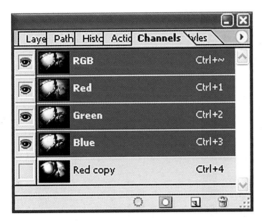

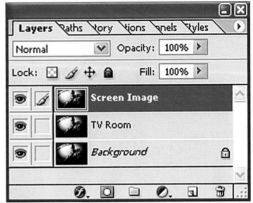

Figure 1.73: Return to the original image and shut off or delete the red copy channel.

Figure 1.74: Set up the Layers palette for the transform operation.

You will now alter the size and shape of the TV Screen layer to fit within the boundaries of the television screen itself. This is done with the Transform commands, found in the Edit → Transform menu. You have several transformations available to you:

- Scale
- Rotate
- Skew
- Distort
- Perspective
- Rotate 180 degrees
- Rotate 90 degrees clockwise (CW)
- Rotate 90 degrees counter clockwise (CCW)
- Flip Horizontal
- Flip Vertical

Transformations can be applied only to layers; they may not be applied to the background. To transform the background, you must first convert it to a normal layer. Double-click the Background layer and rename it to convert it to a standard layer.

For this example, you will be using Distort. Choose Edit → Transform → Distort (see Figure 1.75).

Distort allows you to alter the shape and dimensions of a layer by clicking, then dragging one of the transform points, found on the corners and in the center of the sides of the Transform bounding box. Grab the bottom corners of the Transform bounding box and move the point so that the bottom edges of the layer roughly meet the bottom edges of the TV screen (see Figure 1.76).

Repeat the process for the top corners of the layer. Because the boundaries of the screen are curved, you want to ensure that the entire TV screen is covered. As a result, the transformed screen will be larger than the actual screen (see Figure 1.77). Accept the transformation when you have the layer in place.

The next step will utilize the displacement map created earlier, and warp the TV Screen layer to better match the curve of the actual TV. Choose Filter → Distort → Displace. In the Displace dialog box, enter **10** for both the Horizontal Scale and the Vertical Scale (see Figure 1.78). Click OK.

Now you are asked to find a displacement map to use with the Displace filter. Although Adobe Photoshop comes with a variety of pre-made displacement maps (found in the Presets folder), find the one you created before and click Open (see Figure 1.79).

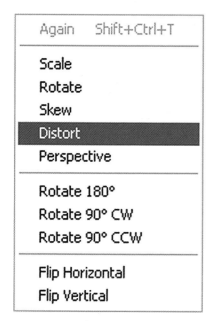

Again	Shift+Ctrl+T
Scale	
Rotate	
Skew	
Distort	
Perspective	
Rotate 180°	
Rotate 90° CW	
Rotate 90° CCW	
Flip Horizontal	
Flip Vertical	

Figure 1.75: Choosing Edit → Transform → Distort

Figure 1.76: Transform the layer by moving the corners and sides of the bounding box.

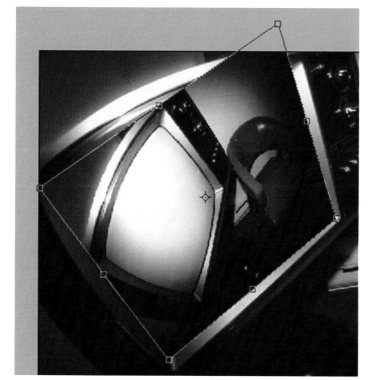

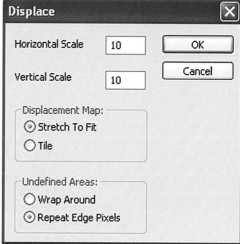

Figure 1.78: Displace settings

Figure 1.77: Resize the layer so that the entire screen, but only the screen, is covered.

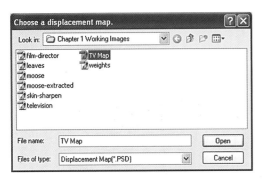

Figure 1.79: Find and open your saved displacement map.

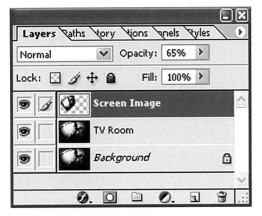

Figure 1.81: Reduce the Screen Image layer's opacity to see the image beneath.

Figure 1.80: Open the displacement map.

Figure 1.82: Polygonal Lasso options

Note that the TV Screen layer now appears warped; the edges are no longer straight as they once were, and the image itself has had a shift in pixels trying to match the variations of light and dark in the map (see Figure 1.80).

You really don't want the excess pixels extending beyond the screen, so reduce the opacity of the Screen Image layer to 65% or so (see Figure 1.81). This way you can see the screen beneath. Select the Polygonal Lasso tool (see Figure 1.82). Make a selection around the screen, choose Select → Inverse, and hit the Delete key to trim away the excess pixels (see Figure 1.83).

Perhaps a change in blending mode will assist in making this appear to be a broadcast image. Change the blending mode of the Screen Image layer to Hard Light, and increase the Opacity to 85% (see Figure 1.84).

Figure 1.85 shows the final image. I'm sure you have seen this mirror effect in advertisements, and now you can perform the process yourself.

The tools found in Adobe Photoshop CS are powerful, certainly, but their true power doesn't really become evident if they are used alone. The tools and functions in Photoshop are meant to work together and complement one another; a little intuition and a dash of experience will help you discern which tools in combination will render the effect you want or give you the best results in a given situation.

Figure 1.83: Delete the excess pixels.

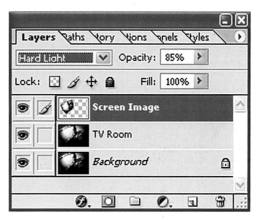

Figure 1.84: Blending mode and Opacity change

Figure 1.85: What's on the TV?

two

Techniques for Embellishing Portraits

"Vanity, vanity, *all is vanity..." Almost nobody likes the way they look in photographs. Here you're going to learn how to help with that.*

This chapter and the next deal specifically with images of people— from light portrait retouching to drastic alterations. The techniques demonstrated are in no way restricted to images of people; these are just a few examples of corrections and alterations with thousands of possible applications that aren't exclusive to a specific photo type. What the techniques will do is help you work through a process (or at least demonstrate one way of doing things), and once you've learned a procedure, you can then find ideas for applying it to your own artistic renderings. Even better, once the right side of your head is tingling with ideas, you will soon find that you can subtly or drastically alter the steps in a technique to generate some pretty amazing results. Who knows, you could revolutionize a new artistic form...or at least generate some interesting pictures to e-mail to family members.

The images referenced as source files for these techniques can be found in the Chapter 2 Source Files *folder on this book's CD.*

Enhancing Eye Color

I love working with eyes. They've been called windows to the soul, and this is close to the truth. You can discern many things from a person's eyes, from emotional state to truthfulness (or lack thereof). I've known people who swear their eye color changes depending on their mood, and after experiencing a couple of foul tempers, I learned to discern those ill moods just by checking to see if the eyes were a soothing hazel or a wicked shade of green. Green is rarely good...any fan of comics can tell you that.

Fortunately for me, my love for tweaking eyes works well here, as eye manipulation is a popular topic in the Photoshop community.

The most popular question, and therefore the most often answered, is how to solve the red-eye problem. As that information can be found nearly everywhere, I'm not going to get into it directly; after you are done with this chapter, you will have figured it out, trust me.

What I'm going to show you first is one way to enhance the existing eye character in a photo. Take a look at Figure 2.1. This is the image `stare.jpg` from this book's CD; it should be open in Photoshop as you begin. Personally I'm a fan of hazel eyes; they have always intrigued me for some reason. Browns mixed with greens or blues—representing complexity? Duplicity, perhaps? In any case, the enhancement you'll add here is to make this mixed color richer and brighter. To do that, you'll use duplicated layers, layer masks, and a couple of different blending modes.

Blending modes, opacities, and masks are going to be your best friends through much of this book, and in the following techniques you will see a lot of them. If you skipped those sections in Chapter 1 and are unfamiliar with those modes, it's a good idea to review those sections before proceeding. If you are familiar with one or all of them but they aren't your strong suit, feel free to bend a corner of the book in those sections.

Figure 2.1:
`Stare.jpg` *from this book's CD. You will enhance the richness of the hazel eye color.*

Duplicate the Background layer and change the blending mode of the new layer to Overlay. You will note that the entire image becomes a bit darker as the new layer blends with the background. This does help enhance the color of the eye, but the skin around the eye becomes darker also. A mask will alleviate this problem quite nicely.

Overlay Blending Mode

This blending mode either screens or multiplies the pixel information, depending on the base color. Even when colors or patterns overlay pixel information, the highlights and shadows of the original pixels are maintained. The base color is not replaced; rather, it is blended into another form of the original color.

At the bottom of the Layers palette, click the Add Layer Mask icon. By default the mask is filled with white, allowing the contents of the entire layer to be seen. You do not want all of the pixels to be seen, however, just those of the iris and pupil. With the layer mask selected, choose Edit → Fill and fill the mask with black set to 100% opacity, blending mode set to Normal. Figure 2.2 shows the Layers palette at this point in the process.

Set white as the foreground color. Select the Paintbrush tool and, with a soft-edged round brush, paint over the iris and pupil. Adjust the brush size accordingly so that you are painting only within the diameter of the iris. Although it's not necessary if you have a steady hand, you may want to create a selection of the area. In this instance the Elliptical Marquee tool will work just fine, because the area being enhanced is round. As you paint, those pixels on this layer will be revealed. The layer is still set to Overlay so the color of the blended layers comes through (see Figure 2.3).

To brighten the eye a bit (the point was to brighten the colors without darkening the eye), create a new layer above the Background Copy layer and set the blending mode to Soft Light. With the foreground color still set to white, paint over the iris in this layer also (see Figure 2.4).

The change is subtle, yet effective. Figure 2.5 gives a before and after shot—before on the left, corrected image on the right. See the difference?

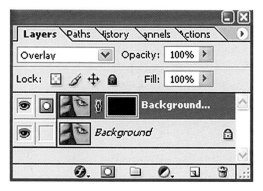

Figure 2.2: New layer and mask in place

Figure 2.3: Painting in the mask

Figure 2.4:
Soft Light with
white paint
brightens the
tone of the eye.

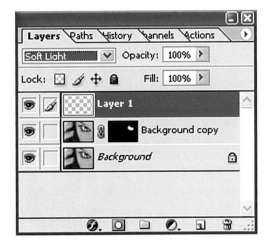

Figure 2.5: The
original eye (left)
and the eye with
enhanced color
(right)

Enhancing Color Variation—Lips

In a manner similar to the eye technique just covered, lips can also be enhanced and given new life digitally. This technique is especially popular for women...they can now look as though they spent hours meticulously applying make-up without even cracking the seal on their lipstick.

One idea I want to work into your way of thinking (if it's not already there) is that techniques you've seen performed on eyes/hair/leaves/concrete or whatever can also be used to enhance other texture types, other subjects, and so forth. Although both eyes and lips reside in the same neighborhood on a body, the characteristics that make eyes recognizable as eyes and lips as lips are very different. But just because the color and texture are different does not mean that similar techniques to color or correct them cannot be used.

Open the image `thought.tif` from this book's CD if you haven't already (see Figure 2.6). The woman in this photo has a certain natural beauty that doesn't really warrant a lot of makeup, but her lips could be a bit richer in tone. This technique will actually use the colors already resident in the image as the foundation palette.

As before, create a duplicate of the Background layer and set the blending mode to Overlay (see Figure 2.7). As the lips are the target of this piece, notice how they take on a deeper shade of red.

Figure 2.6: Woman in thought

To deepen the red even further, select the Burn tool and set the Brush to 70, Range to Midtones, and Exposure to 50%.

Run the brush over the lips, being careful not to linger too long in the same place or burn the same area repeatedly. When you linger in one area or make multiple passes over the same area, the Burn tool will continue to saturate the pixels until they become extremely dark. In nice, easy strokes, run the brush over the lip areas until the richer reds emerge. If you overdo it with this tool the lips will gradually turn black, so take it easy, amigo!

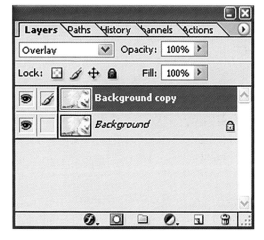

Figure 2.7: Duplicate layer set to Overlay

The Burn Tool

This tool has its foundation in traditional photography. Burning is used in that medium to increase exposure to areas of a print, and the Burn tool in Photoshop works in the same manner. You can use it to increase saturation in a photo, darkening select areas.

Create a mask for this layer and fill it with black. In the mask, paint with white over the lips to reveal the richer tones (see Figure 2.8).

Figure 2.8: Black hides, white reveals.

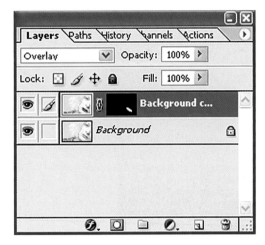

Figure 2.9: Pale to rosy in a couple of quick steps

Figure 2.9 gives a comparison of the original (left) and the corrected (right). The new lips appear to have a light application of makeup, without being over the top. Sometimes it's cool to be subtle.

Altering Eye Color

Altering eye color is simpler than it has ever been, thanks to the addition in Photoshop CS of the brand new Color Replacement tool. This is found grouped with the Healing Brush tool and the Patch tool in the Toolbar. Easy to use, this powerful tool relieves a lot of the stress suffered by retouching amateurs and pros alike, who used to spend a lot of effort wishing such a tool existed.

Before I get into the nuts and bolts of this cool new feature, let me say that it still has a drawback, so it is not a miracle cure for every recoloring ailment. It is destructive to the layer (meaning that it alters the actual pixels), so in the next variation I'll take you through another process that allows you to preserve the original layer. But first let's do some painting!

Open baby.jpg (see Figure 2.10) from this book's CD and find the Color Replacement brush in the Toolbar. Again, it is grouped with the Healing Brush tool and Patch tool in the left-hand column of the Toolbar.

Figure 2.10: I wonder what's going on in the baby's mind...

As with other tools, this one has its own settings that can be changed in the Options bar. For this technique, set the blending mode for the tool to Hue, and ensure that Find Edges is selected for the Limits setting. The Brush size should be 20, the sampling mode should be Continuous, the Tolerance should be 30%, and Anti-aliased should be checked. With the Find Edges setting, Photoshop will look for boundaries to paint within while the new color is being applied, thus allowing only the hue of the iris and not the areas outside it to change.

Hue Blending Mode

This blending mode creates a color based on the luminance and saturation of the base color and hue/tone of the blend color.

Before you change the color of the eyes, you will want to choose a new color. Open the Color Picker (click the foreground color) and select a new color (see Figure 2.11). Click OK.

Duplicate the background layer to keep the original image unaltered and start painting over the iris with an appropriately sized brush. I love the Hue setting, because the color change is subtle yet clearly evident when placed side by side with the original (see Figure 2.12). The reflections are retained, the pupil remains black, and the eye color still looks natural.

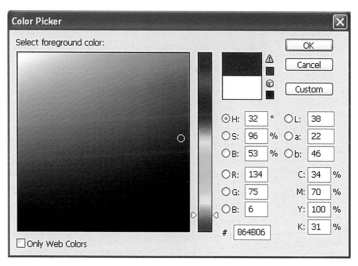

Figure 2.11: Choose the new eye color.

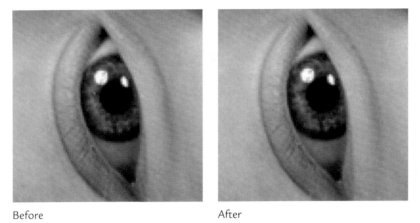

Before   After

Figure 2.12: With the Hue blending mode, the changed color in this example retains a natural appearance.

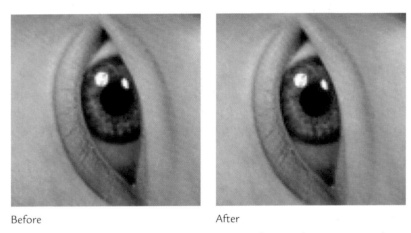

Before   After

Figure 2.13: Replacing the color in Saturation mode gives this image a much more artificial appearance.

   For colors that are richer, change the blending mode of the brush to Saturation. A richer blue is displayed, but the eye clearly looks manipulated and unnatural (see Figure 2.13).

   Delete the previously retouched layer and duplicate the Background layer. Change the foreground color to a light blue hue and change the blending mode of the brush to Color. Those of you familiar with retouching may recognize this mode, because this was a primary mode for retouching in earlier versions of the program.

   Paint over the iris again. Figure 2.14 shows the before and after shot. When I'm working with eyes and lips, the Color blending mode is by far my favorite. The eye color teeters on the edge of natural and unnatural; it could be real, but it could be enhanced. At least that is what viewers will think, and I like to keep them guessing.

   If the brush didn't pay attention to your command telling it to stay within the borders of the iris, a layer mask can fix the problem. Just create a mask for the layer and paint with black over the color that extends beyond the iris.

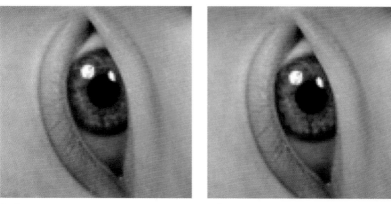

Before   After

Figure 2.14: Enhancing eye color with the Color blending mode

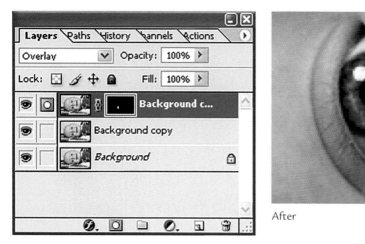

After

Figure 2.15: Creating eyes of deep blue

To really make the eye glow with inner life, duplicate the colored layer and change the blending mode in the Layers palette to Overlay. This will also darken the skin, as seen earlier, so just create a mask, fill it with black, then paint with white in the mask over the eye to reveal it again (see Figure 2.15).

Altering Color Variation—Lips

In some cases, it is still better to use a standard paintbrush (or other technique) than the Color Replacement tool. Changing lip color is such a case.

Why the difference, you ask? The Color Replacement tool is what is called a destructive tool; sounds ominous, doesn't it? What that means is that it alters the actual pixels on the layer you are working on, swapping brown for blue or what have you. The Color Replacement tool needs color before it can work.

*Figure 2.16: Full
red lips*

When you do not want to destroy/swap/exchange the pixels of the original image, but just want to change the color, then painting in a new empty layer over the area to be changed and setting the Layer blending mode to Color gives nearly identical results as the other method; the colored pixels change, the blacks and whites remain untouched. However, the original layer remains intact.

Color Blending Mode

This blending mode creates a color based on the luminance of the base color and saturation of the blend color.

I will also show you a couple of ways to pull out a new color, so let's get into it.

Just for fun, we're going to take some nice red lips and turn them blue. Start by having image `lips.jpg` from this book's CD open and ready to go (see Figure 2.16). If you prefer, you may crop away the rest of the face and just work on the mouth area. Create a new layer and change the blending mode to Color. Select a soft pastel blue as the foreground color and, with the Paintbrush tool, paint over the area where the lipstick is applied (see Figure 2.17).

If you didn't smear the new lipstick, you can skip the next step. As one who's never had to apply makeup to my own face, I tend to be a bit messy when doing so digitally; therefore I will use a mask to help me clean up my mess. Create a mask and paint around the overlap areas with black to keep the color within the boundaries of the lips.

Figure 2.17: Painted layer set to Color blending mode

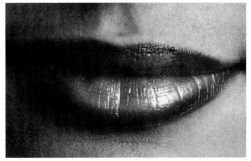

Figure 2.18: Dodge and burn the layer beneath the paint to get the effect shown here.

Figure 2.19: Hue/Saturation adjustment to alter color

Create a duplicate of the Background layer and select the Burn tool set to Midtones. Darken the edges of the lips just a bit. Hold down the Alt/Option key to switch to the Dodge tool and lighten the highlights (see Figure 2.18).

The Dodge Tool

Like the Burn tool, the Dodge tool has its roots in traditional photography. Where the Burn tool increases saturation, the Dodge tool actually decreases it, gradually moving to white.

Another option for coloring portions of an image is to simply apply a Hue/Saturation adjustment layer. In Figure 2.19, I have shut off my Paint layer and created a Hue/Saturation adjustment layer at the top of the layer stack. When tweaking the sliders in the Hue/Saturation dialog box, the portion I'm concerned with assumes the color I'm looking for, but other areas are turned blue. I've filled the mask with black and then painted with white over the lips, hiding the areas of skin turned blue by my adjustment and revealing the lips with the adjustment applied.

Figure 2.20:
Blue-haired
model

Altering Color Variation—Hair

Just to demonstrate that the same processes have multiple applications, and that you shouldn't make things harder than they have to be, let's apply virtually the same coloring technique to altering hair color.

Open the image `punk.jpg` from this book's CD (see Figure 2.20). Duplicate the Background layer and select the Paintbrush tool. Set the blending mode for the brush to Color, with the other options as shown here:

Brush size	100
Opacity	50%
Flow	65%

Select a color and place it in the foreground. Paint over the hair with the brush. Get the sideburns and follow the hairline. Continue painting until all the blue pixels have been swapped with the new color (see Figure 2.21).

I bet you guessed how to clean up the overspill. If you said "Layer mask," you are absolutely right! See how things work together for the common good?

Figure 2.21: These kids nowadays…

Figure 2.22: Masking away the dyed skin

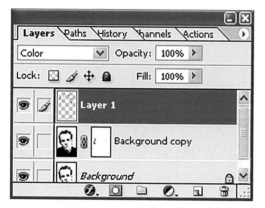

Figure 2.23: New layer set to Color blending mode

Create a mask for the painted layer and, with a black brush resized as needed, paint over the areas of skin that have turned red because of the dye. Work into those nooks and crannies until the flesh returns to its normal color (see Figure 2.22).

For a little added splash, create a new layer above the painted layer and set the blending mode for the new layer to Color (see Figure 2.23). Select varying shades of color for the foreground (green, blue, mauve, stucco…) and paint over a few strands of hair that have been clumped together. Use Figure 2.24 as a reference if you like.

Figure 2.24: Punk rocker or poser?

Figure 2.25: Our hair model

Variation: Subtly Enhancing Highlights and Natural Hair Color

The previous technique showed a pretty drastic alteration, but the majority of alterations that people attempt in Photoshop are subtle—simply enhancing color or changing it slightly. Here's one method for changing color that retains the natural look of the hair.

Open image `retouch.jpg` (see Figure 2.25) from this book's CD.

You will start by adding highlights, so duplicate the Background layer. Select the Dodge tool and change the options to these:

Brush	80
Range	Midtones
Exposure	34%

Figure 2.26: Blending mode changed to Overlay

Change the blending mode for the Background copy layer to Overlay (see Figure 2.26). Using the Dodge tool, brighten a few strands of hair similar to the painting of color done in the previous technique. Do not dodge the hair too much; a few highlighted strands will do (see Figure 2.27).

Next you can add color as in the previous technique, but drastically toned down. Create a new layer and set the blending mode to Color. Select a color somewhere between red, orange, and brown

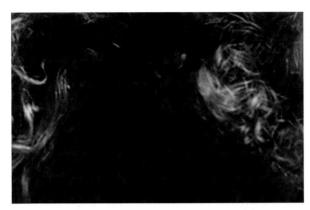

Figure 2.27: Highlights with Dodge

Figure 2.28: New layer in Color mode...again

Figure 2.29: The finished result

as the foreground color and paint over the hair in the new layer (see Figure 2.28). The adjusted image is shown in Figure 2.29. If the color is too harsh for your taste or need, simply lower the opacity of the painted layer.

Whitening Teeth

As of this writing, I'm a smoker (I say that in the hopes of quitting the nasty habit someday). I've given up the cigarettes but not the pipe. I also drink more coffee than the average bear.

That combination of vices makes for a pretty unsightly smile if stringent oral hygiene is not followed. Photoshop, on the other hand, can help you put a sparkle on those pearly whites in no time.

Figure 2.30: Yellow smile?

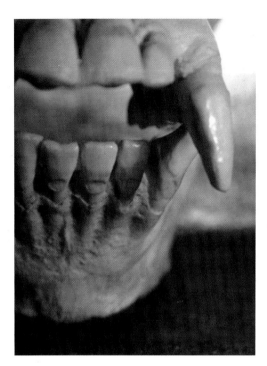

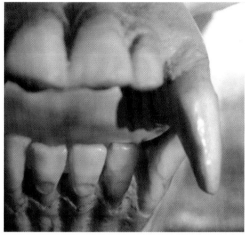

Figure 2.31: Some staining removed

Figure 2.30 shows the teeth you will be working on for this technique. I chose this image in particular because I hate having my real teeth cleaned, and because the teeth themselves are tinted yellow as the result of age.

Open `fangs.jpg` from this book's CD. Duplicate the Background layer and lighten the teeth with the Dodge tool. You need not take out all the yellow…just lighten the teeth a bit.

Next, create a new layer and change the blending mode to Saturation. Select a light gray foreground color and, with the Paintbrush tool, paint over the teeth in the new layer. You may also accomplish this by choosing white, but reducing the opacity of the paint. You will notice the yellow hue disappear as if by magic (or at least a powerful toothpaste). See Figure 2.31.

Saturation Blending Mode

This blending mode creates a color based on the luminance and hue of the base color and saturation of the blend color. Gray produces no change, because there is no saturation associated with gray.

You can whiten the teeth by changing the blending mode of the actual brush to Hue, with these settings:

Brush	100
Opacity	45%
Flow	75%

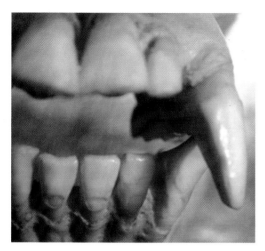

Figure 2.32: Getting whiter

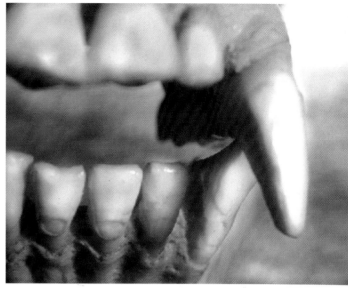

Figure 2.33: A smile made for the movies and politics

Figure 2.32 shows the correction.

If you want to make the teeth look like they have been overbleached, simply select the Background copy layer again and apply the Dodge tool to all the canines, molars, and bicuspids you want until the smile meets with your satisfaction (see Figure 2.33).

Removing Acne and Blemishes

Let's take a break from painting, dodging, and burning, and tackle another issue that appeals to retouchers everywhere. When I was going through those wonderful transition years from boy to grownup, I suffered from a rather active case of acne. I absolutely hated it, and because Photoshop did not yet exist, I had to suffer through far too many photo sessions without any chance of the retouching that kids today have available. Having pictures done for the yearbook was bad enough, but once you became a senior, the pictures were printed in…egad…full color!!!

That particular problem has thankfully faded into the distant past, but a couple of scars remain…both on my face and on my psyche. As with teeth and hair, Photoshop can act as a digital cosmetic surgeon with just a few quick tool applications.

Have the image `skin-rug.jpg` from this book's CD ready in Photoshop. As you can see in Figure 2.34, this lovely young lady has a few minor blemishes apparent on her cheeks, which don't look bad at normal resolution. When you zoom in (see Figure 2.35), blackheads and old acne scars become painfully apparent because of the high resolution of this image. If this shot were part of a model's portfolio, who knows what jobs she might lose?

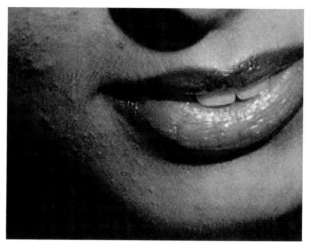

Figure 2.34: In a normal view, the model's old acne scars are barely visible. But zoom in, and...

Figure 2.35: Yikes! Toooo much detail!

Cleaning up the scars is simply a matter of covering them with samples taken from other areas of the face without blemishes. Select the Clone Stamp tool and enter these settings in the Options Toolbar:

Brush	70
Mode	Normal
Opacity	25%
Flow	35%
Aligned box	Checked
Use All Layers box	Unchecked

Hold down the Alt/Option key and take a sample from the woman's chin to apply to the blemished areas (see Figure 2.36). Release the mouse once the sample has been taken and stamp the skin pattern over the blemishes seen to the left side of her mouth (see Figure 2.37). There may be some discoloration...don't worry about that just yet.

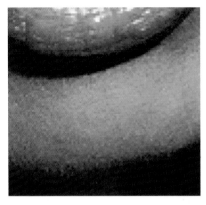

Figure 2.36: Sample taken from clear, unblemished area

Figure 2.37: New skin stamped into place

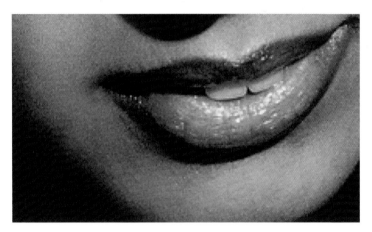

Figure 2.38: Acne and color replaced with new skin

Although they are separate tools, the Clone Stamp tool and the Healing Brush tool often work best in conjunction with each other. Select the Healing Brush tool and enter these settings in the Options Toolbar:

Brush	30
Mode	Normal
Source	Sampled

Again, sample a clear area of skin near where the blemishes were covered, and release the Alt/Option key. Apply the sample to the areas of discoloration (see Figure 2.38).

Figures 2.39 and 2.40 show an area of scarring between the model's eyebrows that is easily corrected using the same technique.

As an added bonus I've decided that, once the skin corrections are done, I'll apply a couple of the coloring techniques we discussed earlier to the final image, seen in Figure 2.41.

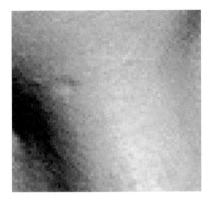

Figure 2.39: Acne scar

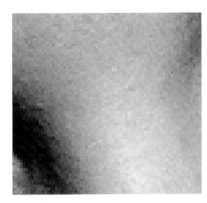

Figure 2.40: Skin smooth once again

Figure 2.41: Lady of the islands

Erasing Wrinkles

This technique is also one close to my heart, and gets cozier there with each passing day. Having officially reached that cumbersome middle-aged mark, I trust that I'll be looking for even more ways to imitate Dorian Gray (or at least in reverse, if that makes sense).

Take a look at Figure 2.42 (`laugh.jpg` from this book's CD). This lady looks like she just heard my favorite "Waiter, there's a fly in my soup" joke, which has brought out a whole lifetime of laugh lines.

I'm sure we can help her out though, and the process is very simple.

Duplicate the Background layer (see Figure 2.43) and with the Clone Stamp tool or the Healing Brush tool (either works just fine) with the settings used in the previous technique, sample clear unwrinkled areas of the skin (see Figure 2.44) and then apply them to the wrinkles. Don't worry if she takes on an unnatural, baby-smooth appearance, such as is the case in Figure 2.45.

To finish this correction, simply lower the opacity of the Background copy layer until some of the wrinkles beneath show through. Figure 2.46 shows my before and after shots.

Figure 2.42: ...and the waiter says, "Shhh! Not so loud, the people at the next table will hear you and want one, too."

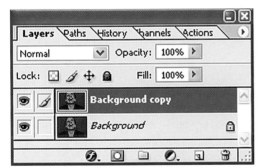

Figure 2.43: Duplicate the Background layer.

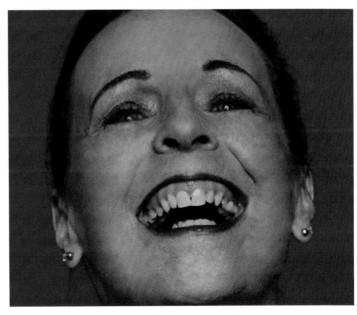

Figure 2.44: Sample the clear skin.

Figure 2.45: Stamp the new skin over the wrinkles.

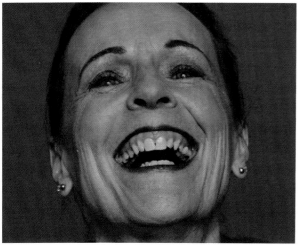

Before

After

Figure 2.46: She looks 10 years younger!

Reverse Cosmetics: Creating a Black Eye

I had a bit of a quandary when outlining this technique. There are so many ways to blemish, cut, or otherwise traumatize the skin using Photoshop CS that I had a hard time choosing which to demonstrate here. I've decided to show you a method for adding realistic bruises using our old friend, the Burn tool. How far you go with tool application depends on the amount of discoloration you need for a given project; Photoshop can tackle the problem.

Open the image `blues.jpg` from this book's CD (see Figure 2.47). This blues singer has just signed with a new record label, and they don't think his publicity still looks like he has suffered enough to be really authentic. We need to beat him up a little; Photoshop can help with that.

Duplicate the Background layer and name the new layer Boxer (see Figure 2.48).

Figure 2.47: Has he paid enough dues yet?

This is the last illustration you'll see of duplicating a Background layer; I've included it here as a last instance to get you in practice so there is no doubt what I mean later.

Using the Burn tool for bruising is by far the quickest method to get those deep tones on the skin. Select the Burn tool and set these options:

Brush	70
Range	Midtones
Exposure	35%

Start with the right eye and run the Burn tool beneath it until the skin darkens as though blood is building up just below the surface (see Figure 2.49). Continue with the other eye, darkening the lids a bit also (see Figure 2.50).

As I close this chapter, I hope that you find ways to use these quick little vanity techniques in your own work. There's still more to cover in the next chapter, so let's keep on movin' and get into some serious alterations. I need 20cc's of Botox, stat!

Figure 2.48: One last look at duplicating the Background layer

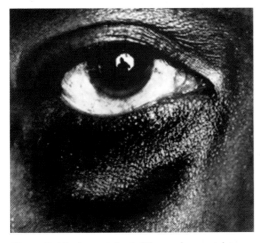

Figure 2.49: A musician's life can be punishing.

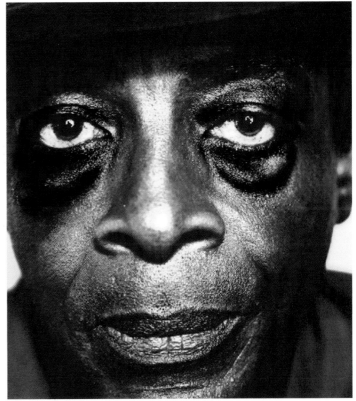

Figure 2.50: Now he's ready for that comeback album with guest spots by Eminem and Shania Twain.

three

Advanced Techniques for Embellishing Portraits

Recently I've read *discussions on the ethics of image correction. The pro side, of course, says there is nothing wrong with a little digital nip and tuck on occasion. The con states that to digitally alter a person in any way for publication or what have you is a boundary that shouldn't be crossed, as the person editing the photo is, in effect, lying to the consumer.*

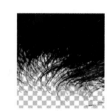

If I were to get involved, I'd probably fall somewhere in the middle. If, for instance, the law enforcement community decided that a crime scene photo could use a little more blood and then added it digitally, that would clearly be a no-no, especially if the accused was invited to court for littering. But suppose a magazine decided to run a big article on the top Photoshop authors? The art director would look at my picture and say, "Gotta do something about that…." As I get older and parts of my body try to move south, I'm thankful for a little digital liposuction.

Digital Liposuction

This technique uses the image `tummy-2.jpg` found on this book's CD. Please open it now.

Notoriously, the camera adds ten pounds, and the belly dancer modeling for this technique (see Figure 3.1) has decided that her publicity stills should look a little skinnier than she actually is. In particular, she doesn't like the love handles in her photos. Whether she needs it or not, the Photoshop physician can help.

One way to trim down the love handles and still keep a natural curve is to generate a path and trim away the excess. Select the Pen tool and, in the Options Toolbar, press the

Figure 3.1: I dream of Jeannie

Path button in the upper left. Select the standard Pen tool (as opposed to the Freeform Pen tool) and set its options as shown in Figure 3.2.

This tool can be tricky, and is pretty daunting to those who don't use it on a regular basis. It really isn't that difficult to work with once you play with it a bit, though.

Take a look at Figure 3.3. First, click the mouse just above where you want the correction to be made. Click another point along the seam of her pantaloons and, holding down the mouse button, drag to the left so that the bars appear, then just manipulate the mouse until you get the curve you want.

> To help you generate perfect curves using the Pen tool, practice dragging the first direction point in the direction the bump of the curve is to go, and the second direction point in the opposite direction. This formula will create an S curve. For more information on curves, please consult "Drawing with the Pen Tool" in the Adobe Photoshop CS Help Files.

Click in the white area to create a new point, and then click the first point to close the path. By closing the path, I mean that all the points of the path will be connected so that a "circle" is formed, leaving no open sides in the path. In the Paths palette, click the Load Path As Selection icon at the bottom of the palette. This will create an active selection following the path (see Figure 3.4).

Figure 3.2: Pen tool options

Figure 3.3: Create a path around the love handle.

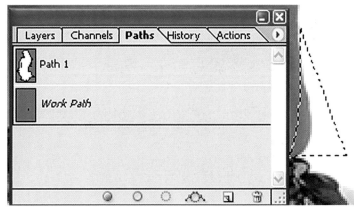

Figure 3.4: Change the path to a selection.

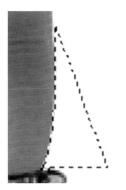

This edit is fairly simple, because the subject is already on a white background. To trim away the love handle, just fill it with white (see Figure 3.5). If the subject were on a different background, there would be additional steps (extracting, and deleting the excess pixels) to complete the retouching. Figure 3.6 shows the before and after images.

Figure 3.5: Fill selection with white to wipe away a couple pounds.

Figure 3.6: Before (left) and after (right)

Digital Liposuction Variation: The Liquify Filter

Another way to tighten up those elusive curves is to use the Pucker Tool in the Liquify Filter dialog box. Using the same image as before, either open a new instance of it or click the original state in the History palette to revert it back to normal.

The Pucker Tool

Found in the Liquify Filter dialog box, this tool moves the pixels within the brush area toward the center of the brush while you either hold down the mouse button or drag. The longer this tool is applied, the more compressed the pixels in the brush area will appear.

Choose Filter → Liquify. Select the Pucker tool on the left, and then set up these options/settings for the tool on the right-hand side:

Brush Size	35
Brush Density	60
Brush Pressure	60
Brush Rate	80

We are reducing the brush size, density, and pressure from their default 100%, as the pinching of pixels that occurs when using this tool needs to be gradual. Reducing the density and brush pressure simply gives you better control and will help prevent harsh distortions. The Liquify tool likes to manhandle pixels, and over-application will quickly stretch and pull the image to the point where the subject is no longer recognizable as a life form.

Now center the cursor over the inside edge of the skin of the love handle. As you click and hold the left mouse button, the pixels surrounding the cursor will be drawn toward its center. Slowly move the mouse up and down the edge to the seam of the pantaloons and watch how the pixels are drawn in. *Do not* linger in one spot for long, because the edge will become lumpy and distorted (see Figure 3.7).

Figure 3.7: Reduce the love handles again…gently!

Another place where women (and some men) want to look more like a fashion model than a belly dancer is the upper arms (see Figure 3.8). Using the same careful technique, pull the fat in on this area also.

Once you have the hang of the process, reduce the exposed shoulder, forearm, and the other side of her waist to keep things in proportion (see Figure 3.9). That is the main problem (but a major attraction for a lot of users) with over-application of this filter: the loss of believable proportions. Using it delicately, however, can create some startlingly realistic results. Please see the tutorial for creating the Alien Boy in Chapter 9, because Liquify will be used extensively.

Now that the model has been trimmed and tucked in her upper areas, she's left with a rather prominent backside. You don't think so? Trust me, if she stood up right now she would be asking for—rather, demanding—her money back (see Figure 3.10)!

To fix this, increase the size of the brush and run it over her derriere until the proportions look right to you. Figure 3.11 shows the before and after shots: another proud customer of the Photoshop Weight Loss Program.

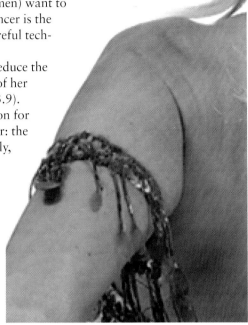

Figure 3.8: Shrink the chicken fat forming on the upper arms in the same way.

Figure 3.9: Slimming

Figure 3.10: One more area to cover

Figure 3.11:
Another happy
customer

Before   After

Digital Face-Lift

This technique uses the image `older-couple.jpg` found on this book's CD. Please open the photo now.

I've already touched on wrinkle reduction in this book, but the changes made there were fairly subtle, more to enhance the photograph rather than the subject of the photo. That was a studio technique a customer would find flattering. This technique takes the process of wrinkle reduction to the extreme, by physically altering the appearance of the subjects to reduce age and give the appearance that they really aren't in their late 60s, but have ceased aging in their mid-50s.

When I first started playing with digital face-lifts, my subjects often ended up looking like some creature that could survive only in the imagination. After numerous failed attempts, I began looking at how real cosmetic surgeons approached their work and altered their clients. Most of the changes a person undergoes are subtle: a slight narrowing of the bridge of the nose, skin removed so that the remaining skin can be pulled back to remove wrinkles, and so forth. If they elect for more trips to the surgeon, the alterations become increasingly apparent until the skin appears stretched, the lips cease moving in a natural way, and the eyes appear in a permanent open state. I won't name any names, but I'll bet you can pinpoint a couple of examples of cosmetic surgery extremes.

Just because it can be done in Photoshop does not mean that a plastic surgeon could get the same results! Playing with pixels is one thing, but my publisher and I accept no liability for what might happen if you alter your picture and then ask a surgeon to duplicate the effect. You're beautiful just the way you are; having known you for over two chapters, I wouldn't change a thing.

On to the technique. The woman in this photo (see Figure 3.12) has excellent skin and structure for digital reconstruction, whereas the man hasn't aged quite as well. Her skin is relatively smooth (although wrinkled); his has fewer wrinkles but the pores and color can be tricky. The other reason I chose this image is to demonstrate that both grandpas and grand-mas can look a few years younger; the editing that it takes to get there may be slightly differ-ent, depending on their skin tone and texture. For example, the lady in the photo has won-derful skin tone, so the primary correction you will do is wrinkle reduction. With the man, the discoloration is the main issue with the skin. Finally, both will receive a once-over with

Figure 3.12: The happy couple

the Liquify tool to tighten up the effects of age. Both subjects in this instance will be subject to everyone's favorite Photoshop toy, the Liquify tool.

Start by duplicating the Background layer. The woman has many fine wrinkles all over her face and neck, but her cheek (see Figure 3.13) has a smooth area that can be used to clean up the rest of her face. Select the Healing Brush tool and with the following options for the tool, take a sample of her smooth skin:

Brush	30
Mode	Normal
Source	Sampled

The Healing Brush Tool

Although similar to the Clone Stamp tool, the Healing Brush not only applies a sample (or pattern) to an area, but also attempts to match the texture, shading, lighting, and transparency of the pixels it is applied to (source pixels). The result gives far better seamless blending than the Clone Stamp in the case of facial reconstruction and other effects.

Apply the sample beneath the woman's eye and on her lid to clean up the minute folds and discoloration seen there. Overlay most of the wrinkles seen in this portion of the face, but leave a couple of tiny crows' feet. Repeat the process around her other eye, and also take out the more prominent wrinkles on her forehead (see Figure 3.14).

Move down to the lower portion of her face, as well as her neck (see Figure 3.15). To correct this area, take another sample from the smooth area on her chin to cover the mole that is being carefully, but not entirely successfully, concealed by makeup. If you recall the touch-up done on the young woman in the previous chapter (removing acne and blemishes), the technique is the same although the wrinkles are more pronounced and frequent. A few wrinkles are needed for realism, but most can go away (see Figure 3.16).

Continue the same technique on her neck (see Figure 3.17). Again, take samples of the smooth areas on her neck and apply the Healing Brush tool in the same manner as before, covering the lines that years of head turning have produced (see Figure 3.18).

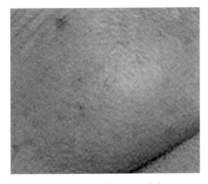

Figure 3.13: Smooth area of skin

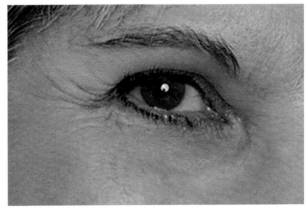

Figure 3.14: Age around the eyes reduced

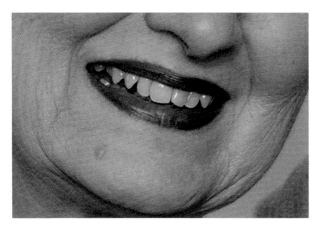

Figure 3.15: Chin and cheeks, pre-alteration

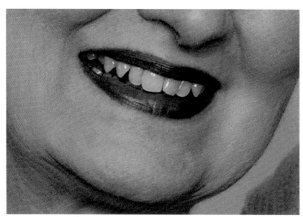

Figure 3.16: Chin and cheeks after new skin is applied

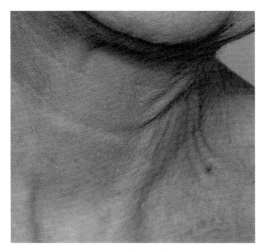

Figure 3.17: And now the neck…

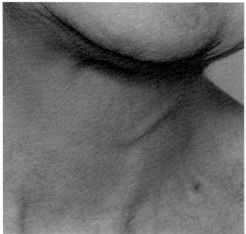

Figure 3.18: The years are melting away.

Grandma has been receiving a lot of attention; it's time to work on Grandpa. His face doesn't have nearly the concentration of wrinkles, but his eyes are showing telltale signs of cobwebs and a few spots of skin discoloration are becoming prominent (see Figure 3.19). Again, wipe these away by sampling a clear portion of his skin and applying the Healing Brush tool as you did on the other subject (see Figure 3.20).

Continue working on the rest of the man's face, removing the age spots and blending the areas of red discoloration. Figure 3.21 shows both subjects after the wrinkle and blemish reduction process.

You will now get a bit more practice with Liquify. The Liquify tool is fantastic for digital face lifting, as long as it isn't overdone. You will use it to tighten the areas of the face that have been pulled and stretched by gravity.

This is going to help shave years off the couple, so choose Filter → Liquify now. As in the previous technique, the size of the brush (no larger than needed to make small corrections),

Figure 3.19: Age spots to be erased

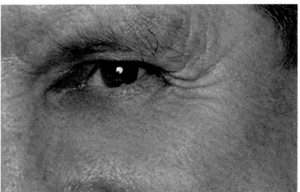

Figure 3.20: Cleaning up the husband

Figure 3.21: A younger pair

reduced density, and reduced pressure will help draw in the flabby skin. These are the settings that I've found work the best:

Brush Size	50
Brush Density	60
Brush Pressure	60
Brush Rate	80

Take a look at Figure 3.22. This is the woman before any Liquify adjustments. What you want to do here is run the tool along the cheeks, much as you would if using the High-lighter during an extraction. Do not linger in one place for long; move the mouse as fluidly

Figure 3.22: Time to reduce those features

Figure 3.23: Ah, to be young again!

Figure 3.24: New layer for hair coloring

Figure 3.25: Photoshop hair treatments

as possible. Reduce the nose size, and pucker the areas above and below her eyes to open them a bit. Also, move along the edges of her neck to slim it.

Work on the man in a like manner. You need not be as detailed with him, because the Liquify would distort his face beyond the point of being recognizable. Reduce his nose, open the eyes, and slim his cheeks, and that should be enough (see Figure 3.23).

Once finished Liquifying, you can employ the hair coloring techniques described in the previous chapter. Note that proceeding with hair coloring will most likely make the image retouching look obvious, so if you want a natural feel to the end result, I'd forgo treating the hair. I'll proceed with hair treatments here, but thought you should be aware of the downside.

As a refresher, I'll step through the process very quickly:

Select a color for the woman's hair and place it in the foreground. Create a new layer (see Figure 3.24).

Change the blending mode of the new layer to Color and, with the Paintbrush tool, paint over the woman's hair in the new layer (see Figure 3.25).

Figure 3.26: Blending mode change for a more natural look

Figure 3.27: Taking the gray out

If the color is a bit stark for your tastes, change the blending mode for the haircolor layer (Layer 1 in this example) to Soft Light (see Figure 3.26).

For the man's hair, create a new layer and change the blending mode to Overlay. The gentleman originally had dark hair, so we need only replace the gray with black. Set the foreground color to black and paint over the man's hair in the new layer. Set the opacity of the layer to 75% to allow just a few of the lighter hairs to show through (see Figure 3.27).

When finished, you will have much younger-looking versions of the original pair. I hope that, when you are done, you will have a greater appreciation for the Liquify filter than when you started. It is a great tool for massive distortions of features, but is also very powerful and masterful at slight alterations. Often the slightest changes can make all the difference in the world (see Figure 3.28).

Before

After

Figure 3.28: Mid 60s to late 40s, thanks to Photoshop

Face-Swapping

This technique uses the image `face-swap.jpg` found on the CD. Please open the photo now.

Have you ever wished you could swap lives with someone else for a day? In Photoshop you can. Perhaps there isn't a lot of call for face swapping in the real world, but it is a fun little feature that friends and family find particularly interesting. Some magazines use this feature to place celebrity faces on the bodies of models for the cover of their respective magazine to increase sales; I'll let you ponder the ethics of this while keeping my opinion to myself.

To swap faces or body parts with another person in Photoshop, the process is fairly simple. Figure 3.29 shows a pair of ladies in close proximity to one another, so the lighting on each is nearly the same. That will help achieve a decent face change.

When changing faces, it is best to use images that have the same dimensions as well as lighting from the same direction. This will help the final image trick the eye of the viewer.

Before performing cosmetic surgery on one of this pair, their faces need to be at the same angle. The woman on the right has a slight tilt to her head, whereas the woman on the left is on a level plane with the horizontal dimensions of the image. In Figure 3.30, I have brought down a guide and placed it just above the left woman's eyes so you can see what I mean.

The eyes of the woman on the right are not level, however. To fix this, first duplicate the Background layer. Select the Magnetic Lasso tool and create a selection around the woman on the right (see Figure 3.31). If you have a problem getting all of her hair in the

Figure 3.29: I wanna be just like you...

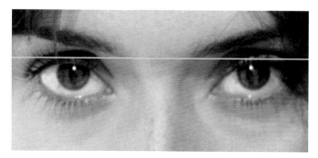

Figure 3.30: A level gaze

Figure 3.31: Select the subject on the right.

Figure 3.32: Rotate the woman so that her eyes are level with the guide.

selection, switch to the Polygonal Lasso after the initial selection is made and click the Add To Selection button on the top left of the Options Toolbar. Then simply create selections around the hair and portions of the woman that did not make it in the first pass with the Magnetic Lasso.

The Magnetic Lasso Tool

This tool is used for making selections around an image. The intent of the Magnetic Lasso is to snap the border of the selection to clearly defined edges. For the best results using the Magnetic Lasso tool, use it to make selections around subjects in high-contrast background, or backgrounds that allow a clear border to be defined around the object being selected.

Once the woman on the right is selected, she needs to be rotated so that her eyes are on the same horizontal plane as the other subject. Quick application of the Transform tools will perform this nicely. Choose Edit → Transform → Rotate and move the selection around until the eyes are on the same plane, or level with the guide, as seen in Figure 3.32. Accept the transform once they are level.

Choose Edit → Transform once again, only this time select Scale. Move the top of the Transform down so that the woman's eyes are level with those of her counterpart. You may need to also adjust the width of her face to prevent distortions (see Figure 3.33). Accept the transformation when you are ready.

While the selection is still active, create a layer mask for the layer. Ensure that the selected area is filled with white and the reverse with black, as seen in Figure 3.34. This sets the image up to wipe away the seams created at the top of the woman's head during the transform process. Switch to the Paintbrush tool and paint over the seams (seen along the sides of the top of her forehead) where the hair no longer matches the layer below. Set the foreground color to black and paint over those seams in the mask until the seams disappear, blending the hair with that of the layer beneath.

It is now time to put the Patch tool into play. Select the tool from the Toolbar and set the options for the tool as shown in Figure 3.35. Ensure that the Patch tool option is set to Source.

Figure 3.33:
Transform the
woman to match
the eyes with the
other subject.

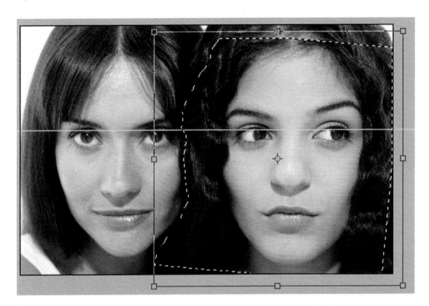

Figure 3.34: A
mask for blend-
ing seams

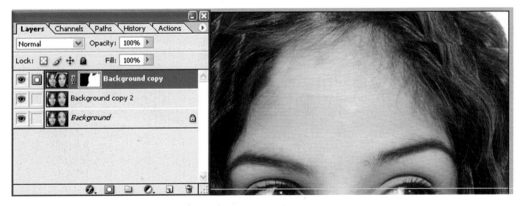

Figure 3.35: Patch tool options

Initially the Patch tool acts just like the Marquee tool in that you draw a freeform selection around the area you want to edit. Make a selection with the tool around the eyes, nose, and mouth of the woman on the left (see Figure 3.36). Although the Patch tool is set to Source, this can be a bit confusing because this is the area that will be replaced. Why the switch? Only the gurus at Adobe know, but I suspect that an evil joke is being played on the left-brainers.

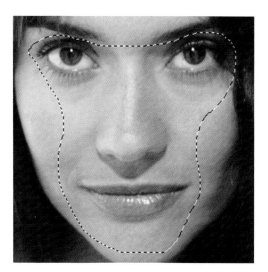

Once the selection is made, just click and drag the mouse to the right. Notice that the face goes away, and it appears that a new copy of the women is being moved around within the selection. Continue moving the mouse until the facial features of the woman on the right appear within the selection in the same spots as the left woman's original features. When you have it in place, the Patch tool will automatically match the color, texture, lighting and seams to the original face, blending it in to appear natural. If you find a few areas where the tool didn't quite do its job, simply load the Healing tool and clean up the edges to merge the new face with the old head. Figure 3.37 shows the final alteration.

Figure 3.36: Patch tool selection of the source (area to be replaced)

Figure 3.37: Not twins, but sisters certainly

Adding Hair

Open `balding.jpg` from this book's CD (see Figure 3.38). This guy is clearly happy about something, and for our purposes let's just say he recently joined the Hair Club for Men. 'Tis a smile of anticipation for successful results and renewed youthful vigor that only hair replacement can achieve. The gentleman in `hair.jpg` (see Figure 3.39), also on this book's CD, seems much more serene; he has reached middle age with a full head of furry real estate. If photos are all one is concerned about, then Photoshop can help once again. It is an easy process to take the hair from one individual and affix the entire mop to another, and this technique will show you how it is done. Remember to try to use images where the head sizes are relatively the same and of the same disposition (facing forward, lighting, and so forth). You may certainly resize as needed, but using photos already of similar dimension and orientation helps cut down a few steps.

Figure 3.38: Anticipating new hair

Figure 3.39: No toupee for me!

It's time for a little extraction action. Select the `hair.jpg` image and duplicate the Background layer. With the duplicate layer active, choose Filter → Extract. Enter these settings in the Extract dialog box:

Tool Options:	
Brush Size	34
Highlight	Green
Fill	Blue
Smart Highlighting	No

Extraction:	
Textured Image	No
Smooth	0
Force Foreground	No

Preview:	
Display	None
Show Highlight	Yes
Show Fill	Yes

When using the Extract Filter, you can toggle through the controls on the right on both the Mac and the PC by hitting the Tab key to cycle from the top, or pressing Shift+Tab to cycle from the bottom. If you need to move the image around while highlighting, hold down the spacebar to temporarily activate the Hand tool, move the image into place, and release the spacebar.

There are a few stray hairs seen along the edge, so use the highlighter to cover these as you proceed (see Figure 3.40). Just highlight the edges of the hair, but along the forehead where the hair can be seen coming from the follicles, you will certainly pick up some skin during the extraction. Don't worry, because this can be cleaned up shortly. Once the hair has been completely outlined, fill the area with the paint bucket (see Figure 3.41).

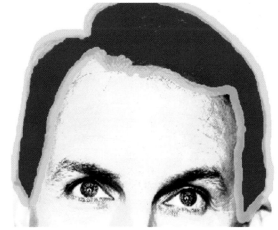

Figure 3.40: Highlight the fine hairs.　　*Figure 3.41: Highlight and fill the highlighted area.*

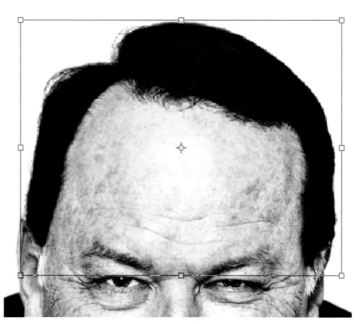

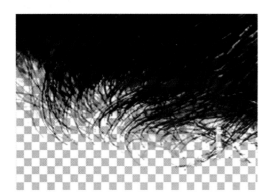

Figure 3.42: Hair extracted from the follicles   *Figure 3.43: Transform the hair to fit the head.*

Click Preview. Take care to look along the hairline of the forehead to ensure that the fine hairs coming from the follicles have been picked up in the extraction (see Figure 3.42). If not, you may need to backtrack and try again.

Once the extraction is satisfactory, hit Return/Enter to accept it (or just press OK). Copy the layer and paste it into a new layer in the `balding.jpg` image. Use the Transform tools to resize the hair to the man's scalp (see Figure 3.43). When you have it resized and in place, hit Return/Enter to accept the transformation.

There was a stark difference in color and luminance between the two images, as is now apparent with the hair on the new head. This can be corrected easily enough with the new Match Color dialog box. Choose Image → Adjustments → Match Color.

Match Color

What is Match Color, you may ask? It is new to Photoshop CS, so a brief description is warranted. Basically, it allows you to match tone and luminance between layers in the same image. The image works as both source and destination for the tonal correction, so you can actually match layers that normally do not belong together (in this case, the hair with the head) so that they appear to be from the same original image. Very cool stuff, if I may interject a little praise Adobe's way.

This tool is very powerful, but in the wrong hands it can be disastrous! OK, maybe not that bad. The thing for you to note is that it works differently for every image combination, so experimentation with the sliders is a must. In this example, the following settings seem to give a good overall match:

Luminance	185
Color Intensity	80
Fade	80
Neutralize	unchecked
Source	`balding.jpg`
Layer	Background

Keep an eye on the image while making the adjustments. When you have a good match, hit OK. When using this command, you will note that some of the skin pixels picked up by the extraction have now blended with the natural skin tone of the balding man (see Figure 3.44). Figure 3.45 shows the final effect.

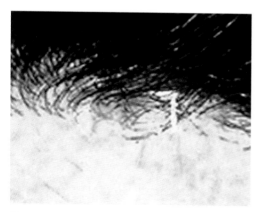

Figure 3.44: Roots fit to the new scalp

Figure 3.45: A happier man

Tattoo Removal

As a former submariner, I am often asked the question "Do you have any tattoos?", to which I answer in the negative. I had considered it on occasion, but just never made the leap. There was a time when tattoos had a negative connotation, labeling those who had them as either sailors or bikers. Tough guys wore them as a badge, even if their message was as simple as "Mom."

Times have certainly changed. Take a walk through the local shopping mall and note all the young women, some still in high school, brandishing tattoos across the small of their backs, their shoulders, or other places better left covered. I often wonder what those young people will do when the fad wears thin and they age a bit and have children of their own. Tattoos aren't like bell bottoms that disappear and then reappear 30 years later when they become fashionable again. I foresee a new wave of cosmetic surgery around the corner: skin grafting will be making a comeback.

And even before young Susie changes her mind about those tattoos, she still might think twice about sending pictures of them to rich Aunt Clara in New Canaan (who's going to leave her millions to somebody, after all). This technique shows one way to remove such selective body art from photos, such as that in `tattoo.jpg` on this book's CD (see Figure 3.46).

With Photoshop's extremely useful Clone Stamp tool, you can take a sample of a portion of the image and actually apply the sample to other portions of the image. In this instance I can capture small areas of bare skin around the tattoo and use those samples to make the offending blemish disappear.

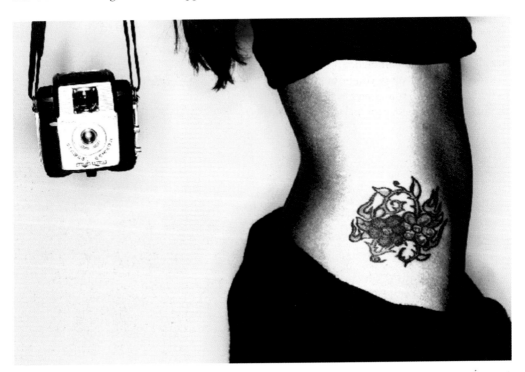

Figure 3.46: What was I thinking putting a tattoo there?

Select the Clone Stamp tool from the Toolbar. Set these options:

Brush	Feathered, Round, 200
Mode	Normal
Opacity	100%
Flow	100%

To adjust the brush diameter and hardness, click the small arrow to the right of the brush icon on the left side of the Options Toolbar. A window opens, allowing you to change the slider positions for diameter and hardness, or you may simply type in the settings (see Figure 3.47).

Once the brush is set up, you are ready to begin cloning. Move the cursor to an area next to the point where you wish to start covering. Hold down the Option/Alt key and click with the mouse on a portion of the bare skin next to the tattoo. Release the Option/Alt key, move the mouse over the tattoo next to where you took the sample, and click with the mouse. The tattoo will begin to disappear, as shown in Figure 3.48.

Continue sampling and cloning around the perimeter of the tattoo. Try to use samples that match the tone of the area adjacent to the portion that you are working on (see Figure 3.49).

Continue sampling and stamping until the entire tattoo is covered. Don't worry if an unsightly crease appears down the side of her abdomen, as seen in Figure 3.50. The next few steps will show you how to blend that in with the surrounding flesh. Increase the size of the Clone Stamp brush to 300 and decrease the opacity to 65%.

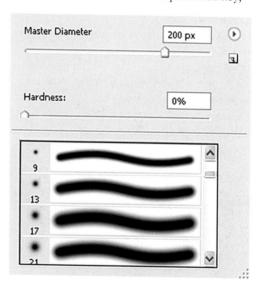

Figure 3.47: Adjust the brush diameter and hardness.

Figure 3.48: Begin applying the Clone Stamp tool.

Figure 3.49: Sample and apply the Clone Stamp tool around the perimeter of the tattoo.

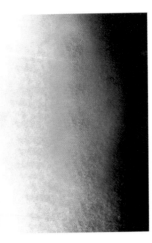

Figure 3.50: Cloned, yet not perfect.

Begin sampling neutral areas of skin (spots that appear to be somewhere between the two contrasts on either side of the crease). Apply the Clone Stamp and smooth out the crease. You'll note that the area covered may appear blurred compared to the skin prior to application of the stamp.

This can be corrected by using a tool similar to the Clone Stamp tool, namely the Healing Brush. They work in a similar manner, although the Healing Brush is intended to sew together those areas distorted by editing and blend them together seamlessly.

Select the Healing Brush from the Toolbar. Set these options for the Healing Brush tool:

Brush	300
Mode	Normal
Source	Sampled

In the same manner you used to sample with the Clone Stamp, sample areas of skin that have definite skin textures, such as pores, goose bumps and so forth, and apply those to the blurred area. In this case, I've taken samples from her ribs below the top. With the Healing Brush, it doesn't matter as much that the section sampled is darker or lighter than the area where the sample will be applied, because the Healing Brush will attempt to match the color of the sample to that of the area it is being applied to.

As you did with the Clone Stamp, apply your samples to the blurred area. When you are done, you should have a fresh patch of baby-smooth skin, sans tattoo (see Figure 3.51).

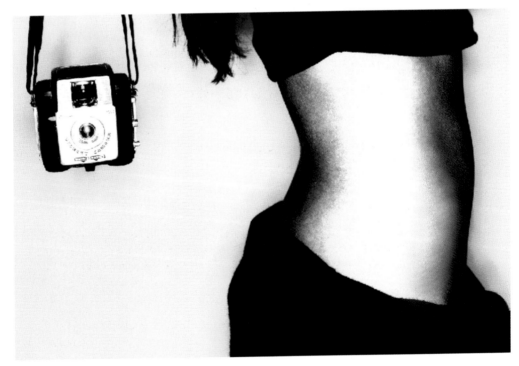

Figure 3.51: Look, Aunt Clara...no tattoo!

Figure 3.52: Pride cometh before the fall.

Before Braving the Needle: Digital Tattoo Application

Although I have no interest in having ink driven beneath my skin repeatedly with a needle on any part of my anatomy, there are quite a few people willing to subject themselves to the procedure. Perhaps I could offer my services to tattooists, allowing customers to see, in advance, what they will look like after the tattoo is complete? Photoshop will certainly allow me to do this.

Personal perspective out of the way, let me show you how to apply a tattoo to skin. Start with image `muscle-man.jpg` on this book's CD (see Figure 3.52). Here you see a rather beefy individual who evidently trains with weights on a regular basis. Perhaps he isn't quite satisfied with his progress thus far, and would like a cartoon reminder of his dream body forever etched into his skin. Duplicate the Background layer and rename it Muscles.

Before applying the other image as a tattoo, it is evident that an displacement map will be required in order to conform the tattoo image to the curve of the flexed arm.

Displacement Maps

Displacement maps are images that are used with the Distort filter. They determine the amount of distortion that takes place when the filter is applied by mapping the layer to conform to the light and dark areas of the map; the amount of displacement is determined in the Displace Filter dialog box.

Switch to the Channels palette. Starting with the red channel, select the red (see Figure 3.53), the green (see Figure 3.54), and the blue (see Figure 3.55) to see which gives the

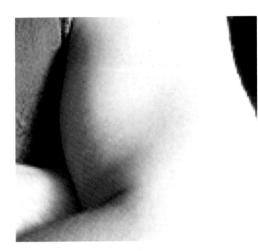

Figure 3.53: Red channel

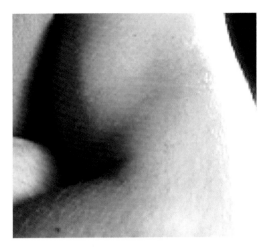

Figure 3.54: Green channel

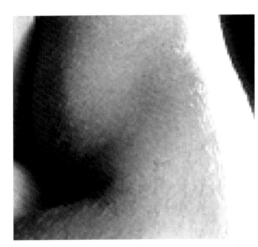

Figure 3.55: Blue channel

Figure 3.56: Duplicate the channel to be used for the displacement map.

best contrast between the light and dark areas. You can cycle through the RGB channels and see each by selecting the Channels palette and hitting the shortcut keys:

- RGB: Command/Control+~
- Red: Command/Control+1
- Green: Command/Control+2
- Blue: Command/Control+3

In this instance, I've chosen the blue channel. Duplicate the channel that you've chosen by dragging it to the New Channel icon (see Figure 3.56).

Choose Image → Adjustments → Brightness/Contrast. Decrease the brightness of the copied channel to about –18 but increase the contrast to about +70.

You may need to increase the contrast a bit more in order for the displacement to work properly. This can be accomplished by burning the dark areas and dodging the lighter areas and reflections, especially (if not exclusively) on the arm where the tattoo will be applied (see Figure 3.57).

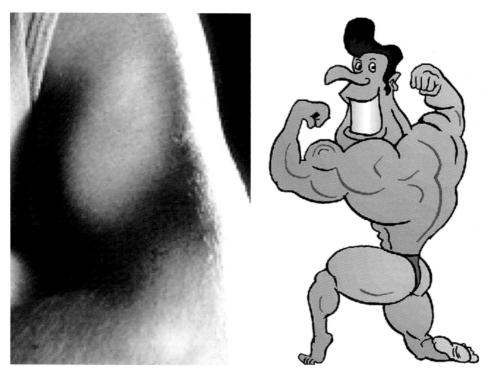

Figure 3.57: Highlights and shadows intensified   *Figure 3.58: Open the clip art to use as the tattoo.*

Select Filter → Gaussian Blur. Use a setting that takes away the rough characteristics of the skin while retaining the definition implied by the shadows and highlights. Use a setting of about 3 pixels, which in the viewer window appears to give the amount of blur/contrast that will work well for the map.

Right-click the blue copy channel and select Duplicate Channel from the pop-up menu that appears. In the Duplicate Channel dialog box, duplicate the channel as Muscle Map. Set the destination to a new document and name the new document **Muscle Map**. Click OK and save the new displacement map to your hard drive as a grayscale PSD file. I've chosen to simply place mine on the Desktop for easy retrieval.

Return to the Channels palette and activate the RGB channel group, deselecting the copied channel used for the map. This will allow you to view the original image in the Layers palette. If you like, you can delete the blue copy channel.

Once the displacement map is created, saved, and ready to be applied, you will need something to apply it to. I've found that digital tattooing is an excellent utility for using clip art that has been residing on my computer, unused.

Clip art reminds me of the denizens on the Isle of Misfit Toys in "Rudolph the Red Nosed Reindeer." Most clip art might have the luxury of being played with once, then are left forgotten or sent to the Isle of Deleted Items. Some clip art never find a home. Tattooing is one way in which Photoshop allows you to recycle these poor, once loved but underappreciated pieces of art.

When I need clip art in a hurry, I head over to my friends at Clipart.com (http://www.clipart.com). That line may sound like a commercial of some sort, but it's true.

For this portion of the tutorial, select image `clipart.jpg` (see Figure 3.58).

Figure 3.59: Transform the clip art to fit the arm in size and angle.

Figure 3.60: The clip art finds a new home.

The resolution/size differs from the muscle man photo, but that is fine in this instance. Press Command/Control+A while the clip art image is active to generate a selection of the entire image. Hitting Command/Control+C copies the image (do that now). Return to the muscle man photo and press Command/Control+V to paste the clip art bodybuilder into his own layer.

Click the Move tool. Drag the clip art to the area of the arm where the tattoo will be applied. In this case, place the clip art over the bicep/tricep. Decrease the opacity of the clip art for a minute…just enough to see the arm beneath so you can better position the new art. Then use the Transform tools to resize (Edit → Transform → Scale) and rotate (Edit → Transform → Rotate) the clip art to match the size and angle of the upper arm (see Figure 3.59). When the move is to your satisfaction, increase the opacity of the layer to 100% again.

Now you will erase the unwanted white pixels surrounding the clip art. Choose the Magic Wand tool from the Toolbar. With the Magic Wand tool, click on the white area around the bodybuilder and hit the Delete key. Deselect. See Figure 3.60 for the result.

You will now get some use out of the displacement map. Go to Filter → Distort → Displace. In the Displace dialog box, enter a horizontal scale of 10 and a vertical scale of 10. Because the displacement map is the same size as the bodybuilder image, the Displacement Map setting does not matter. Also, the clip art is small enough and placed in such a way that the Undefined Areas setting will not matter either (see Figure 3.61). Click OK.

The Choose A Displacement Map dialog box opens. Find and open the displacement map created a few steps ago. Click Open and the displacement map will be applied to the clip art layer. If the distortion is not to your satisfaction, you may run the Displace filter again with both settings set to 5.

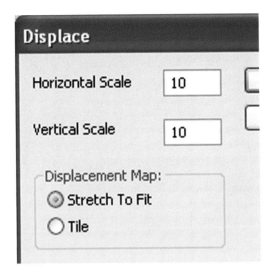

Figure 3.61: Adjust the Displacement Map settings.

Figure 3.62: Blending mode and opacity change

Now that the clip art has been properly distorted and conformed to the muscles of the upper arm, it is time to start blending the clip art into the skin. Note that the object is to have the drawing appear as though it is part of the skin. This is done effectively with a combination of Layer blending modes and Blend If settings.

Rename the clip art layer **Tattoo** in the Layers palette. Set the Layer blending mode to Color Burn, and reduce the opacity of the Tattoo layer to 85% (see Figure 3.62).

Click the Add A Layer Style icon at the bottom of the Layers palette. From the menu, select Blending Options from the top of the list.

In the General Blending section at the top of the dialog box, the blending mode and opacity settings just applied are displayed. The settings of concern now are the Advanced Blending settings further down in the dialog box. Open the Blend If drop-down menu and select the red channel. The bottom of the Blending Options dialog box contains two sliders that control how the selected layer will blend into the layer beneath it. Hold down the Option/Alt key and click the left slider point on the right side of the This Layer adjustment area. With the mouse, drag the slider until the top setting (the black adjustment) reads 0 on the left and the bottom setting (the red adjustment) reads 1 and 255 (see Figure 3.63). Click OK

Figure 3.64 shows the result of the blending adjustment. The bodybuilder clip art now appears to be embedded in the skin somewhat; it could use a bit more definition.

A few further enhancements are needed to really get this tattoo looking good. Duplicate the Tattoo layer and change the blending mode to Darken. Reduce the fill opacity to 60% (see Figure 3.65).

Open the Blending Options dialog box for this layer. Keeping

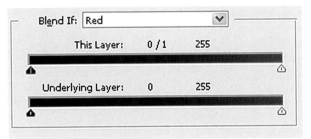

Figure 3.63: Blend If settings

Figure 3.64: Faded tattoo

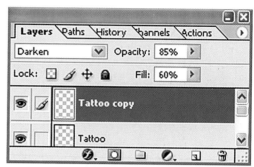

Figure 3.65: Duplicate the Tattoo layer.

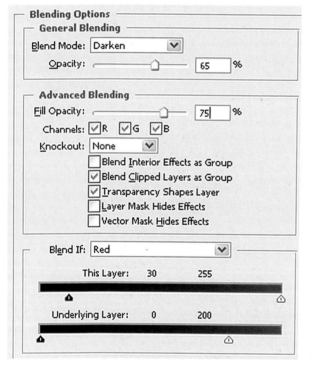

Figure 3.66: Adjust the Blending options.

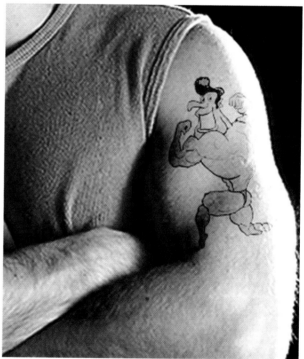

Figure 3.67: The tattoo thus far

an eye on the image, tweak the Opacity setting and the Blend If sliders on the bottom to darken the lines of the tattoo but make them still appear faded into the skin. See Figure 3.66 and use those settings as a reference. Figure 3.67 shows the result of this adjustment when applied: some color is still retained in the boundaries of the tattoo, but the lines have been darkened considerably.

As a final touch to help the clip art seem part of the arm, a mask can be applied to soften the dark lines where the clip art fades into the shadow. Select the Tattoo layer. Click the Add A Mask icon at the bottom of the Layers palette and select the mask. Click the Gradient tool and in the Options Toolbar, choose a gradual white-to-black gradient (the default gradient). Click the Radial Gradient button, with the mode set to Normal and the opacity set to 100%.

Click the Tattoo layer. Starting in the center of the clip art, draw the gradient out so that the dark edges receding in shadow begin to fade. When applied correctly, the layer mask will appear as it does in Figure 3.68.

To help enhance the blending and give the image a bit more realism, you need not work on the tattoo but rather sharpen the bodybuilder himself. To do this, run the High Pass filter trick from Chapter 1 on the bodybuilder layer.

My final image is seen in Figure 3.69. Try this with any old clip art; the effect works well on faces, wet skin, and pretty much any piece of human real estate you can think of. With practice, you just may find a hidden income: tattoo consulting!

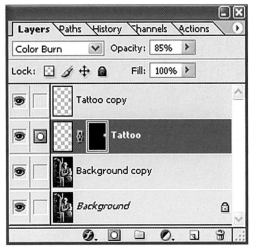

Figure 3.68: Gradient applied to the layer mask

Figure 3.69: Final tattoo image

four

Techniques for Artistic Effects

This chapter, *like the previous one, deals primarily with images of people; and again these techniques can be used on photographs where people are not present. The effects presented here can be applied to just about anything you can wrap your right brain around.*

My pocket dictionary describes artistry *as being ability attained by study, practice, and observation. I might add* imagination *to that list; once the ability is there and the observations are made, if there is no imagination, there is only duplication of what surrounds you or inspires you. A true right-brainer will get past this hurdle of imitation and begin creating new forms of art on old ideas. Likewise, an artist working with Photoshop can create new genres using tools intended for entirely different purposes.*

Although it continues themes already introduced, this chapter will break new ground, covering a few ideas not touched on yet as well as dabbling in what is fast becoming a very popular genre: Dark Art.

Adding Color to Black-and-White Images

In some circles, colorizing black-and-white images may be almost as controversial as retouching portraits. But we're not talking here about Ted Turner and classic Hollywood movies; we're talking about you, the Photoshop artist working with images that might become more interesting when you add some color.

There are two simple ways of adding color to black-and-white: with a color cast or by tinting individual colors.

Method 1: Adding a Color Cast

At times, especially when dealing with black-and-white images, just a simple overall color cast can have a striking effect. For this first technique, you will learn how to create a quick tone change on a black-and-white photo.

This technique uses the image elderly.jpg (see Figure 4.1) from this book's CD. Please find and open it now.

I love the expression in this image. Even though we are given only a portion of the man's face, the eye carries a definite spark of some emotion or intense scrutiny.

Duplicate the Background layer in the Layers palette. Later we will work with non-destructive Adjustment layers, but for this example I'm working directly on the layer (actually editing the layer pixels) to ensure that both processes are covered. Rename the background copy layer **aged,** as seen in Figure 4.2.

Choose Image → Adjustments → Hue/Saturation. When the Hue/Saturation dialog box opens, check the Colorize check box in the lower-right corner. Then adjust the sliders as seen in Figure 4.3 and click OK.

HSB, or Hue, Saturation, and Brightness, are the three fundamental characteristics of color. Hue is the color reflected from or transmitted through an object. Saturation is the strength of that color. Brightness is, of course, how light or dark the color appears. For more information on HSB, refer to the Photoshop help file on "HSB model".

This adjustment will give you a general tone resembling sepia. I am not going for an exact sepia effect, but just wanted to give an earthier feel to the image.

Figure 4.1:
"What are you
looking at?"

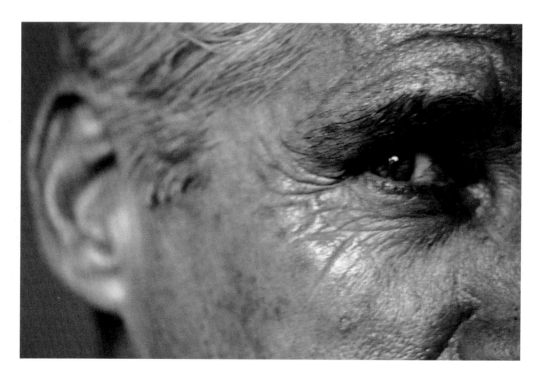

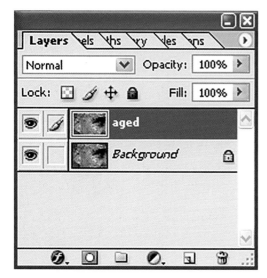

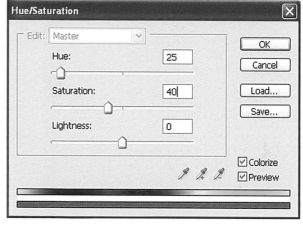

Figure 4.2: Duplicate the background layer, and rename the duplicate.

Figure 4.3: Adjust the hue/saturation of the new layer.

Painting Selected Areas in a Color Cast

Sometimes one adjustment you make to an image will suggest another. In this case, once I had tinted the image, I decided that painting the eye in a contrasting color would add even more interest. To do that, you'll revisit a technique in the previous chapter: painting with the Paintbrush tool in Color blending mode. Double-click the foreground color on the Toolbar to open the Color Picker dialog box. Find a light brown and click OK.

Select the Paintbrush tool and give it these settings:

Brush Size:	100
Mode:	Color
Opacity:	70%
Flow:	65%

Notice that I'm using a Soft Round feathered brush. The important thing here is, again, to change the blending mode to Color.

In the Aged layer, paint directly over the iris. Painting over the reflections (white) or pupil (black portion) won't matter; in Color blending mode, whites and blacks are not affected. Only the color information in the painted area, other than black or white, will change (see Figure 4.4).

Sometimes, depending on the color and the thickness of the application of the brush, the tone comes out a bit dark. By going over the colored area

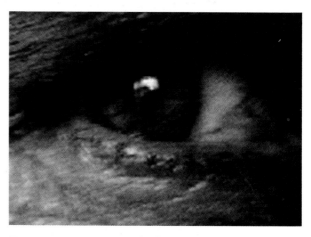

Figure 4.4: Painting in Color blending mode changes only the color information, leaving black and white areas unchanged.

with the Dodge tool set to midtones, you can lighten the color a bit. This adds extra life to the eyes; depending on how strongly you apply the tool, the eye can take on a mystical quality, burning with inner life. Select the Dodge tool and set the options to these:

Brush Size	44
Range	Midtones
Exposure	32%

Apply the Dodge tool to the irises, brightening the midtones. Don't linger too long in one spot, but just give it a general swipe around the perimeter of the pupil (see Figure 4.5).

Figure 4.5: Use the Dodge tool to brighten the colored area.

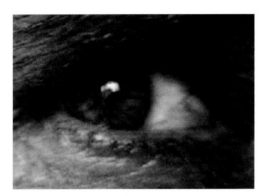

Occasionally you may desire a more vibrant or shocking color, and a simple re-application of the Paintbrush tool with a different hue can have a striking effect.

For instance, change the foreground color again, this time using a yellowing green. Select the Paintbrush tool again and, using the same options set up previously, paint over the iris. This setting changes the hue of the eye to a striking green, contrasting the eye with the overall tone of the rest of the image (see Figure 4.6).

Figure 4.6: Youthful spark in a wizened face

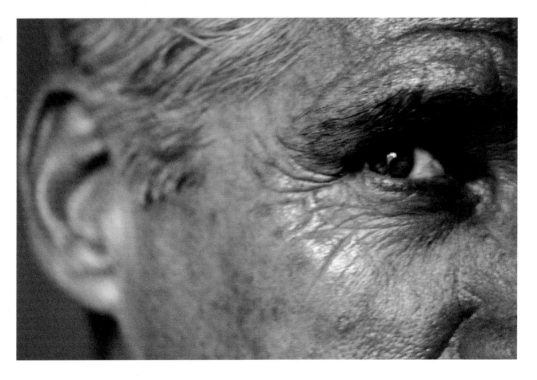

Method 2: Recreating the Hand-Tinted Look

Not every black-and-white image can be colored by something as basic as a hue/saturation adjustment and some painting. Some images require a bit more to bring out natural tones.

I'm not certain this technique renders what you might call natural tones, however. This technique is more in the style of methods used years ago to color photographs of their time. Color film wasn't commonplace 60+ years ago (yes, I realize that is the understatement of the year); so much of the color seen in old photos was added later. It gives the photo a retro feel, and I love retro.

Take a look at the image `BW-Portrait.jpg` on this book's CD (see Figure 4.7). Is that a cute kid or what? It is somehow hard to envision that this youngster would now most likely be in his seventies.

The first layer you will work on will correct the frame, giving it an aged paper feel. Create two copies of the Background layer, and make the topmost copy invisible. Select the layer just above the original background (see Figure 4.8).

I often switch back and forth between creating Adjustment layers (which applies the adjustment to all the layers beneath it) and actually applying adjustments directly to a specific layer. If I don't want the adjustment to be destructive, then an Adjustment layer works perfectly. If I don't care if the pixels on the layer are altered, or if I don't want the change to apply to the layers beneath, then I may just apply the adjustment directly to the layer. In this instance, I'm going to use an Adjustment layer. Create a new Hue/Saturation Adjustment layer and move the sliders as seen in Figure 4.9. This will give the image a slightly browned (sepia) appearance, implying age.

Select the topmost layer; this will be the second duplicate of the background created earlier. Create a mask for the layer. Using a black brush with the opacity for the brush set to 60%, paint around the frame edges in the mask. This will hide the black-and-white frame and reveal the colored frame beneath. The child will remain without color to this point (see Figure 4.10).

If you revealed a portion of the background also, don't worry about it in this case. The overall effect is to be one of age, so having the brown show through on the photo backdrop is permissible. The main thing is that the boy still be grayscale (see Figure 4.11).

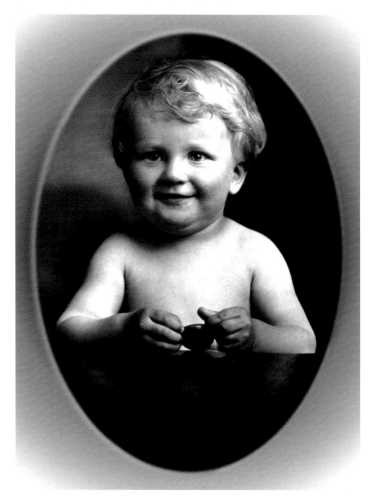

Figure 4.7: Somebody's grandpa

Figure 4.8: Background layer duplication

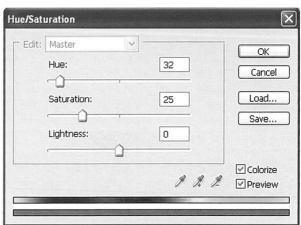

Figure 4.9: Hue/Saturation adjustment

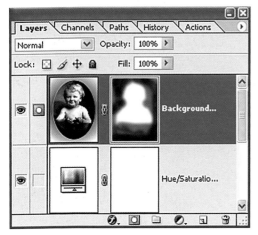

Figure 4.10: Mask away the black-and-white frame.

Figure 4.11: Child in grayscale

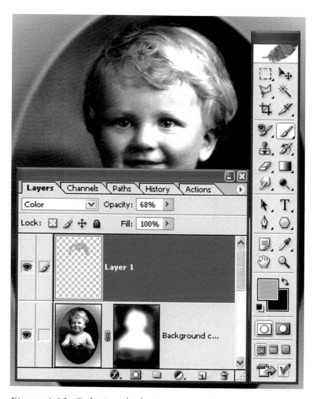

Figure 4.13: Coloring the hair

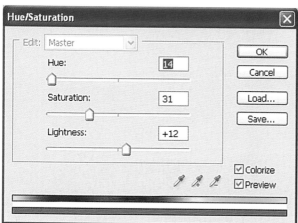

Figure 4.12: Hue/Saturation values…again

You will be making another Hue/Saturation adjustment, but this time to the actual layer. Choose Image → Adjustments → Hue/Saturation and enter the values seen in Figure 4.12. Click OK. This is going to give the child some color, albeit faint.

Create a new layer and change the blending mode to Color. As you should be well familiar with by now, select a foreground color for the hair and paint over the hair with the Paintbrush tool in the layer set to Color blending mode. If the hair appears too well colored, simply lower the opacity of the layer (see Figure 4.13). When the hair has been tinted, change the foreground color again, this time to a tone that will likely match his skin color (see Figure 4.14). In the same layer as the hair color, paint over the skin areas of the child (see Figure 4.15).

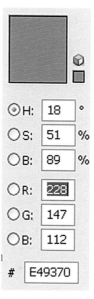

Figure 4.14:
A new hue for
the skin

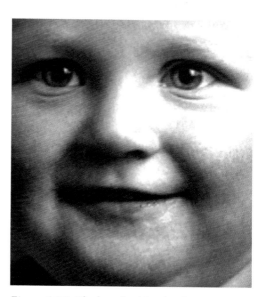

Figure 4.15: Black-and-white slowly comes to life.

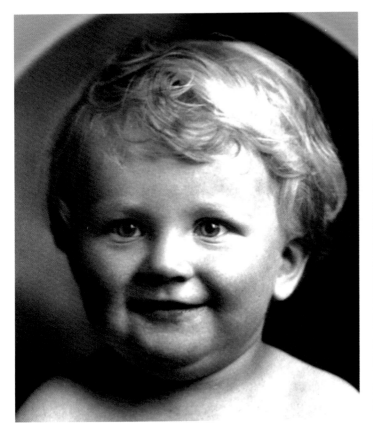

Figure 4.16: Boy with eyes, cheeks, and face tinted

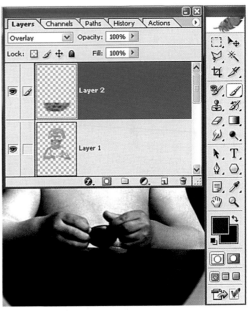

Figure 4.17: Painting the tabletop

Continue coloring in this layer, but change the foreground color to red to add some rose to the boy's cheeks. Switch to a light blue and paint over the irises…you should be well versed in this by now! Figure 4.16 shows the updated image of the child. It certainly looks like the old hand-colored photographs from years ago! Note that there may be some bleed-over of color beyond the borders of the hair and so forth. If you take a close look at this style of photograph, that was quite common and adds to the effect (so long as it isn't overdone).

For the final step, add some color to the table. Select a dark brown/red for the foreground color. Create a new layer at the top of the layer stack and set the blending mode to Overlay (see Figure 4.17). Now simply paint over the table surface. Figure 4.18 shows the final image, complete with a newly varnished table and the boy's reflection off the surface.

If you aren't sure what to do with a technique like this, I submit to you that photo restoration and coloring is becoming very popular, especially among people of the older generations. You might be able to work a little digital magic and make an elder smile…that is reward in itself. Chances are, though, they will pay you for it as well.

Figure 4.18:
Grandpa's baby
photo, fully
restored

Applying Textures

As with colorizing, there are two methods of applying textures that you should be familiar with: using displacement maps and duplicating mask layers. Here you'll try examples of both methods.

Method 1: Using Displacement Maps

This tutorial will help make you familiar with the process of conforming a pattern to the varying depths of an image.

This technique requires images `eye4texture.jpg` and `scales.jpg` from this book's CD. Please have them open and ready to proceed. Select image `eye4texture.jpg` (see Figure 4.19) and duplicate the Background layer. Rename this layer **Eye** in the Layers palette. Go to image `scales.jpg` (see Figure 4.20). Hit Command/Control+A to select the entire image, and then press Command/Control+C to copy the image. Return to the eye image and hit Command/Control+V to paste the texture into a new layer. Rename the newly pasted layer **Texture** and reselect the Eye layer, as seen in Figure 4.21.

Set the blending mode of the Texture layer to Overlay to gauge how the pattern looks when laid on top of the eye image. As you have not yet told the layer to conform to the face, the texture retains its stark straight lines (see Figure 4.22). It still looks cool, but it can certainly look better.

To conform the pattern to the face, you need to create a displacement map from the face and use it in conjunction with the Displace filter to warp the texture. Turn off the Texture layer (by clicking its icon in the Layers palette). This layer needs to be rendered

Figure 4.19: The foundation image

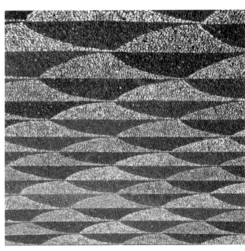

Figure 4.20: The texture to be applied to the face

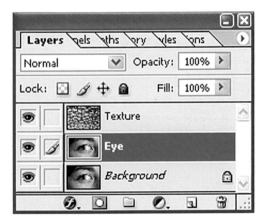

Figure 4.21: Layers palette set up

Figure 4.22: Pattern with the eye peeking through

invisible so that a map can be made of just the eye. If the layer remains visible, it will also be visible in the channels, and that won't do for the map. Select the Eye layer.

Open the Channels palette. Create a duplicate of the blue channel, because this is the one with the most contrast and will best serve for the map. Ensure that only this channel is active, as seen in Figure 4.23.

Figure 4.23: Duplicate the blue channel.

Choose Filter → Blur → Gaussian Blur. The edges need to be softened a bit so that when you apply the map with the Displace filter, the displacement of the texture will be smooth and conforming. Set up the Gaussian Blur as seen in Figure 4.24 and click OK.

In order to use this black/white/blurred version of the face as a map, it needs to be an image separate from the original. Right-click the blurred channel and select Duplicate Channel from the menu that appears. The Duplicate Channel dialog box will open. The top field in the dialog box really isn't too important for this particular tutorial, but the lower portion is. Change the Document field to New, and enter a name for the image. In this case, I've named it Eye Map.

Next, the new document needs to be saved to the hard drive so that the Displace filter can utilize it. Select the new document and save it in .psd format to the hard drive, in a folder that you can recall easily (see Figure 4.25). Now the displacement map is ready for use in the next step.

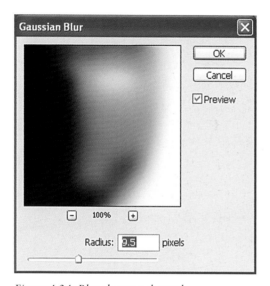

Figure 4.24: Blur the new channel.

Figure 4.25: Save the displacement map image.

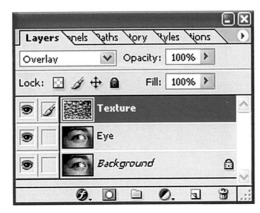

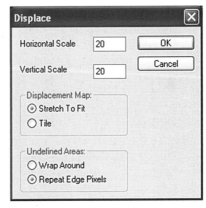

Figure 4.26: Activate the Texture layer again.

Figure 4.27: Adjust the settings for the Displace filter.

Figure 4.28: The texture now conforms to the curves of the face.

With the displacement map saved, it can now be used on the texture of the original image. Return to the eye image, and in the Channels palette you may either delete the blue copy channel or just render it invisible the same way you would for a layer. Click the RGB channel to restore color to the rest of the image.

Open the Layers palette again and make the Texture layer visible once more, again with the blending mode set to Overlay (see Figure 4.26).

Choose Filter → Distort → Displace. Set both the Horizontal Scale and Vertical Scale settings to 20, select Stretch To Fit for the Displacement Map style and Repeat Edge Pixels for Undefined Areas, as seen in Figure 4.27. Click OK.

Photoshop will now ask you to select a displacement map. Select the one that we just created from your hard drive (`Eye Map.psd`) and click Open.

Take a look at the eye image. Note that the lines in the texture have warped a bit, giving the effect of the texture traveling over the curves of the face (see Figure 4.28). Pretty cool stuff!

Figure 4.29: The new image with the eye color changed

As a final touch, I'm going to repeat the process of coloring the eye: adding a mask to the Texture layer, blotting out the eye with black paint applied to the mask, then painting a new hue over the eye in the Eye layer with the Paintbrush tool set to Color mode. Figure 4.29 shows my final image.

Method 2: Duplicating Layers (Inspired by Dark Art)

One of my favorite genres to spring from the creative founts of right-brained imaginations lately is the style becoming known as Dark Art. Inspired by the Goth movement, Dark Art gives the artist an outlet to imagine in shades other than calm and serene pastels. Some can be a bit tasteless, and I leave that aspect alone. However, darker moods can make for decent art that reflects emotion just as true (truer in some respects) as any frilly art house piece.

What you will find on many art websites with darker themes (a personal favorite of mine is Deviant Art at http://www.deviantart.com) is a form of texturing the subjects of portraits that is both shocking and fascinating at the same time. This tutorial will explore one way in which texture can be applied to a person with startling effect.

Take a look at `Brent-1.jpg` (see Figure 4.30) from this book's CD. I took this photo with a Minolta DiMage 7Hi camera of my good friend Brent. I should note here that Brent is one of the nicest people I know; the end image is no reflection of his personality. Duplicate the Background layer.

Figure 4.30: My good friend Brent

Figure 4.31: The working texture

Switch over to `cracked-earth.jpg` (see Figure 4.31), also on this book's CD. Select the entire image (Command/Control+A), copy it (Command/Control+C), and return to the Brent photo. Paste the texture into a new layer (Command/Control+V).

Rename the new layer **Texture Layer.** Create a mask and with a black paintbrush set to about 60% opacity, paint away the texture outside of the skin boundaries. You need not make these areas totally transparent, but just so that most of the cracks in these areas disappear. Set the blending mode for this layer to Soft Light (see Figure 4.32).

This applies the texture lightly to the face, but the effect you are shooting for here is to actually make the texture appear etched into the face. Duplicate the masked layer, this time changing the blending mode to Overlay (see Figure 4.33). The effect is taking shape, but still needs some cleaning up (see Figure 4.34).

First, let's do something about that color cast; the reds are coming through a bit harsh at the moment. Create another duplicate of the Background layer. Choose Edit → Adjustments → Hue/Saturation and move the sliders as seen in Figure 4.35. This will give the new layer a greenish tint. Click OK and change the blending mode for this layer to Overlay too (see Figure 4.36).

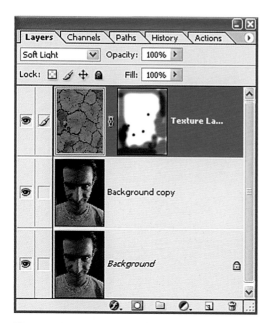

Figure 4.32: First Texture layer: Soft Light

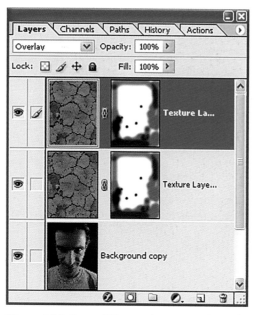

Figure 4.33: Second Texture layer: Overlay

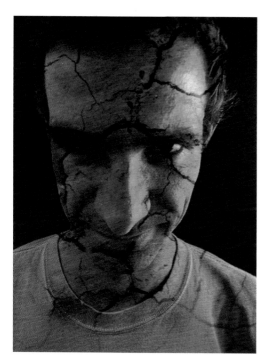

Figure 4.34: Still have some work to do…

Figure 4.35: Changing the hue to a green color cast

Figure 4.36: Green Brent, set to Overlay

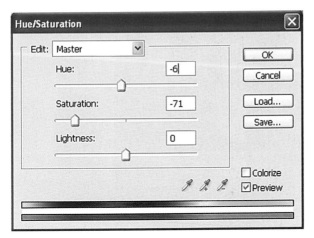

Figure 4.37: Reduce the saturation of the green layer.

Figure 4.38: Using a mask to reveal the eye beneath

The entire image is a bit bright—remember, this is intended to be dark, not cheery. Make a new Brightness/Contrast Adjustment layer beneath the texture layers but above the Brent layers and enter the following values in the Brightness/Contrast dialog box. Click OK.

Brightness	–20
Contrast	+41

Select the green layer and make a quick Hue/Saturation adjustment to it, as seen in Figure 4.37. Basically you just want to reduce the saturation to around –70. All that green is a bit overwhelming to the rest of the tone.

The eye could use a color change to make it stand out a bit. In the end effect, the left eye should be totally wiped out and the right eye should have an eerie glow. First, create a mask on the green layer and paint with black over the eye/iris on the mask to reveal the eye in the layers beneath (see Figure 4.38). On the layer beneath the green layer, use the Dodge tool to enhance the iris color as seen in the previous chapter.

Now select the Burn tool and enter these options:

Brush Size	400
Range	Midtones
Exposure	50%

At this point in the project, the face shadows, in particular on the left-hand side, are made darker by simply burning each face layer (with the exception of the background).

You may also darken the areas beneath some of the cracks to give them emphasis. The final image should look like Figure 4.39. Another option for making the cracks conform to the face is to create a displacement map, as you did in the previous technique. Experiment on a family member or friend...you will never look at them the same way again! If you show them the finished image, they may regard you with some suspicion as well....

Figure 4.39:
"Yes, I've had a
bad day. Why do
you ask?"

Painting with Gradients

This next technique is built on the idea of melding realism and art into the same photograph in the form of a transition. Granted, we have done a lot of transforming photos thus far, in particular photos of people. This technique employs yet another type of Adjustment layer to achieve the alteration: the gradient map.

The Gradient Map

This feature looks at the grayscale range of an image (transition of white to black and everything in between) and then uses a gradient to recolor those areas. The more colors involved in the gradient, the more color variations applied to the shadow and highlight transitions in the image.

Figure 4.40:
Sleepy child

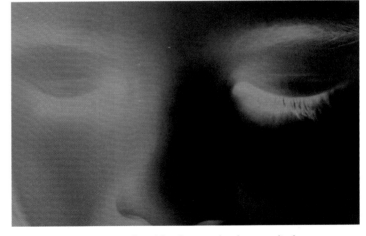

Figure 4.41: Create a gradi-
ent map Adjustment layer.

Figure 4.42: Foreground and background colors applied as a
gradient map

 Start with the image `sleepy child.jpg` from this book's CD (see Figure 4.40) and duplicate the Background layer.

The Gradient Map Adjustment layers are added from the same menu as the other Adjustment layers you have worked with. Open the menu at the bottom of the Layers palette and select Gradient Map from the list (see Figure 4.41).

When the Gradient Map Adjustment layer is created, it will load a default gradient using the foreground and background colors that you have selected. In the image seen in Figure 4.42, I had a tan hue for my foreground and black as my background. Note that the tan was actually applied to the darker areas of the child's face, and the black makes a gradual transition to the lighter areas.

With the Background Copy layer selected, choose Image → Adjustments → Desaturate (see Figure 4.43).

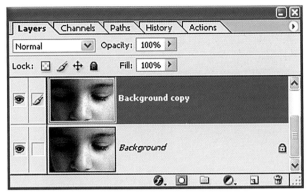

Figure 4.43: Desaturate the Background Copy layer.

Figure 4.44: Working with the mask

Figure 4.45: Mix of masking, blending mode, and gradient map

A really cool trick for making instant art from an image is the Difference mode. Change the blending mode of the Gradient Map layer to Difference.

The Difference Blending Mode

This blending mode looks at the brightness values of the base and blend colors, then subtracts the lighter. Blending with white inverts the colors; black leaves the pixels unchanged.

Difference blending is actually a personal favorite of mine, especially when working with gradients set to Difference mode. Try running a gradient over an image multiple times in alternating directions while in Difference mode. The patterns are pretty crazy, and can be extremely helpful when working in photo-realistic metal images.

Paint in the mask for the Adjustment layer with gray/black to hide the color change/gradient over the brow and eye on the right side of the face (see Figure 4.44). Note the changes, as seen in Figure 4.45.

Changing the gradient to a soft mix of pastels (see Figure 4.46) and continuing to darken the right side of the mask (Figure 4.47) will give some very interesting and stylish results. Experiment! That is the key here. This technique is not intended to achieve a specific end result, but rather to get those of you unfamiliar with gradient mapping into the swing of using this powerful tool for artists.

The results of the edits performed here are seen in Figure 4.48.

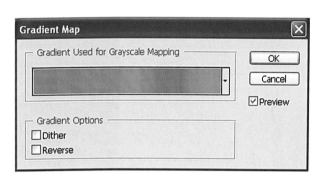

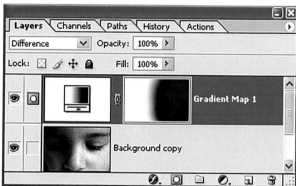

Figure 4.46: Pastel gradient

Figure 4.47: Darkening the mask further

Figure 4.48: Soft transitions

Lightening, Darkening, and Coloring

Before moving on to techniques that focus on in-depth projects and specific genres, I want to show you a fun way to transform stone into radiant glass. The techniques seen here are actu-ally variations of one used to lighten and darken standard photographs, but a little imagination can take any tutorial/technique and warp it into something completely dif-ferent, which frequently renders some unex-pected results.

From this book's CD, open `stone.jpg` (see Figure 4.49), which shows a hand holding a plain smooth stone of the type used in homeopathic healing. There isn't much to say about it as it is; the image just isn't that exciting. A few layers can spice this up a bit, hopefully saving the photo from the trash bin.

First, duplicate the Background layer. The thought here is to give the stone quali-ties that will make it appear translucent and glowing, so some highlights can be added with the Dodge tool on the surface to get things started (see Figure 4.50).

Next, change the foreground color to a dark gray (see Figure 4.51). This color will be used to darken the washout of most of the image.

Figure 4.49: A pretty boring image

Figure 4.50: Add a few highlights with the Dodge tool.

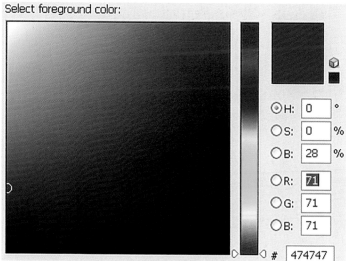

Figure 4.51: Dark gray for darkening

Figure 4.52: Starting to look glassy

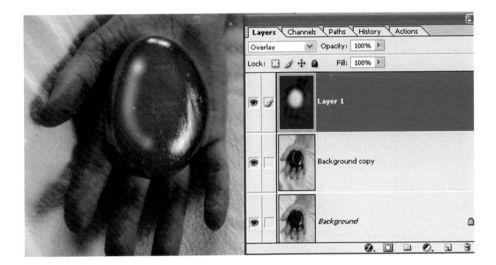

Figure 4.53: New foreground color

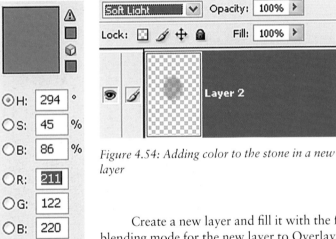

Figure 4.54: Adding color to the stone in a new layer

Create a new layer and fill it with the foreground color. Set the blending mode for the new layer to Overlay. This will increase the contrast of the hand image and darken the washout a bit. However, you are trying to brighten the stone. That will be fixed in a second. First, select the Burn tool and run it over the fingers in the gray layer to darken the hand a bit. Then select the Paintbrush tool and set the foreground color to white. This is where it begins to get interesting! Paint over the stone in the gray layer with white. The stone begins to take on a glassy quality (see Figure 4.52).

Change the foreground color to a pink/purple hue, as seen in Figure 4.53. In a new layer, paint the color over the stone. Change the blending mode for the new layer to Soft Light (see Figure 4.54).

Make another layer and fill this with a lighter gray than the previous gray layer. Set the blending mode to Overlay again, and paint over the stone with white. This time, however, don't paint stark white over the entire stone, but just run the brush over one side so that it glows more than the other. A bit of paint in the other areas of the stone is fine, but concentrate on the left side of the stone (see Figure 4.55).

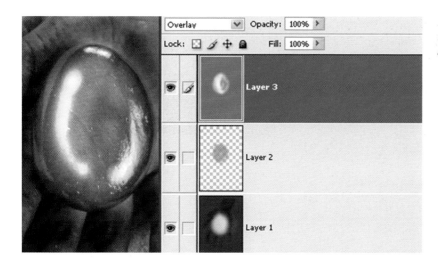

Figure 4.55: Further highlights and glow

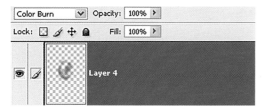

Figure 4.56: Deepen the color.

Create another layer and change the blending mode to Color Burn. Paint in this layer directly over the stone also, but don't cover the entire surface. This will make one side of the stone appear to have more depth of color than the other side (see Figure 4.56). The final image is seen in Figure 4.57.

That sums up the short effects. As we go into the next chapters, the techniques will be divided into specific genres, using all the techniques seen in the first few chapters plus a lot not covered yet. Now that you are warmed up, let's tackle photography art specific to your interest.

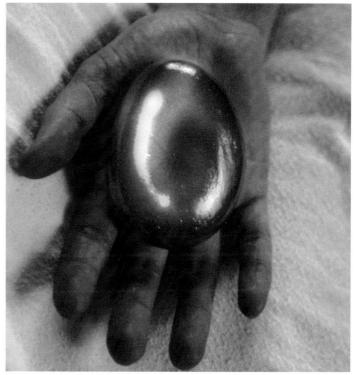

Figure 4.57: Glowing stone

two

PART

Digital Intensive: Photography as Art

An artist is the definitive right-brainer, yet artists have left-brained skills also in that they have spent some time learning and working with the tools of their respective genres. A sculptor who uses metal as a medium will know something about metallurgy. A photographer will know their equipment and how to make that equipment capture their subject in the best possible situation. An artist uses left-brain resources to reveal their right-brain dreams. In the following chapters, you will see a few ways that this artist (if I may be called such) processes ideas and realizes them. The process is broken down into three stages: Conceptualizing, Visualizing, and Realizing.

five

Landscapes and Nature

As children, *we have all sometimes looked up at the sky and seen misty ships, crocodiles, or riders on horseback in the clouds. It may seem fanciful, but to me these cloud-shapes are examples of how patterns repeat in nature. Over the last few years, the emerging science of fractals—colorful patterns generated by mathematical formulae that repeat endlessly—has begun to show us the significance of these patterns. All things physical seem to be tied to similar mathematical formulae.*

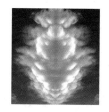

Our world consists of similar (in many cases identical) patterns and formulae, whether calculating the rotation of solar systems around a central point or studying the arc of a single rotation of a strand of DNA. The universe is a wondrous combination of fractals built with a specific design in mind, using math as the foundation to tie all things together and dictate the boundaries that keep everything in operation. To those who stand too close to the canvas, it may seem chaotic and random. Stepping back, one can see the entire picture, and begin to appreciate what the designer, as artist, envisioned when the first stroke of paint was lovingly applied.

Symmetrical Landscaping: Digital Manipulation

Concept Create a landmark using natural elements to warn travelers of danger.

Visualize In my mind, I see a tumble of stones displaying an unnatural symmetry. I'm sure you have seen stone faces in cliff sides; one of the more famous of these was recently overcome by nature and fell in New Hampshire. Another extreme and somewhat dubious case is the face seen in photos of Mars.

Realize You will create a natural-seeming landmark with unnatural symmetry using duplicate layers and masks. You will also generate a figure of clouds using a popular lineart technique variation.

To begin creating my landmark, I've chosen the photo shown in Figure 5.1. This is of a large stack of boulders that will work well to warn our fellow travelers, especially after we have our warning in place.

To proceed with this tutorial, please open the image `stones.jpg`, found on this book's CD. Once your image is open, duplicate the Background layer. Some of the process will be very similar to other effects in the book. No worries...this tutorial is about to take a decidedly different turn.

Choose Filter → Extract to open the Extract dialog box. This tool takes some practice, but once you get some extract time under your belt it goes much easier. This is far more powerful than the Background eraser, especially for dealing with hair, grass, shrubs, and so forth.

I realize that Extract was covered in Chapter 1, but because many Photoshop users have a lot of trouble with this feature, I'm going to walk you through the process one more

Figure 5.1: A natural landmark

Figure 5.2: Area to be extracted

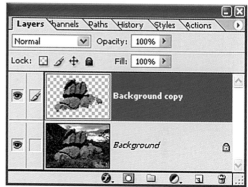

Figure 5.3: New layer for extracted pixels

time. On the left-hand side of the Extract dialog box, you will see a series of tools stacked vertically. The first of these is the Highlighter; use this to draw your selection. On the right-hand side of the view screen, you will see the attribute settings for the selected tool. Set the size of the Highlighter (diameter of the brush) so that very little overlap occurs on either the rock, which we will extract, or the landscape and sky that will be left out of the extraction.

Once you have the area outlined that you want to extract, there is one more thing you need to do prior to clicking OK. First you must select the Paint Bucket tool on the left side of the Extract dialog box and "fill" the area enclosed by the Highlighter, indicating to Photoshop that this area should be placed in its own layer. Select the Paint Bucket tool and click within the highlighted area. The selected area will turn blue (or whatever color you have set in the Paint Bucket options on the right side of the dialog box) (see Figure 5.2). Click OK.

Now the area selected by the Highlighter will be on its own layer, as seen in Figure 5.3. We can now manipulate the stone separate from the background, which will serve us well for the effect we are trying to achieve.

Duplicate the new layer in the Layers palette. Choose Edit → Transform → Flip Horizontal.

Take a look at the stone structure now (see Figure 5.4). We are beginning to get some nice symmetry, but because we have not yet applied a mask, the stone is still just a bit too natural.

What do I mean by "too natural"? Again, it has to do with personal aesthetics. I want my landmark to appear carved by nature, and not only look interesting but also surreal—something people native to the area might consider spiritual simply because of its uncanny appearance. A layer mask combined with the gradient 48-52 BW Gradient.grd on this book's CD will help us on our way to achieving this.

Create a layer mask for the new layer, and select the Gradient tool. Ensure that 48-52 BW Gradient.grd from the Gradients folder on this book's CD is loaded and ready to go. Draw the gradient straight across the mask horizontally. The resulting image (see Figure 5.5) is closer to what I'm looking for, but now it is a bit too unnatural. Am I ever satisfied with anything?

Figure 5.4:
A tumble of
boulders

Figure 5.5:
Unnatural stone

Because the edifice appears too unlikely to have been naturally carved, we can work with the layer mask to restore some of the original features, the trees, the post, and even cracks to give it a more natural appearance.

With the mask selected see (Figure 5.6), click the Paintbrush tool. If black is no longer the foreground color (it should still be), type **X**. Begin painting in the mask with black to reveal portions of the image that will give it its natural appearance back—for instance, the post (see Figure 5.7), the bush (see Figure 5.8), and so on.

Continue adding features by painting black on the mask. I've painted to restore nearly all of the lower-right portion of the original stone, keeping the symmetry of the top untouched (see Figure 5.9).

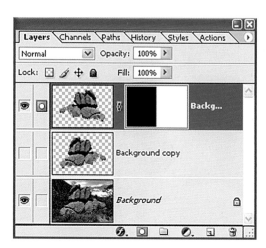

Figure 5.6: The mask selected

Figure 5.7:
Revealing the
post

Figure 5.8: Revealing the shrub

Figure 5.9: The new landmark

Figure 5.10:
Grizzly bear
headshot

Adding an Image in the Clouds

Now that our landmark has taken shape, we need to warn fellow travelers that they are heading into dangerous territory. Rather than a man-made warning, this image will have the message displayed in the clouds above the edifice. To create this effect, you will use the same steps that are more often used to create the effect of a pencil sketch from a photograph.

First, you will need a headshot of a bear, saved as `bear.jpg` on this book's CD (see Figure 5.10).

With the bear image open, duplicate the Background layer.

In order for the sketch effect to work, we will convert the image to Grayscale mode. Choose Image → Mode → Grayscale. When the dialog box opens (see Figure 5.11), select Don't Flatten.

Figure 5.11: Select Don't Flatten.

Figure 5.12: Applying the Gaussian Blur

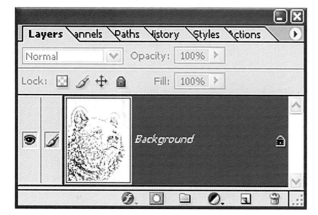

Figure 5.13: Merge all the layers.

Choose Image → Adjustments → Invert. Change the blending mode of the inverted layer to Color Dodge. Your image should now appear nearly all white.

The next step to this effect (keep this in mind for creating lineart images) is to apply a Gaussian Blur. Choose Filter → Blur → Gaussian Blur. In the Gaussian Blur dialog box, enter a blur amount of 30 pixels (see Figure 5.12) and click OK.

Press Command/Control+Shift+E to merge the visible layers together into the background (see Figure 5.13). The new bear image should look like an extremely well-done pencil drawing, as seen in Figure 5.14. Try this technique on some of your family or personal photographs.

Next, we will convert the sketched bear image into clouds for our original landmark project. Choose Select → Color Range. With the eyedropper, sample the white (see Figure 5.15) so that when you click OK, a selection of the white areas will be active. Don't worry about the unselected white or gray areas, because we have a use for them also. Choose Select → Inverse; you should now have the dark-to-light gray portions of the image selected.

Figure 5.14: The bear photo as a pencil sketch

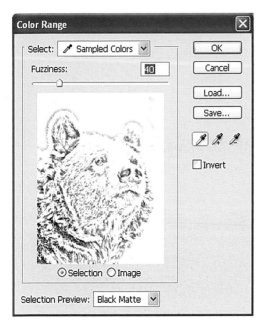

Figure 5.15: Selecting the color range

Figure 5.16: Paste bear into the original image.

Now move the selection to the original image. Press Command/Control+C to copy the selection. Go to the Landmark image and press Command/Control+V to paste the selected pixels into a new layer (see Figure 5.16).

Choose Edit → Transform → Scale. Grab a corner of the bounding box and move it toward the center of the transformed area to decrease the size. See Figure 5.17 and use those dimensions as a guide.

Select the Move tool. Drag the new bear layer beneath the masked layer, as seen in Figure 5.18. We do not want the clouds to appear in front of the rock, but rather want them to take their normal place in the sky. Also, change the layer blending mode to Screen.

To complete the cloud effect, first move the bear to the upper right of the rock. Next, open the Layer Styles dialog box for the bear layer. Select Inner Glow and enter the following attributes for the new bear cloud (see Figure 5.19):

Blend Mode	Multiply
Opacity	50%
Noise	0%
Color	Gray
Technique	Softer
Source	Edge
Choke	0%
Size	7-9 px
Anti-aliased	unchecked
Range	50%
Jitter	0%

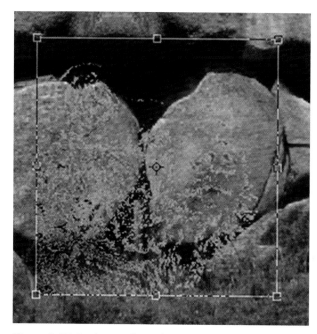

Figure 5.17: Reducing the scale

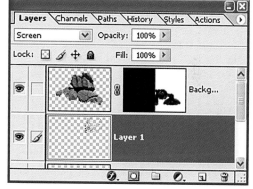

Figure 5.18: Move the bear layer.

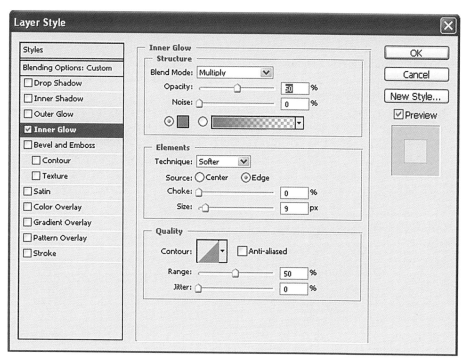

Figure 5.19: Adding an inner glow

Figure 5.20: A sign in the clouds

Click OK. The final image (see Figure 5.20) demonstrates a right-brain view of how a natural warning might appear. Did I really see what I just thought I saw? If not, Photoshop will certainly help me bring that imaginary vision to life.

Patterns in the Sky: Calendar Imaging

Concept Using a natural cloud formation, create an image of unnatural symmetry.

Visualize For this piece, I see a spectator staring skyward at a scene he or she simply cannot understand. Using the techniques learned previously, I see a cloud scene duplicating itself from a central line, the portents known only to the mind behind the pattern. This image can then be used in a variety of applications.

Realize Using the masking techniques that have been covered in earlier chapters and the previous tutorial, it will be a simple thing to realize this vision. You will simply take techniques learned earlier and apply them to a different scene.

I love clouds—always have and always will. I'm not sure what the attraction is exactly. Finding patterns in the sky as a child certainly helped feed my imagination—watching pirate ships transform into wispy horses chasing dragons across an expanse of blue. It was then when I began my first experiments in creating stories around the scenes.

Every culture looks to the sky for inspiration or an omen. What will mankind do if or when such a sign does appear in the expanse above?

Figure 5.21: A beautiful sunset on the beach

This technique uses the image `surf.jpg` from this book's CD (see Figure 5.21). Please open it now. For this technique, I've selected an image that gives a good foundation: a young boy standing in the surf, gazing at the sunset. It looks nice enough, but if you've seen one sunset, you've seen them all, right? Maybe not. Photoshop will allow you to change the scene that he's gazing at in short order. This technique is actually gaining in popularity; people love symmetry in asymmetrical situations, especially in photographic art.

When duplicating scenes in nature—or rather, when folding scenes over on one another—experimentation is certainly your friend. What do I mean? Simply that you shouldn't settle for the first version, but should try the following techniques in more than one way, such as reversing the direction of the gradient, swapping the black and white colors, and so on. There are literally hundreds of variations that can be achieved in the same image simply by altering the Gradient used in the gradient map. Allow me to demonstrate.

First, duplicate the Background layer and create a mask for that layer (see Figure 5.22).

Select the Gradient tool and load the Gradient `48-52 BW Gradient.grd` found in the `Gradients` folder on this book's CD.

Starting from the left side of the mask, draw the gradient across the entire image in a straight horizontal line. Figure 5.23 shows the result. Don't mind the foreground just yet, but take a look at the cloud formation that is created. Interesting, but it is good to check the other option available: what would happen to the sky if the mask were inverted?

With the mask active, choose Image → Adjustments → Invert. This will swap the black to white and white to black, mirroring the other half of the image and rendering an entirely different blend in the clouds (see Figure 5.24).

Figure 5.22: *Putting the mask in place*

Figure 5.23: *New scene with the first pass of the gradient*

Figure 5.24: *Same scene with the mask colors swapped*

Personally, I like the second rendering of the sky better, so I'll leave the sky as it is for now. Now you can work with the mask to reveal a single beach scene, leaving the sky folded over on itself.

Select the Paintbrush tool and set the foreground color to white. Paint over the black portion of the mask that covers the beach, revealing the rest of the scene in the masked layer. (Figure 5.25 shows the Layers palette.)

As stated in the title of this tutorial, the vision is to have this rendering show up on a calendar. Keeping with the theme of reflections and symmetry, create two text layers on the lower portion of the image. Use the first as a title (in this instance, Reflections) and the month and year on the other side. Space them equidistant from either side; use a guide to ensure that they are on the same horizontal plane also (see Figure 5.26).

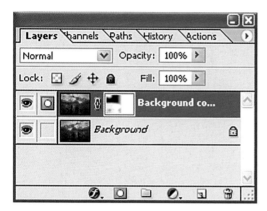

Figure 5.25: Use the mask to reveal a single beach.

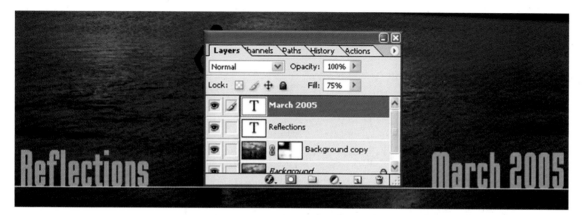

Figure 5.26: Create the calendar text.

Figure 5.27: Generate reflected versions of the text.

Figure 5.28: Transform the reflected text.

The right side of my cranium is telling me that the text still needs some work—how about reflecting the type? To do this, just duplicate the text layers (I'm starting with the Reflections layer) and choose Edit → Transform → Flip Vertical. With the Move tool or the Down arrow key, move the type to just below the guide (see Figure 5.27). Rasterize the layer so all the Transform commands become available and then transform the layer to appear as though it is reflected away from the light source (see Figure 5.28). I know this should be a shadow in reality, but this isn't exactly a real scene, so a little artistic leniency is warranted.

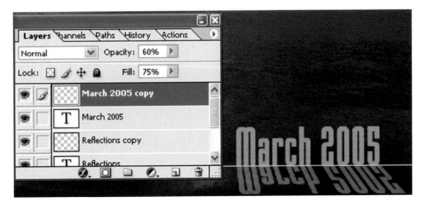

Figure 5.29: Reduce the opacity of the reflected text.

Figure 5.30: Strange horizon

Repeat the process for the type on the other side, and then reduce the opacities of the reflected type layers so that they are a bit faded compared to the original type layers (see Figure 5.29).

The final scene (Figure 5.30) shows the boy gazing at a scene that isn't quite ordinary, and is oddly beautiful and captivating. I see a crab on the horizon…how about you?

Figure 5.31 and Figure 5.32 show two more examples using the same process. I use this technique frequently, and have been able to generate images that are very interesting to behold. Try applying this technique to photos of tree branches, water reflections, or even cityscapes.

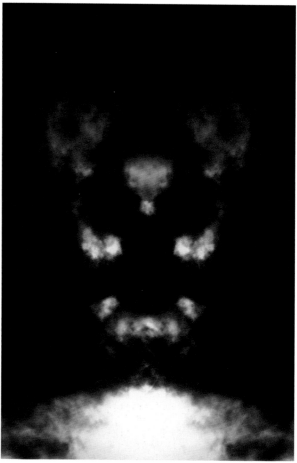

Figure 5.31: Cloud variation 1

Figure 5.32: Cloud variation 2

Neon Reflection on Water: Perspective Art

Concept Create a scene of a wet street with reflections of a neon sign evident in a pool of water.

Visualize As I consider this image, a hundred memories of nights long past traversing wet streets to get to a watering hole pop into my brain. I think of one of my trips to England when it rained constantly. So the scene I see is in the evening or sometime after dark, with water in the streets and reflections of neon playing on the surface of standing water in the street.

Realize To realize this vision, two images will be required: one of a street or sidewalk and another of neon. To realize the vision, you need not have a photo where water is present; the image you will use here is bone dry. Photoshop is going to provide the water.

This technique uses images `access.jpg` and `neon.jpg` from this book's CD. Please open them now.

Figure 5.33:
Recessed access
plate in a side-
walk

To start, select access.jpg (see Figure 5.33). When I first considered this piece, I imagined a cobblestone street or walkway with a few stones removed, the recessed area serving as the puddle of water. The access.jpg image, however, is even better suited to this purpose, because the access cover is recessed into the surrounding walkway and will hold a puddle nicely.

Duplicate the Background layer. Select the Polygonal Lasso and create a selection around the cover (see Figure 5.34). The area to the top left of the selection will be somewhat jagged, because the broken stones around the plate are more evident. You need not include the broken recesses in the selection, but don't simply create a straight-lined selection in this area either.

Figure 5.34:
Selection of the
cover plate

Move the selected plate to its own layer by choosing Layer → New → Layer Via Cut.

Next you will prepare the neon image to use as the puddle reflection. Go to the image neon.jpg (see Figure 5.35), select the entire image, copy it, and paste it into its own layer in the

Figure 5.35: I love the blues.

Figure 5.36: Paste and flip the neon image into the sidewalk image.

Figure 5.37: Transform the shape of the Neon layer to fit in the cover plate area.

sidewalk image. Flip the image (it will be a reflection so it needs to be reversed) by choosing Edit → Transform → Flip Horizontal. Reduce the scale of the new layer to fit over the plate area. If the plate extends beyond the edges of the neon layer pixels, don't fret; that will be corrected in short order (see Figure 5.36).

Now use the Transform commands to adjust the size and shape of the neon image to fit within the boundaries of the plate (see Figure 5.37). Once the transformation fits the correct dimensions, accept the transformation.

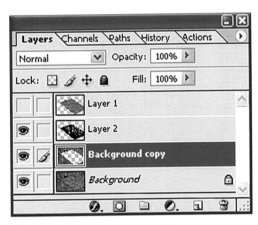

Figure 5.38: Select the Sidewalk layer.

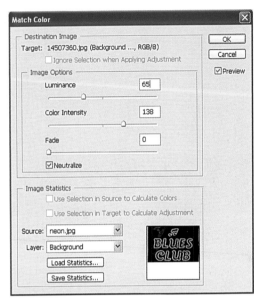

Figure 5.39: Match color settings

Figure 5.40: The sidewalk at night

Now you can start working to make the image match the neon, appear to be after dark, and look as though it is wet. How? Well, let's look at that. First, select the layer containing the sidewalk with the plate removed (see Figure 5.38). The neon image should still be open in the background of Photoshop. If not, you will need to reopen it and then return to this image and layer.

Choose Image → Adjustments → Match Color. This step will do a couple of things for you: you can darken the image to make it appear as though the photo was taken at night, and you can also create the illusion that the stone is wet. Before playing with the sliders, look at the bottom of the Match Color dialog box, at the Image Statistics section. Set the source to `neon.jpg`. The neon image will appear in the viewer to the right. Set the Layer to Background.

Now you can adjust the Luminance, Color Intensity, and Fade sliders. Use the settings seen in Figure 5.39, and keep an eye on the image itself. You will see it take on a blue hue with the lighter stones embedded in the brick becoming lighter, making it appear as though the sidewalk is wet. Click OK (see Figure 5.40).

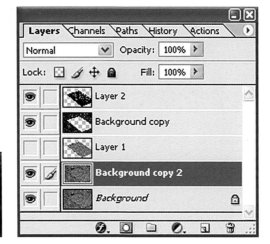

Figure 5.41: Darken the edges of the Neon layer.

Figure 5.42: Select the Sidewalk layer.

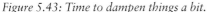

Figure 5.43: Time to dampen things a bit.

Figure 5.44: Use the Burn tool to add water to the cracks in the stone.

Select the Burn tool and set it to darken the Highlights:

Brush size:	125
Range	Highlights
Opacity	78%

First, darken the edges of the Neon layer so that the light edges blend into the dark recesses of the sidewalk (see Figure 5.41).

Next, select the Sidewalk layer (see Figure 5.42) and take a look at the cracks and seams where the bricks come together (see Figure 5.43). By burning these areas, you can make it appear that the seams are wetter than the stone exposed more prominently to the air. Run the Burn tool over these cracks, and also around the edges where the plate recesses into the sidewalk (see Figure 5.44).

The stone looks wet, but there is still some moisture that can be added. The neon is reflecting off a pool of water, at least in my brain, so that effect can be simulated with a few ripples. Select the Neon layer and make an oval selection with the Elliptical Marquee tool (see Figure 5.45). Choose Select → Feather and feather the selection by 5 pixels. Click OK.

Open the Filters menu and select Distort → ZigZag. Take a look at Figure 5.46 and enter the settings seen there to generate some ripples. Click OK. Make four or more oval selections across the surface and repeat the rippling process each time. Alter the width of the selections each time to indicate variation in the size of the raindrops hitting the surface (see Figure 5.47).

As the pool consists of water, some of the cover plate should be seen beneath the surface. To do this, make the cover layer visible once again and select the Neon layer. Reduce the opacity of the Neon layer to 70% (see Figure 5.48).

Reducing the opacity will wash out the color of the Neon layer, but a quick adjustment of the Brightness/Contrast will fix that.

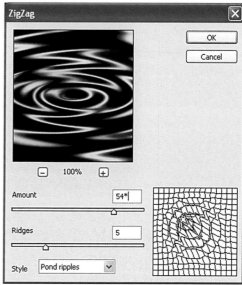

Figure 5.46: Use ZigZag to apply a few ripples.

Figure 5.45: Elliptical selection

Figure 5.47: Raindrops

Figure 5.48: Add transparency to the water.

Choose Image → Adjustments → Brightness/Contrast and enter the settings seen in Figure 5.49. Click OK.

The neon could be a bit brighter, as could the reflections on the ripples. Duplicate the Neon layer and set the blending mode to Screen. Increase the opacity of this layer back to 100% (see Figure 5.50). Figure 5.51 shows the final image. Does it look like water to you? Did the vision stay true to that mentioned in the beginning of this section?

Some possible applications: Transforming objects to conform to other molds is a good thing to know. You can conform labels to products, fit buildings to scenes where they do not belong, and so forth. Water and ripples can help you transform outdoor shots into pond reflections; you can add liquid to an image without a drop of fluid.

Figure 5.49: Brightness/Contrast adjustment

Figure 5.50: New Screen layer

Figure 5.51: Final water image

Enhancing the Flora

Concept Take a standard photo of a flower and dress it up to appear professionally retouched.

Visualize For this image, I see something simple. A quick color adjustment (or color change) of a flower, and then have that flower displayed in a stylish way—say, with a black faded border to make the color of the petals stand out.

Realize I'm willing to bet that you already have the process in mind. To realize this concept will take only a few steps of techniques already covered in this book. Specifically, you will use colorizing methods seen in Chapter 2, and place emphasis on the subject (Soft Focus) with the addition of a partially filled layer.

Nature photographers, in particular those who do not do it professionally or have the money to buy expensive equipment, often want to dress up their photos just a bit. Here's one way to do that. Again, this is not a recipe book for learning the program or a new trick in every section. This book is meant to show you how to apply effects in a variety of applications to enhance your photos and display them artistically.

This project uses the image `rose.jpg` found on this book's CD (see Figure 5.52). Please open it now.

Go to the flower image and duplicate the Background layer. My grandmother used to love yellow roses; this rose seems to be uncertain what color it wants to be. I say pick one and be

Figure 5.52: Washed-out flower

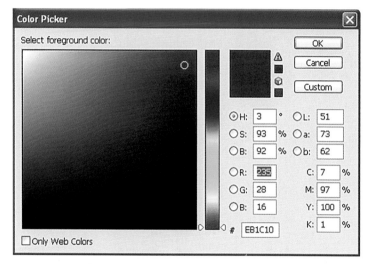

Figure 5.53: Select a new flower hue.

Figure 5.54: Recolor the petals.

happy already! Because this is just a flower, I suppose I'll have to pick a new color for it. Open the Color Picker for the Foreground and select a nice rosy red, as seen in Figure 5.53. Click OK.

Remember the different ways to recolor covered earlier in the book? This is the same general idea. This time you will be using the Color Replacement tool. Select the tool now and enter these settings:

Brush	175
Mode	Hue
Sampling	Continuous
Limits	Contiguous
Tolerance	30%
Anti-Aliased	Yes

Paint over the petals of the rose with the new color, changing them to a soft pink (see Figure 5.54). Continue until the entire flower takes on the new hue (see Figure 5.55).

The rose is a refreshing pink now, but the addition of another copy of the Rose layer set to Soft Light blending mode will darken the median and darks areas to bring out a bit more color (see Figure 5.56).

To create a darkened frame for the rose, create a new layer beneath the top layer set to Soft Light. Click the Gradient tool and set the Gradient to Transparent to Black, with Radial selected in the Options Toolbar (see Figure 5.57).

Figure 5.55: Recolor the entire flower.

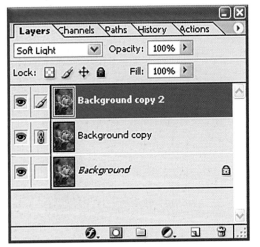

Figure 5.56: Soft Light flower layer to enhance color

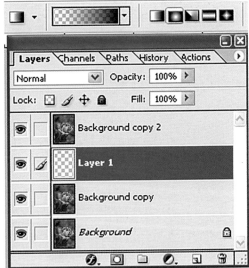

Figure 5.57: Gradient options

Click in the center of the flower and draw the gradient out toward the edge of the flower. Actually, you need to draw the gradient beyond the petals a bit so that the black doesn't cover the flower itself. Set the opacity for the Gradient layer to 75% to allow the greenery to be seen (see Figure 5.58).

Figure 5.59 shows the final image. Compare it with the original to see the changes; which appeals to you more?

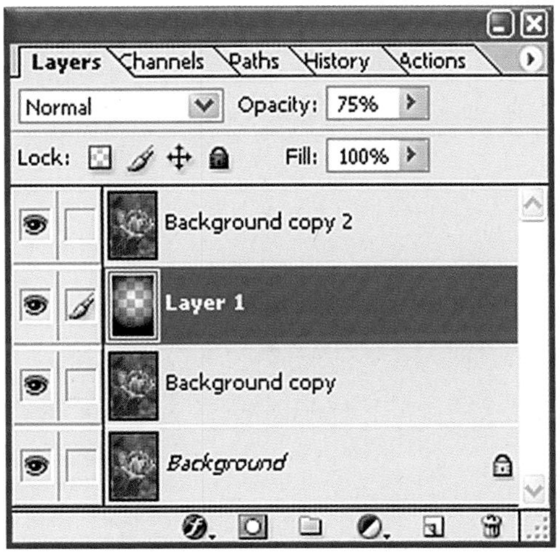

Figure 5.58: Reduce the opacity of the Gradient layer.

Figure 5.59: Finished product

Changing the Mood (Background Alteration, Tone): Dark/Goth

Concept The idea behind the next two effects is to take a photo of an area and turn it into a darker version of itself. I've chosen two examples: a graveyard, which is already fairly dark by nature, and a serene wood at sunset.

Visualize As there are two effects to be presented here, my brain has conjured two results. The first, to be centered on a graveyard photo, is to create a world of combined texture and lineart that will render a stark, gloomy version of the original photograph. The second, centered on a calm woodland path, is to re-create my version of a forest sense in nightmares and horror movies—a place devoid of color, warmth, and hope, where ghostly images may appear at any moment on the path before you.

Realize Both techniques will follow the same path to their fruition, although the effects are quite a bit different from one another. These will be realized by a combination of Difference layers, Adjustment layers, and a liberal application of curves. The next two techniques can be lumped together, because the technique to create the effects is similar, although the results are completely different. Here we will dip into the realm of the night, letting the phantoms of our imaginations show us their world: stark and cold and...dark.

These techniques will use the images `graveyard.jpg` and `forest.jpg` from this book's CD. Please open them now.

We will start with the graveyard photo (see Figure 5.60). Although some daylight is evident in this photo, the scene still appears bleak, with the stone faces in shadow. To start

Figure 5.60: Graveyard at sunset

creating the effect that I have in mind, duplicate the Background layer. Choose Image → Adjustments → Invert (see Figure 5.61).

Create another copy of the Background layer. Place this new layer at the top of the layer stack and change the blending mode to Difference (see Figure 5.62). This will draw out much of the color in the sky and clouds, as well as darken the edges of the tombstones and the chapel in the background. Why is that important? Because it will give the curve some darker areas to work on, as you will see (see Figure 5.63).

Before you get to the Curve Adjustment layer, first create a Hue/Saturation Adjustment layer with the settings seen in Figure 5.64. Click OK. I realize that this setting will take most of the color away that was created before, but what I mainly wanted there wasn't the color at all, but better definition to the lines in the image.

Now create a Curve Adjustment layer, as seen in Figure 5.65. If creating curves is still a bit tricky for you, I've included `GraveyardCurve.acv` in the `Curves` folder on this book's CD. Simply load and apply that curve from the Curves dialog box.

Lastly, take away some of the effects that the curve had on the clouds by painting in the cloud area with black, directly in the mask for the Curves Adjustment layer (see Figure 5.66).

Figure 5.67 shows the final image. Compare this to the original, and see that this effect brought even the text on the stone out of the shadows, where in the original photo this side of the church and headstones was in darkness.

Figure 5.61: Graveyard inverted

Figure 5.62: Difference layer

Figure 5.63: Inverted scene, more color, better definition

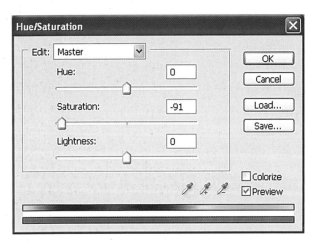

Figure 5.64: Hue/Saturation settings

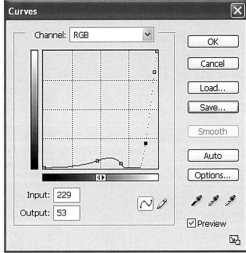

Figure 5.65: Curve adjustment

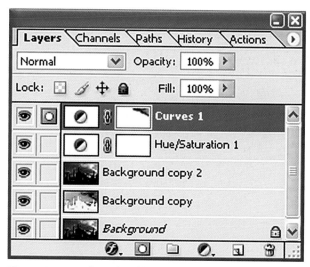

Figure 5.66: Reduce the effect of the curve adjustment on the cloud.

Figure 5.67: Gloomy surreal boneyard

Figure 5.68: A pleasant walk in the woods

Switch over to the image `forest.jpg` (see Figure 5.68). Using the same, or nearly the same, technique, this can be turned to a scene out of *The Blair Witch Project*, *The Ring*, or any other popular horror movie of recent years. Actually it reminds me of the woods in the Evil Dead movies. Ash Rocks! (Something for my fellow Deadites out there…)

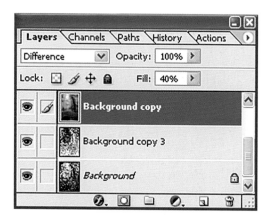

Figure 5.69: The
Background
layer duplicates
and their alter-
ations

Figure 5.70: Nature through an interesting lens

As before, create two copies of the Background layer. Invert the first (Image → Adjustments → Invert), and set the blending mode for the second to Difference. This time, reduce
the fill opacity of the Difference layer to 40% (see Figure 5.69). Figure 5.70 shows the new
forest…very pretty in an odd sort of way.

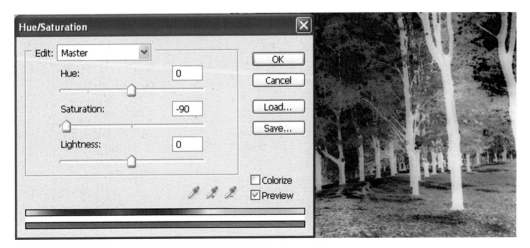

Figure 5.71: Hue/Saturation adjustment

Create a Hue/Saturation Adjustment layer again, with nearly identical settings to those seen in the Graveyard tutorial (see Figure 5.71). Next, create a Curves Adjustment layer, this time using the curve `DarkwoodCurve.acv` found in the `Curves` folder on this book's CD. Or you can simply re-create the curve seen in Figure 5.72 by hand.

The result is an image that almost appears to have been done with ink on a harsh negative (see Figure 5.73).

This closes out the chapter on Nature, although we are far from done working on natural images. Next we move on to animals...let's see what sort of right-brain mischief we can come up with in the animal kingdom. The Crocodile Hunter would be proud!

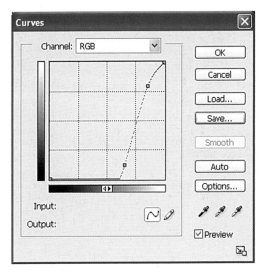

Figure 5.72: Dark wood curve

Figure 5.73: Haunted woods

six

Animals

At times, *photos lend themselves to the creative process simply by being what they are. Photographers are always trying to capture their subjects in the perfect light, the perfect pose, the perfect situation that conveys a mood, delivers a message, and so forth. The photographer reaches out with their art to invoke a response in the viewer.*

Photoshop can work with the digital artist to enhance the connection, to reinforce the link between artist/photographer and viewer. Whether the artist is going for shock value, emotion, or comfort, Photoshop can be used to enhance the mood of a photo using textures and pigments resident in the original, or combine images to change the mood of the message that the image conveys. This chapter takes natural elements and creatures from the world around us to demonstrate these points.

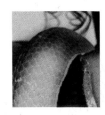

Comical Critter Alteration: Greeting Card Art

Concept If you have ever purchased a greeting card of some sort, I'm sure you have seen those with the humorous animal manipulations that have clearly been run through the Photoshop mill. Kittens and puppies in comical situations and poses can put a smile on the face of the most hardened, disgruntled card buyer. The vision for this project is to take a generally ugly creature (by most standards) and give it a human expression...literally.

Visualize Somewhere in the course of maneuvering through our teen years, my friend Brian Brown took to calling people Fish Lips. With that inspiration, I see a denizen of the deep that isn't the sharpest pencil in the box, but is too painfully dense and happy to care.

Realize Take a photo of a repulsive-looking fish and apply a human smile to the photo. To do that, you'll use a number of techniques that should be very familiar by now, including layering and the Clone Stamp tool. You'll also revisit the new Photoshop CS tool, Match Color, from Chapter 3.

Figure 6.1: A face only Momma can love

To start, open the images for this tutorial from this book's CD: uglyfish.jpg and smile-3.jpg (see Figures 6.1 and 6.2).

First you need to take the smile from the girl in the second image and copy it. In this case, the Magnetic Lasso tool should work just fine. Select the Magnetic Lasso tool and give it a slight feather of 2. Enter the following settings for the tool in the Options Toolbar:

Selection Type	New selection
Feather	2 px
Anti-aliased	Selected
Width	10 px
Edge Contrast	10%
Frequency	40

With the lasso, draw a selection around the perimeter of the girl's smile, taking in the lips as well as the teeth. If the selection doesn't grab all of the lips, switch to the Polygonal Lasso, change the selection type to Add To Selection, and simply include the portions of the lips that were omitted in the first pass. When your selection is complete, it will look like Figure 6.3.

With the selection active, press Command/Control+C to copy the selected portion of the face to the Clipboard. Return to the fish image.

Duplicate the Background layer on the fish image and name the new layer **Fish**. Paste the lips (Command/Control+V) into a new layer at the top of the layer stack and name this layer **Lips**.

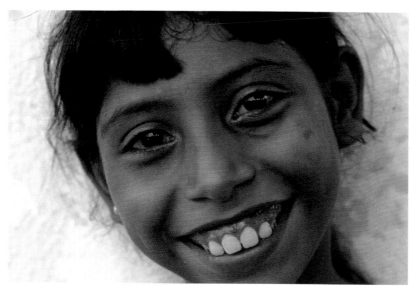

Figure 6.2: What a pretty smile!

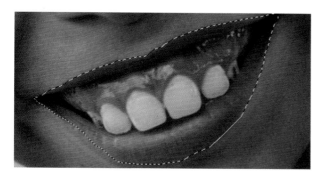

Figure 6.3: Select the girl's smile.

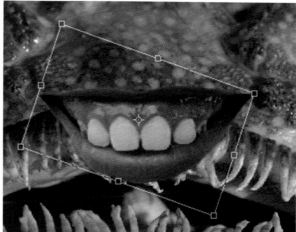

Figure 6.4: Paste the smile onto the fish image and rotate the smile.

You need to do a couple of things to get the lips in place and change them to the right dimensions to match the mouth of the fish. First, choose Edit → Transform → Rotate and with the mouse, grab a corner of the box and reposition the lips so that the top lip is parallel with the top of the image. Press Enter and accept the change once it is in position (see Figure 6.4).

Next, the smile needs to be resized to match the dimensions of the fish image. Choose Edit → Transform → Scale and change the size of the smile so that the corners of the mouth are positioned beneath the eyes of the fish (see Figure 6.5).

You'll see portions of the fish mouth peeking out from behind the smile; these need to be corrected to make this image as realistic as possible. In the Layers palette, turn off the

Figure 6.5: Lips to fit the face

Figure 6.6: Reducing the size of the fish mouth

Lips layer and select the Fish layer. Click the Clone Stamp tool and set the options as follows:

Brush	Round, Feathered, Size=250
Mode	Normal
Opacity	65%
Flow	100%
Aligned	Checked

Basically, the technique here is identical to that of the tattoo-removal tutorial in Chapter 3. Take samples from around the outside of the fish mouth and begin cloning the edges in so that they will be covered by the Lips layer. You need not cover the entire mouth, but just the areas that extend beyond the lips (see Figure 6.6).

In the Layers palette, turn on the Lips layer again and take a look at the image. If you need to clone away more of the fish mouth, do so now. Remember while cloning to take your samples as close to the area you will be covering as possible. Figure 6.7 shows the altered fish face with the Lips layer on.

It is now time to revisit one of my favorite features in Photoshop CS: Match Color. As you learned in Chapter 3, this is one handy tool for making images that don't normally belong together mesh in tone. Choose Image → Adjustments → Match Color and in the Match Color dialog box, enter the settings seen in Figure 6.8.

You may have to do some tweaking to your settings other than what you see in the figure. Just eyeball it until you get a good match between the layers. Once you are satisfied with the tone of the lips, click OK to accept the change.

Adobe gives you the option of saving Match Color settings for use later. To save the Match Color settings, first make your adjustments. In the Image Statistics area of the Match Color dialog box, click the Save Statistics button. Then simply name the setting and save it to a folder on your computer.

Figure 6.7: All layers on with the smile in place

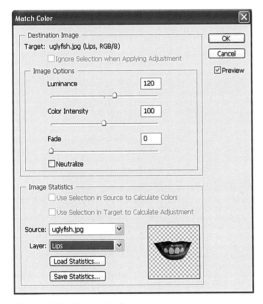

Figure 6.8: Match Color settings

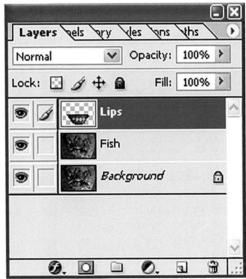

Figure 6.9: Choose the Lips layer.

Now use the Burn tool around the perimeter of the lips on the Fish layer to darken the area somewhat and increase the illusion that the lips belong on the fish. Here are the settings:

Brush	Round, Feathered, Size=175 (adjust size as needed)
Range	Midtones
Exposure	36%

Next, click on the Lips layer (see Figure 6.9) and begin to run the Burn tool around the perimeter. You may need to darken the highlights as well, so simply change the range to Highlights for the Burn tool and apply as needed.

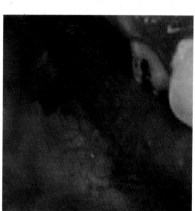

Figure 6.10: Using the Burn tool

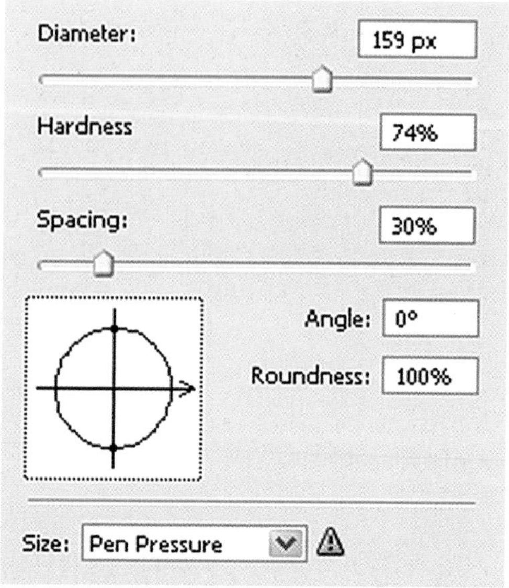

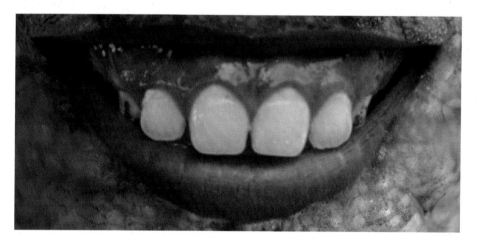

Figure 6.11: Adjust the Healing Brush settings.

Figure 6.12: Happy fish!

Continue working with the Burn tool until it appears that you have a good merge between the tone around the mouth and the edge of the lips (see Figure 6.10).

With the Lips layer selected, press Command/Control+E to merge it with the layer beneath.

Select the Healing Brush tool and adjust the hardness, spacing, and diameter of the tool (see Figure 6.11). Reduce the opacity of the tool to about 30%; take samples from around the mouth and lightly overlay them on the edge of the lips. Work around the perimeter of the mouth and gently blend the lips in with the scales (see Figure 6.12).

There are only a couple more steps to go now. Rename the merged layer to **Fishlips**. Duplicate the Fishlips layer in the Layers palette. Next, select Image → Apply Image and enter the settings seen in Figure 6.13. Once your settings are entered, click OK. What this

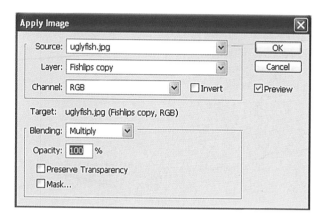

Figure 6.13: Apply image settings for blending the fish and lips more completely.

Figure 6.14: The missing link? Photoshop helps blend images from two worlds together.

Figure 6.15: I think I know this guy...

does is effectively use the image itself to increase the contrast and further make the lips appear as though they belong on the fish. Check out Figure 6.14.

Click the Healing Brush tool again and do some touch-up work as needed around the lips and on the fish. Reduce the Brush size to 90 or so, but keep the rest of the previous settings.

When you are satisfied with the image, you may want to add a message at the bottom and send it to friends, family members, and anyone else you care to give a smile to (or simply annoy with e-mail attachments). Figure 6.15 shows the completed image with text message included.

Animal Photographic Display: Website

Concept Create a full-page image to use as an Image Map for a themed website dealing with a group of animals.

Visualize There are so many ways to present images on the Web, choosing the perfect display for any single site is a difficult choice. I've chosen big, ferocious cats as the subject, and want the web page to reflect that. So what I envision is a large background cat with a few effects applied, some thumbnails for navigation, and a text title that has elements of the theme applied to it.

Realize Realizing this project will require one primary image, several for use in navigation, and some type. The primary image will be used as the background, and secondary images will represent links or categories available on the website. The type will serve as the logo for the page.

Figure 6.16: Panthera tigris

This technique is just one idea for displaying themed images on a web page. Chapter 10 looks specifically at web-related art, including sites targeted to different audiences and creating a functioning web gallery, so consider this project a teaser.

For the primary background image, open `white-tiger.jpg` found on this book's CD (see Figure 6.16) and duplicate the Background layer. Name the new Background Copy layer **Tiger-Main**.

This image is going to be used as a web page, so it needs to first be trimmed to a manageable size. As the monitor generally sees only 72 dpi and this is a large image, it can be reduced quite a bit. First, grab the Crop tool and trim down the photo, as seen in Figure 6.17.

Next, choose Image → Image Size. Deselect Constrain Proportions at the bottom of the Image Size dialog box and change the resolution to 72 dpi. Change the Width and Height to 800 pixels and 600 pixels, respectively (see Figure 6.18).

Figure 6.17: Cropped to a manageable web page shape

For an excellent reference and learning tool to help understand image size and resolution, refer to the Adobe Photoshop CS Help Files under the category (naturally) "Understanding image size and resolution."

I'm thinking that some increased contrast in the dark stripes and shadows will give me the drama I'm looking for, and to pull this off, a simple Threshold adjustment applied to a new layer should do the trick.

The Threshold Tool

This tool takes a grayscale or color image and converts it to a high-contrast version in black and white. The Threshold tool determines which pixels will be white (those lighter than the threshold) and which will be black (those darker than the threshold). Try using this command for converting photos to B&W Bitmap style art.

Duplicate the Tiger-Main layer in the Layers palette (see Figure 6.19). With the new layer selected, choose Image → Adjustments → Threshold. Move the slider so the Threshold level is 120 and click OK (see Figure 6.20).

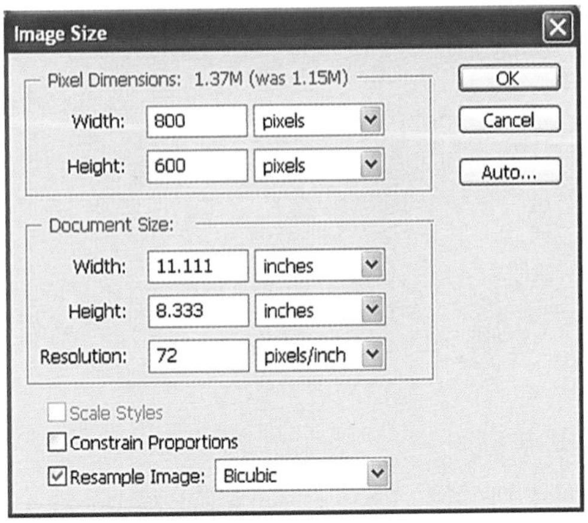

Figure 6.18:
Image size reset to
resolution/pixel
dimensions for
the Web

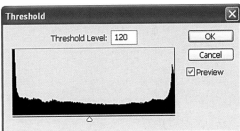

Figure 6.19: New
layer for the
Threshold
adjustment

Figure 6.20: Tweaking the Threshold slider

You will want to see the tiger beneath the layer the Threshold adjustment was performed on, so change the blending mode of this layer to Multiply. Even with the new blending mode, the eyes could stand out a bit more (I mentioned my addiction to eyes earlier), so create a mask for the top layer (see Figure 6.21) and paint with a black brush over the eyes in the mask, revealing the unaltered layer beneath.

Figure 6.22 shows the resulting image/effect. This gives an interesting merge of Photo and Art…you see natural fur and eyes, but the stripes and shadows appear painted.

At this point, you've created the background image for the site's home page. For the next step, adding thumbnail images to use as buttons on the image map, I'm going to give you a practical exercise using the File Browser and the new Automate features added in this version. Actually the features (most of them, anyway) have been around for a while, but now they can be accessed directly from the File Browser. What I'll have you do is generate thumbnails from within the File Browser itself, without having to manually open the images being turned into thumbnails.

Figure 6.21: Revealing the eyes with a mask

Figure 6.22: Merging paint with fur

Figure 6.23: Selecting thumbnails in the File Browser

The following example uses several images that, for copyright reasons, are not included on the CD. To proceed with this technique, you can simply use any folder of images on your computer to replace the one I use here.

Continuing with the idea that this image is to serve as a web page—in particular, one in which to display photos of animals—select a folder of images to go on the web page and open it in the File Browser. The File Browser allows you to flag specific files to be used for a specific purpose. First, select the images in the folder you want to convert to thumbnails by holding down the Command/Control key and clicking each thumbnail to be reduced (see Figure 6.23).

For ease of management, Photoshop allows you to flag specific images in a folder when you want to set them aside for a specific purpose. You will now flag those images selected moments ago by going to the upper left of the File Browser, just above the area with the folders list. You will see several menus: File, Edit, Automate, Sort, and View. Select Edit and choose Flag from the menu that opens (see Figure 6.24).

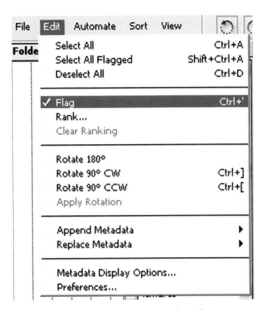

Figure 6.24: Flagging images in the File Browser

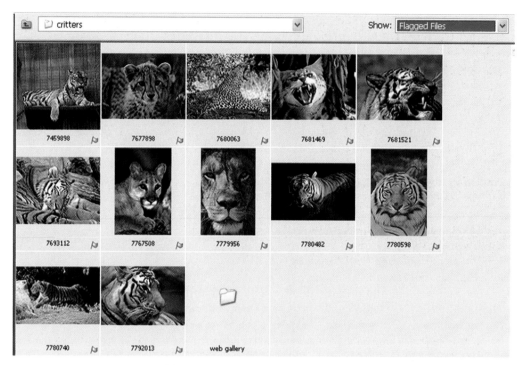

Figure 6.25: Create a manageable group of flagged images.

Now, on the right-hand side of the File Browser at the top above the thumbnails, you will see another drop-down box called Show. Open this menu and select Flagged Files from the list (see Figure 6.25). All of the files that were not selected will disappear, leaving only those that were flagged. This leaves a far more manageable group, and I'm sure you can readily see other applications for this feature. In short, it is a very handy feature.

It is time to create a few thumbnails. To do this, you will use the Contact Sheet II. Go to the Automate menu in the File Browser and select Contact Sheet II from the list.

The dialog box for the Contact Sheet is rather large, so I'm not giving an example. Here are the settings that you need be concerned with:

- In the Source Images area, open the Use menu and click Selected Images From The File Browser.
- In the Document area, set the proportions to a standard 8 inches wide by 10 inches high, resolution 72 pixels/inch.
- In the Thumbnails area, set the placement to 5 columns and 6 rows.
- Click OK.

Once you click OK, a new document is generated with two layers—a Background layer and a layer with the thumbnails and their information. I suggest saving this document somewhere on your computer.

Select the Rectangular Marquee tool and make a selection around the first thumbnail. Don't worry about the text below it; simply select the picture. Copy the selection (Command/Control+C), create a new document (Command/Control+N), and paste the thumbnail into the new document (Command/Control+V).

The thought here is to dress up the thumbnails a bit. Because this is a site on photography, perhaps giving the thumbnails characteristics of paper photographs will work well. I'm sure you have seen tutorials or images in advertising where the photo is displayed as a Polaroid-style picture. Let's give that a try.

With the new thumbnail document selected (the single thumbnail just created), ensure that the background is white; if not, fill it with white now and have white set as the Background color in the Toolbar.

Choose Image → Canvas Size. Increase the Width and Height settings so that the background extends beyond the border of the thumbnail, as seen in Figure 6.26. Click OK.

Chances are that the background is now huge compared to the thumbnail. You will want to trim that down. Grab the Crop tool and move the points so the area that will remain resembles a Polaroid snapshot (see Figure 6.27).

Select the Background layer. To add to the impression that this is a physical photo that you can reach out and pick up, draw a slight white-to-light gray gradient across the background. Set up the Gradient Toolbar as shown in Figure 6.28. Draw the gradient

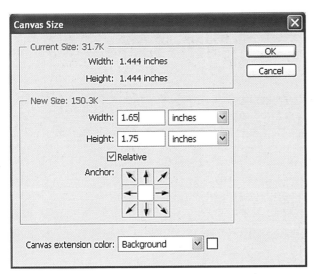

Figure 6.26: Increase the size of the canvas.

Figure 6.27: Crop the edges of the thumbnail image.

across the background, starting in the center of the image and drawing it to the upper-right corner. The change is very faint, as seen in Figure 6.29.

Once you have the thumbnail done, merge the layers together. Select, copy, and paste the thumbnail into the original Tiger document. Repeat the thumbnail process for a few more images (see Figure 6.30).

When I visualized the project, I mentioned a text logo using elements of an actual tiger. My thought is to borrow the fur from one of the creatures and apply that pattern to the logo. Find the image `tigerleap.jpg` on this book's CD and open it. Select the Crop tool and trim the image down so that only the fur on the side of the cat remains (see Figure 6.31).

Now you will save this image as a pattern. Choose Edit → Define Pattern. In the Pattern Name dialog box, name the pattern and click OK (see Figure 6.32). By making a pattern, you are creating an instance of the fur that can be applied to text, backgrounds, and so forth, and may be reused over and over again without the need to copy the pattern from a photo each time. The pattern is saved as a preset.

Figure 6.28: Slight change in gradient color

Figure 6.29: Gradient applied to thumbnail background

Figure 6.30: Paste the thumbnails into the original document.

Create a Text layer and enter some large type to use as a logo. I've named this, appropriately, Big Cats. The font doesn't matter much; use one that suits your taste. Place the new text in the lower-right corner; you may reposition it with the Move tool (see Figure 6.33).

Now you will apply the pattern to the text. Open the layer style for the Type layer and select Pattern Overlay. Select the pattern you just created using the tiger stripes, with the settings seen in Figure 6.34.

Next, select Color Overlay from the left side of the Layer Style dialog box. Choose black as the fill color and change the blending mode to Hue. This will wipe away the color in the stripes, leaving only black, white, and gray. The reason I've opted to wipe away the color

Figure 6.31: Selecting fur for a pattern

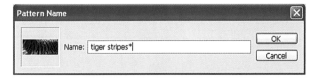

Figure 6.32: Define the pattern.

Figure 6.33: Create a text logo.

has to do with aesthetics: the fur on the primary tiger image is black and white, and I want the text to reflect that (see Figure 6.35).

> When working with a type layer, you can change the color quickly to either the foreground or background by using the shortcut keys. To fill with the foreground color, hit Alt+Backspace (Windows) or Option+Delete (Mac). To fill with the background color, hit Ctrl+Backspace (Windows) or Command+Delete (Mac).

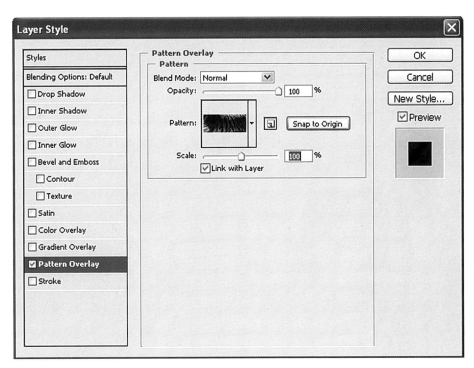

Figure 6.34: Apply the tiger pattern to the type.

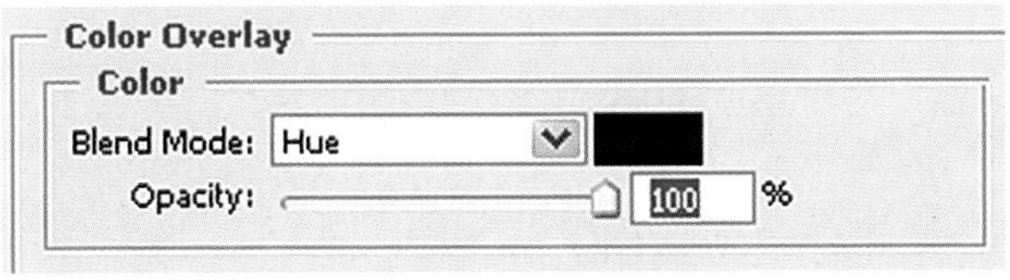

Figure 6.35: Overlay the text with black; set the blending mode to Hue.

Before you apply the layer style, select Stroke from the left menu. Use these settings:

Size	3
Position	Outside
Blend Mode	Normal
Opacity	100%
Fill Type	Color
Color	White

This will give a nice border so that the white areas of the fur don't blend directly with the white areas on the text.

Figure 6.36 shows the final page, complete with text below the thumbnails to indicate a few links. This is just one way out of millions of possibilities to create a themed home page layout from a few images. For more on the subject, please refer to Chapter 10.

Figure 6.36: Big Cats website image

Drastically Lost Creature out of Place: Collage

Concept Take an animal from one habitat and place it in another image where it doesn't (but could) belong.

Visualize What I want to do here is take a photo of a snake and place it on a person. Granted, people handle snakes all the time—but only by choice. However, Photoshop will let us perform the feat without having the model come in contact with the snake personally.

Realize With a combination of the right photos, a little extraction actions, and some blending and lighting manipulations, Photoshop will allow you to pull this off in no time.

Start with the images `treesnake.jpg` and `bareback.jpg` found on this book's CD (see Figures 6.37 and 6.38).

Figure 6.37: Snake on a tree

Figure 6.38: Reach!

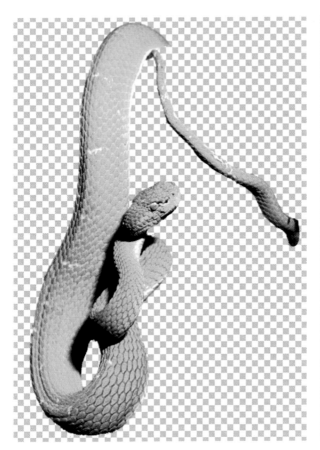

Figure 6.39: Extract the snake from its environment.

Figure 6.40: Place the snake in its new home—the model image.

Start with the snake photo and extract it from the background. (For more on extractions, please see the Extractions section in Chapter 1.) Figure 6.39 shows the snake after it has been removed from the background.

Now you will wrap the snake around the model. To do this, you first need to place the snake in the model image. Copy the snake from his document and paste it into a new layer in the model image. Duplicate the Background layer in the model image (see Figure 6.40).

Use the Transform tools to match the size of the snake to the model. Reduce the size and move the transform bars (scale works good for this) so that the tail of the snake wraps around the rib cage of the model, with the bulk of the snake hanging from her left shoulder.

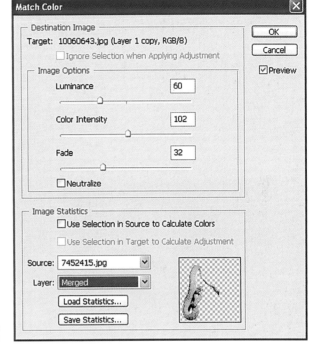

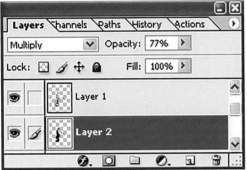

Figure 6.41: Create a Shadow layer.   *Figure 6.42: Match Color settings*

When the snake is in place, create a new layer directly beneath the Snake layer. Command/Control+Click the snake to generate a selection, then fill the selection with black in the empty layer. This will be used as a slight drop shadow. Once filled, deselect and apply a Gaussian Blur of 4 to the black. Set the blending mode for the Shadow layer to Multiply, and reduce the opacity of the layer to 75–80% (see Figure 6.41).

Select the Snake layer and choose Image → Adjustments → Match Color. Use the Match Color settings seen in Figure 6.42 to alter the tone of the snake a bit. When you are done, click OK.

Select the Burn tool and run it around the snake in the shadowed areas to take away some of the brightness and darken the shadow. Take a look at how the light falls on the model and where the shadows are on her, then darken the corresponding areas on the snake (see Figure 6.43). Darken any areas on the snake where they appear too bright, especially around the neck (see Figure 6.44). You also want to see where the shadow of the woman's head falls on the snake and darken this area.

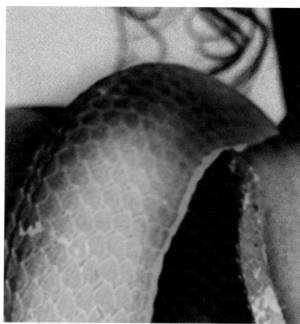

Figure 6.44: Create a shadow for the woman's head on the snake.

Figure 6.43: Burn in some shadows.

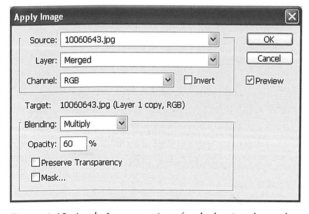

Figure 6.45: Apply Image settings for darkening the snake

You may want to darken the snake a bit more; running Apply Image on the Snake layer will help complete this. Choose Image → Apply Image and enter the settings seen in the Apply Image dialog box in Figure 6.45.

As a final step, try applying some lighting effects to the overall image (see Figure 6.46). Note in the final picture that the snake's shadow now appears on the woman's hip. You can do this by simply using the Burn tool on the model's layer in the same manner that you burned shadows onto the snake skin.

Figure 6.46: They don't pay her nearly enough for this job…

Crossbreeding Species: Digital Manipulation

Concept Combine two photos to generate an entirely new creature.

Visualize What I see in my mind is a combination of human and feline. We have dealt with both separately in this chapter, so the vision is a merging of those two worlds. I'd like to see features of both a lion and a person incorporated into the same face.

Realize Although it sounds as though this could be very complicated to pull off, that isn't the case at all. Using some of the masking techniques already learned (you are probably pretty well versed in masks by now), combining a lion with a person will be a cakewalk.

Although I'm usually working until the wee hours of the morning, when I can, I try to watch Late Night with Conan O'Brien. The humor is often rather base, but I'm a little off in my sense of humor. There is one bit they do on the show that combines photos of people to see what their children would look like. This is an offshoot of that.

Begin with two images from this book's CD: `leo.jpg` and `intense.jpg` (see Figures 6.47 and 6.48). Make a copy of the woman image and paste it into a new layer in the Lion document. Reduce the opacity of the woman layer to 60%; this way you can see the lion beneath to line up the images in the next step (see Figure 6.49).

Figure 6.47: King of the jungle

Choose Edit → Transform → Scale and increase the size of the woman's face so that her eyes overlay those of the lion. Also position the lips so that the lower lip extends below the pleat in the lion's upper lip below the nose (see Figure 6.50). When everything is in its proper place, accept the transformation.

It's time to meld the two faces with a mask. Create a layer mask for the woman's face layer (Figure 6.51). Select the Paintbrush tool and set black as the foreground color. Using a fairly large, round, feathered brush, begin painting in the mask to hide portions of the woman's face, such as the nose, cheeks, and so forth. Leave her lower lip visible, as well as her eyes and strands of hair hanging down on the left side of the image (see Figure 6.52). Continue working on the mask with black paint until most of her face is hidden, leaving only the eyes, eyebrows and the lower lip visible (see Figure 6.53).

Figure 6.48: Queen of the business world

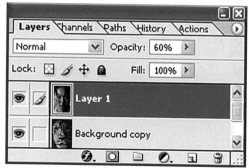

Figure 6.49: Preparing layers for the merge

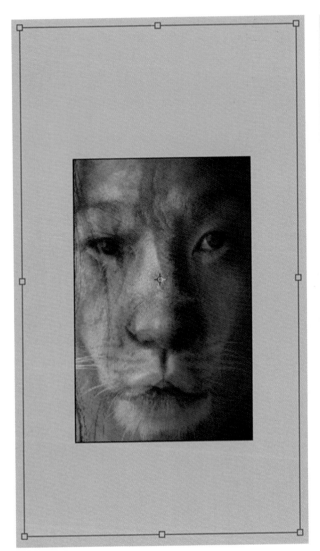

Figure 6.50: Match facial features between the two photos.

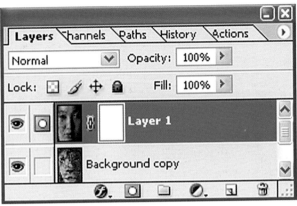

Figure 6.51: Create a mask for the female face.

Figure 6.52: Hide portions of the woman, revealing the cat beneath.

Figure 6.53: The lioness revealed

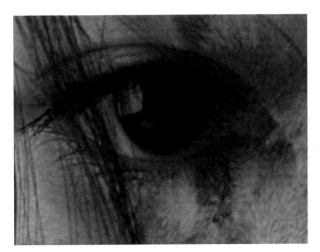

Figure 6.54: Add color to the eyes.

For a few final touches, add some color to the irises as you did in the coloring tutorials in Chapter 2. I love emerald on cats, so I've applied green to the eyes here (see Figure 6.54). Also add some color to the lips (see Figure 6.55).

Increase the size of the woman's eyes a bit with the Liquify filter. You need not make them too large, but a little enhancement goes a long way.

Lastly, increase the richness of the color of the overall image. You can do this with Apply Image (Image → Apply Image). Use the settings seen in the Apply Image dialog box in Figure 6.56. Once the settings are ready, click OK.

Figure 6.57 shows the final lioness photo. I love the color of this piece, as well as the seamless melding of facial features from both photographs for a combined whole.

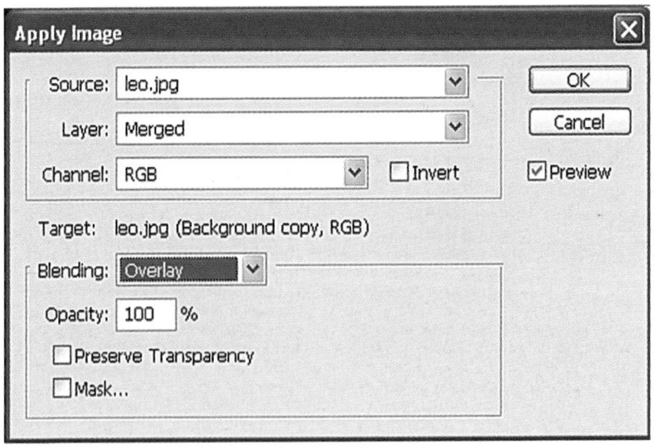

Figure 6.55: Add some red to the lips.

Figure 6.56: Apply Image settings for enhancing color

Figure 6.57: The lioness realized

seven

Objects

When I was younger, *everything art-related fell into two general categories: Cool or Dumb. I didn't understand then the spirit behind the art. I'd see a broken cup glued to a wall and, rather than appreciate anything the artist may be trying to convey, I'd chuck it into the latter category (I'm still not sure about that piece). Anything by Boris Vallejo—air-brushed, semi-nude women with giant winged reptiles—was Good Art, and anything else was decidedly Lame, Dumb, so on and so forth.*

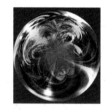

I still love Boris (www.borisjulie.com), *but now appreciate other forms of artistic expression. I never used to understand stationary objects or common household items taking prominence in photographic art, but can see that they actually play a vital role in advertising (yes, even advertising can be considered an art form), illustrating retro styles and making simple statements about our lives in the new millennium. Displaying a product to render it appealing isn't an easy process; an artist needs that right-brain imagination. This chapter deals with photos of objects used in art. There are a couple of pretty standard takes, and a couple that are possible only because Photoshop is in the darkroom. Let's get into it, shall we?*

Chrome Sphere: Digital Manipulation

If you are familiar with any of my online work or previous books, then you already know my attraction to metallic effects. I just love working with metal, and I'm not the only person out there with a metal addiction. Chrome effects especially draw a lot of interest, and Photoshop is an excellent tool for working in the medium without ever stepping into a forge or spending time with a welder.

Concept Using elements from a photograph, create a photo-realistic object completely unrelated to the original photo.

Visualize Through past experience, I realize the power Photoshop has for generating realistic spheres and orbs of all types, simply working with the existing filters. Spheres are easily generated from scratch, but can a photograph with reflective elements such as chrome be turned into a sphere using the same metallic color variations and reflections as the photo? You bet.

Realize To realize this project, a photo using an object that is highly reflective should give the desired reflective sphere effect. As an added touch, an additional reflection of a photographer will be added to the face of the final image. Your key Photoshop tools will be the Polar Coordinates filter and the Transform menu, along with some layer masking.

First things first: You will need a highly reflective metallic image. Because the end effect is a chrome sphere, the image will need a lot of chrome and the stark highlights produced by the process. For this technique, open WheelChrome.jpg (see Figure 7.1) from this book's CD.

To set up the Layers palette, convert the Background layer to a standard layer by double-clicking it in the Layers palette and renaming it. Name the layer **Wheel Chrome**. Duplicate the Wheel Chrome layer, and create a new Background layer filled with a dark color. I'm using a dark blue in this case. Make the original Wheel Chrome layer invisible, because you will be working with the Wheel Chrome Copy layer (see Figure 7.2).

If you have worked with creating spheres before, then perhaps you have used selections, Spherize, 3D Transform, and so forth. These

Figure 7.1: Reflections of chrome

are excellent tools for generating spheres, but this tutorial is a bit different: You are not creating a sphere from nothing, but want this photo to become a sphere. Photoshop allows for that process as well, and the trick resides in the Polar Coordinates filter.

Choose Filter → Distort → Polar Coordinates. You will actually run this filter a couple of times to generate the sphere, but for this first pass select Polar To Rectangular in the Polar Coordinates dialog box and click OK (see Figure 7.3).

That makes for a pretty strange-looking warp, but at this point you are nearly halfway to the sphere shape. The image requires a little perspective change before the sphere can be completed, so choose Edit → Transform → Flip Horizontal and accept the transformation. Then flip the same image vertically (Edit → Transform → Flip Vertical) and accept the transformation again.

Return to the Polar Coordinates filter, this time selecting Rectangular To Polar in the Polar Coordinates dialog box. In the viewer window, you need to reduce the image size in order to see the whole sphere (see Figure 7.4). Click OK.

The edges of the sphere are a bit messy, so select the Elliptical Marquee tool and create a selection around the sphere, leaving out the rough edges (see Figure 7.5). Select Inverse, then hit the Delete key. Remember, if you need to move the layer while using the Marquee, hold down the spacebar as a quick way to bring up the Move cursor.

The reflections are coming together, but by using a quick masking technique they can

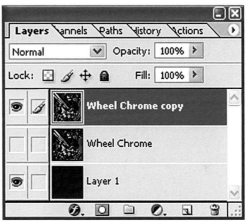

Figure 7.2: Set up the Layers palette.

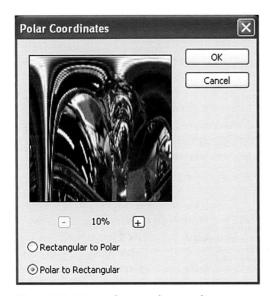

Figure 7.3: Manipulating polar coordinates

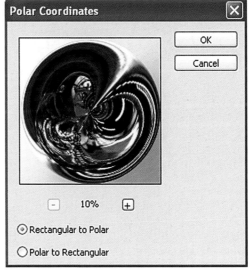

Figure 7.4: Sphere in progress

Figure 7.5: Erase edge pixels from the sphere.

Figure 7.6: Add a mask.

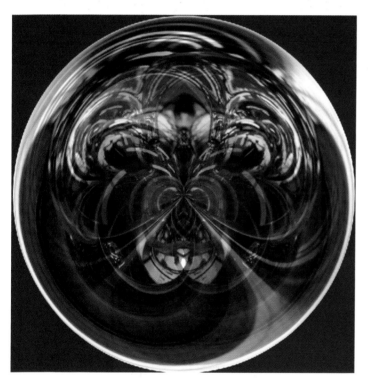

Figure 7.7: Reflective sphere

be maximized even further to enhance the chrome effect. Duplicate the Wheel Chrome Copy layer, and flip the new layer vertically with the Transform tools. Create a layer mask for the new layer and with a black-to-white gradual gradient, fill the mask from the lower-left corner to the upper-right (see Figure 7.6).

Take a look at Figure 7.7. Your reflections may not match mine exactly, but that's fine. It is extremely tricky to duplicate another person's masking effect. The point is that you should have a sphere with a highly reflective surface, with nearly identical duplication of the reflection across the face.

Let's rotate the sphere a bit. Rather than separately rotate each layer that makes up a portion of the sphere, simply link them together in the Layers palette and select Edit → Transform → Rotate. Grab a corner and rotate the sphere counterclockwise (see Figures 7.8 and 7.9).

As it stands, the sphere is pretty straightforward, but could use some depth of color, shadows, and additional reflections. For one thing, there is no apparent light source from any given direction. Command/Control+click one of the sphere layers to generate a selection and create a new layer. Using a white-to-black/dark blue gradient set to Radial in the Options Toolbar, fill the

Figure 7.8: *Link the sphere layers before rotating them.*

Figure 7.9: *Rotation complete*

selection with the gradient starting in the upper-left quadrant of the sphere and moving down to the lower right. Set the blending mode for the layer to Soft Light (see Figure 7.10).

To enhance the impression that this is a metal object, a touch of gray added to the point closest to the viewer will help. Set the foreground color to gray and in a new layer, draw a foreground-to-transparent radial gradient out from the center of the sphere (see Figure 7.11). Reduce the opacity for this layer to 85%.

Now you can use the Dodge and Burn tools to add additional highlights and shadows. Select the Dodge tool and, in the Options Toolbar, set the following attributes:

Brush size	250, round, feathered
Range	Highlights
Exposure	50%

The Dodge and Burn tools find their roots in photographers' need to regulate exposure in specific areas of their images in the darkroom. Either light is held back (Dodge) to lighten areas of a print, or exposure is increased (Burn) to darken areas of a print.

Merge the two sphere layers containing the actual reflections together. Select the newly merged layer and dodge in highlights in opposing quadrants. Start with the upper left, add a few to the lower right, and so forth. Keep in mind that the reflections will get narrower toward the center of the sphere (see Figure 7.12).

Steel and chrome have a subtle blue-gray quality that the eye may not realize initially, but it is present in most metallic reflections. Rather than add more blue (that was accomplished with

Figure 7.10: Blending mode change

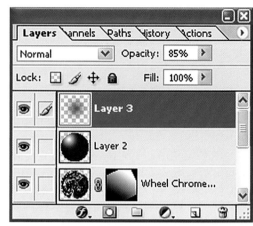

Figure 7.11: Metal gray added

Figure 7.12: Dodging reflections

the radial gradient layer), you can simply remove some of the color to help the effect along a more natural path. To emulate this and assist in the realistic quality of the sphere, create a Hue/Saturation adjustment layer at the top of the layer stack with the following attributes:

Hue	0 (no adjustment)
Saturation	–40
Lightness	0 (no adjustment)
Colorize	unchecked

Click OK to accept the change to the saturation of color in the overall image. You still want to retain the blue from the gradient layer, so simply drag the gradient layer to the top of the layer stack above the Hue/Saturation adjustment layer (see Figure 7.13).

Now you just need to add the reflection of the photographer. Open photographer.jpg from this book's CD (see Figure 7.14).

Extract the cameraman from his background and copy and paste him into the sphere document (see Figure 7.15). If you need a refresher on extractions, please take another look at that section in Chapter 1. Now the man needs to conform to the curve of the sphere. Choose Filter → Distort → Spherize (see Figure 7.16), setting the Mode to Normal and the Amount to 100%.

Place the man's layer beneath the Hue/Saturation adjustment layer in the layer stack so that the blue will overlay his reflection and the saturation will be reduced

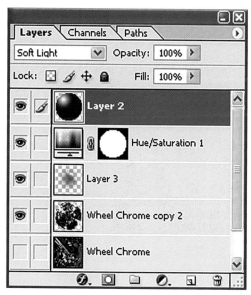

Figure 7.13: Layer rearrangement

Figure 7.14: Caught on film

Figure 7.15: Layer for the cameraman

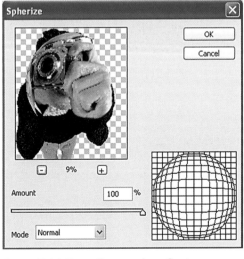

Figure 7.16: Rounding out the reflection

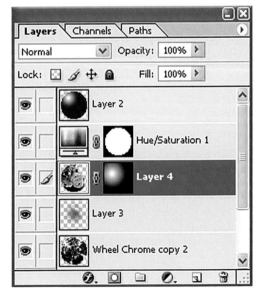

Figure 7.17: Get rid of extra pixels.

Figure 7.18: Chrome sphere

for this layer as well (see Figure 7.17). Create a mask for the layer and, using a white-to-black radial gradient, fill the mask so that the area where the man resides is visible, gradually fading over the face of the sphere. Command/Control+click one of the sphere layers to generate a selection, select the inverse on the man's layer, and hit Delete. Be sure you are deleting the actual layer pixels and not the mask.

Figure 7.18 shows the final result.

Digital Woman: Advertising

In the introduction to this chapter, I mentioned advertising as being an art form—or at least artistic elements are used in the advertising medium. They are called Graphic Arts, after all. To reflect that point, this tutorial will show one way to build an ad from an idea, using Photoshop, your own gray matter, and a whole lot of imagination.

Concept Create a unique advertising piece, reflecting objects, people, and the digital world. This piece should use the logo prominently as well as displaying the product.

Visualize As my mind works out the details for this, one thing is clear: I want to ensure that the logo sticks out in the piece, so I'll use it repetitively (or in more than one instance). The idea should not only display the logo, but should also encapsulate the company slogan.

Realize To realize this technique, you will require a logo, a computer photo, and a face. You will capture a photo using a converted text layer and combinations of masks, blending mode changes, and colorizing techniques (see Chapter 2) to complete the final image. You will also be working with the Transform tools again.

To start the ad, let's first create a digital image. I can hear it already…"Wait a minute, Al, aren't we already working with digital images?" Sure we are, but that isn't really what I have in mind. How about if the main character consisted of ones and zeros, literally? It's worth a try.

Open the image `glasses.jpg` from this book's CD (see Figure 7.19). This photo has elements that I think will fit nicely in the final image, in particular the reflections on the large lenses. You'll soon see what I have in mind, but first let's really make this lady digital.

Figure 7.19: Reflective with reflections?

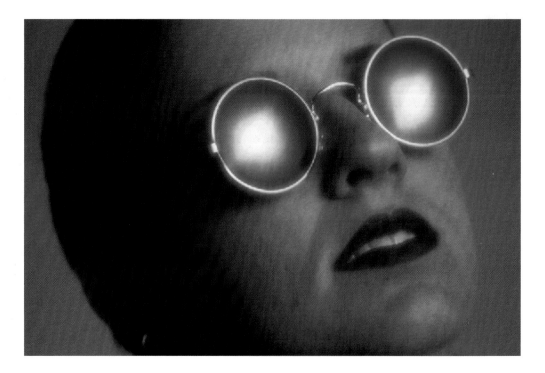

Now that the primary image is open, it is time again to set up the Layers palette. Create a new layer just above the background and fill it with black. Next, duplicate the Background layer and place it above the black layer. Rename the new copy of the woman **Glasses-1**, and move the layer to the left about one-third the width of the image. This will give some space on the right for additional ad copy once the primary image is complete (see Figure 7.20).

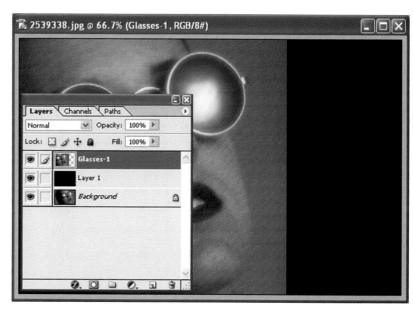

Figure 7.20: Leave space for the ad text.

You need a layer consisting of ones and zeroes to use in the image conversion, so select the Vertical Type tool. In the Options Toolbar, set the font to Arial Black, Regular, 12 pts, Top Justify, and the color for the font to white. Starting in the upper-right corner, make four columns of ones and zeroes, typed randomly (see Figure 7.21). Rasterize and duplicate the Type layer, move the new layer to the left to create four more columns, and merge those layers together to create an eight-column layer. Repeat the process until the entire face is covered (Figure 7.22). Rename the final merged-character layer **Numbers**.

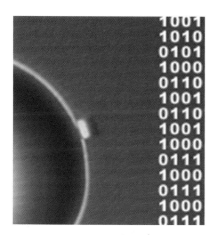

Figure 7.21: Ones and zeroes

Figure 7.22: Digitized

Command/Control+click the Numbers layer to select all of the type, then choose Select → Inverse. Select the Glasses-1 layer and copy it (Command/Control+C). Paste the pixel information into a new layer, then name the layer **Face-Numbers**. Duplicate the layer and set the blending mode for the new layer to Overlay (see Figure 7.23).

Return to the Glasses-1 layer. My thought is to use the reflections on the glasses to display a glowing logo, which is the primary reason this photo was so appealing to me. In order to do that, the lenses need to be visible in their entirety while the rest of the face remains digitized. You guessed it: A mask is about to come into play.

Create a layer mask for the Glasses-1 layer and fill it with black. Set white as the foreground color and using the Paintbrush tool, paint over the lens areas in the mask (see Figure 7.24).

The process just applied needs to be reversed for the Face-Numbers layers. What I mean is that the numbers need to be hidden from the lenses, but revealed on the face so that the numeric construct is still visible. Create a mask for each Face-Numbers layer and fill the mask with white. Paint over the lenses with black in the masks, and also reveal the wire frame around the lenses, as seen in Figure 7.25.

The numbers bordering the faces aren't needed either, so continue to paint in the Face-Number layers' masks and hide the characters that do not compose the face (see Figure 7.26).

Now for the logo. In considering the theme of this exercise, I worked in reverse: I knew the technique that I wanted to demonstrate before I had the product in mind. The image/effect you're creating here is attempting to suggest something digital and somewhat futuristic, so a computer company would be a perfect fit. So what sort of logo would work for a computer company? What would be unique but easily associated with computers? After a bit of thought, I decided on the nearly universal On button icon. Most PCs and Macs have it embedded on the face of the button.

In the real world, of course, you'd be working with an established company; and they would usually supply their logo and information about their products for your design.

Figure 7.23: Numbers construct the face.

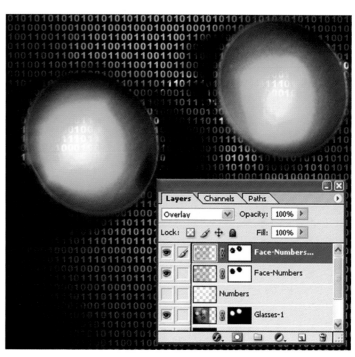

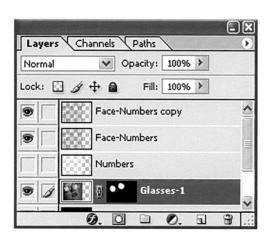

Figure 7.24: A mask reveals the lenses.

Figure 7.25: Hide the numbers in the logo area.

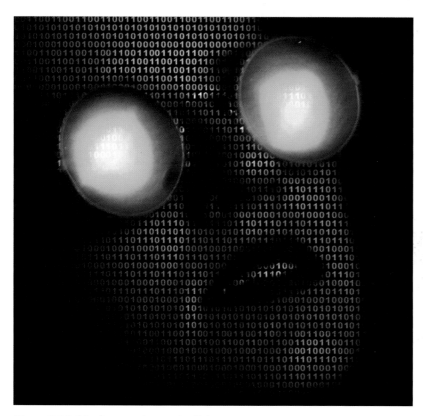

Figure 7.26: Mask away the excess digits.

Figure 7.27: A PC On button

Figure 7.28: The glowing logo reflected on the glasses

Let's get to the logo placement. Open the image on button.jpg (see Figure 7.27) from this book's CD. The logo needs to be transferred to the face image. Here's the process:

Use the Elliptical Marquee tool to select the glowing logo and glowing circle around the On button.

Copy the logo to the clipboard (Command/Control+C).

Paste the logo into the digital face image at the top of the layer stack.

With the Transform tools, conform the logo to one of the lenses.

Duplicate the Logo layer and move this instance of the logo to the other lens.

Merge the two Logo layers together.

After all those steps, the logos should appear on the digital face image as seen in Figure 7.28.

Create a mask for the Logos layer. The idea is to reveal some of the reflection seen on the original lenses, but to still retain the logo. Select a median gray foreground color and paint in the mask over the center of the lenses (see Figure 7.29).

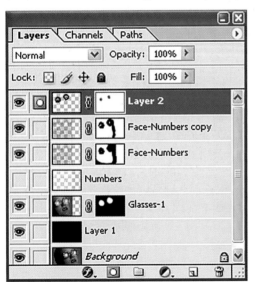

Figure 7.29: Revealing light beneath

If you retained the glowing ring around the button when it was copied to the face image, then you followed the instructions correctly. However, I don't want the ring to glow; rather, it might look cooler if the glowing ring were turned to metal to appear to be new frames for the lenses. How do you accomplish that?

It isn't as hard as it may sound, really. The reflections are already present in the lights; take the color away and you should have a nice metallic frame. Create a new layer at the top of the layer stack, and set the blending mode for the new layer to Color. You should already have gray set as the foreground color, so reduce the size of the paintbrush to compensate for the width of the frame. Then just paint away the color on the frame (see Figure 7.30).

To enhance the reflections, simply select the Dodge tool and apply the Dodge to taste on the lower-right and upper-left quadrants of the logo rings. You may also need to do this to the actual Logo layer to enhance the effect, as seen in Figure 7.31.

Figure 7.30: Remove the color to reveal metal.

Figure 7.31: Metallic highlights

Most computers already display our logo.

Wishful thinking.

ACME Computers.
What other PCs want to be when they grow up.

Figure 7.32: Complete advertisement

In the final image (see Figure 7.32), I've simply added another instance of the logo, a company slogan, and information. Something to think about when doing ad pieces (as I've tried to reflect here) is how to tie the text to the image or vice versa—for instance, the wistful look on the digital woman paired with the "Wishful Thinking" statement in the text.

Enticement: Reverse Advertising

Something that has always baffled me is the connection of personal vices with selling a product. I understand why advertisers take the vice approach, but why in the world would the consumer connect, say, beer with sports? If a quarterback showed up for a game drunk out of his gourd, he certainly isn't going to perform very well. Yet alcohol advertisements and sports are intricately woven together in the minds of the public.

It boggles the mind. Consider ads in magazines that show construction workers enjoying a brew after work. There is nothing wrong with that in the minds of most people, but what about the next morning when the workers return to work hung over after a night of too many relaxing beers? If the crew in a shipyard were to enjoy a few refreshing shots of tequila during their lunch break, would you want to ride on the completed ship?

Some of these ads have evolved to the point of being ridiculous, but have bred and fed another advertising art form: the public service message. Recently many commercials have been appearing that, initially, seem to be promoting a product, but as the ad ends some tragic result ensues due to overindulgence and negligence. That is the point to this technique.

Concept Create a faux advertisement displaying a product and a situation where the product should not be used.

Visualize Alcohol was a problem for this writer for years, so that is what I see in my mind: an ad using some enticing image of alcohol combined with a situation where consumption could prove not only dangerous but deadly.

Realize To get this message across, you'll use some standard Photoshop techniques, extracting part of one image and placing it in another image. This technique will also show you one way of extracting the reflections from glass: a very cool thing to know!

Open the image `powerlines.jpg` (see Figure 7.33) from this book's CD. At first glance, it may appear to be a serene desert sunset, but what if the man in the photo is a lineman? Taking a break next to his work vehicle to enjoy the sunset is one thing, but adding alcohol to a dangerous job is something else entirely.

The secondary image reflects the vice. Open the image `scotch.jpg` (see Figure 7.34) from this book's CD. The glass needs to be extracted from this photo and placed in the other one.

The edges of the glass are a bit blurry, so you may want to run the High Pass filter trick from Chapter 1 to sharpen those edges before proceeding. This will help ensure a cleaner extraction.

Choose Filter → Extract, and outline the glass as you would any other extraction (see Figure 7.35). This extraction is slightly different, because the glass is meant to be transparent. That means a little extra thinking is involved when selecting areas to extract. You certainly do not want the room in the background to carry through to the other image, yet you still need the reflections to show that this is indeed glass. Take a look at Figure 7.36. Highlight around areas within the boundary of the original highlighted area that you want to omit, leaving the reflections intact but removing the room seen through the glass. Leave the

Figure 7.33: A hard day's work

Figure 7.34: What could it hurt?

liquid alone…that will be needed in the final image also. Fill the highlighted area with the Paintbucket and hit Preview.

The extraction will probably be a bit rough, so some edge cleanup will be needed (see Figure 7.37).

Once you have the glass fairly well cleaned up, copy and paste it into the power lines image. Use the Transform tools to resize the glass to fit the image, and move the glass to the left side of the image so that part of it is lost beyond the image. Also, move the glass down so that the base is partially obscured. This will create a little less work in cleaning up the glass, yet still get the message across. Again, the free space on the right will serve for the ad copy (Figure 7.38).

Create a mask for the Glass layer and hide any offending pixels by painting over their corresponding area in the mask (see Figure 7.39). Work within the boundaries of the glass also, hiding any jagged edges along the reflections carried over during the extraction. Once cleaned up with the mask, your image should look like Figure 7.40.

Figure 7.35: Initial area for extraction highlighted

Figure 7.36: Room omitted, highlights retained

Figure 7.37: Clean up the extracted object.

Figure 7.38: Place the glass in the original document.

Figure 7.39: Mask the jagged pixels.

Figure 7.40: Cleaned-up image

If you look at the liquid, you will notice a couple areas of red that were retained from the room in the original glass image. There isn't any red in the sunset, so this needs to go. You can clean this up quickly by selecting the Clone Stamp tool, sampling where the liquid has the proper golden tone, and stamping the sample over the red areas (see Figure 7.41).

Figure 7.41: Omit the red.

Now that the reflections are cleaned up and the glass, for the most part, appears to belong in the power lines photo, one more item needs to be addressed to make the glass truly look at home. Curved glass has a lens effect on objects seen through it, so the power lines behind the glass need a bit of tweaking. To do this, use the Magic Wand tool and select the area outside of the glass in that layer. Choose Select → Inverse and click the Background layer. Copy the selection and paste it into a new layer beneath the glass (see Figure 7.42).

*Figure 7.42:
Background for
the glass*

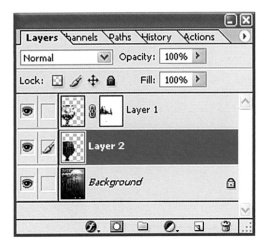

Activate the selection (Command/
Control+click the new layer). Now choose
Filter → Distort → Spherize. Set the Mode
to Horizontal Only and the Amount to
100% and click OK. Open the Spherize
filter one more time, set the Mode to
Normal and the Amount to 100%, and
click OK again. The background behind
the glass will appear warped, as though
seen through a lens or, go figure, a glass!
Now simply add your message, and hope
that someone, somewhere, will pay
attention (see Figure 7.43).

*Figure 7.43: Pub-
lic awareness
message*

Common Images in Art

Concept Most photographic art does not use or require a lot of digital manipulation to inspire, to evoke, and to appeal. For this piece, simply apply two similar images to a background to reflect a theme.

Visualize I was a thespian in my high school days (an actor, to those unfamiliar with the term). The Comedy and Tragedy masks were commonplace on the stage and in posters we created to advertise upcoming plays. I see such an image, using masks of Comedy and Tragedy on a simple background.

Realize The process for realizing this will be a piece of cake, and with some help from Photoshop we can have a professional-looking poster done in very little time.

To start, open the image `roughBG.jpg` (see Figure 7.44) from this book's CD to serve as the background.

Figure 7.44: Background for the poster

The background looks pretty good as it sits, but maybe just some shadow could be added to imply a border and take the emphasis away from the background in the final image. This is done easily with a quick layer style. Duplicate the Background layer and open the Layer Styles palette, selecting Inner Glow. Enter the following settings for the glow in the dialog box:

Blend Mode	Multiply
Blend Color	Dark Brown
Opacity	75%
Noise	25%
Technique	Softer
Source	Edge
Choke	0%
Size	220%

Don't worry about any of the other settings; just click OK. This will darken the border of the background gradually, as seen in Figure 7.45.

Open the image tragedy.jpg (see Figure 7.46) from this book's CD. For this project, you can omit the extensive extraction described for previous exercises, because the background is a solid color and the mask is clearly defined. Use the Magic Wand to select the areas of white (press the Add To Selection button in the Options Toolbar), select Inverse, choose Select → Contract → 2 px, and copy and paste the mask into the background image. Use the Transform tools to reduce the size of the mask if you need to, and then move it to the right side of the background until only half of the face is showing (see Figure 7.47).

Make the mask appear to float above the background with the application of a drop shadow. Use the following settings for the shadow:

Blend Mode	Multiply
Opacity	50%
Angle	50 Degrees (with Global Light turned OFF)
Distance	385 px
Spread	0
Size	100 px

Figure 7.45: Darken the border.

Figure 7.46: Tragedy mask

Figure 7.47: The mask finds a new home.

The edges of the mask could be darkened as well, just like the Background was. With the Layer Styles dialog box still open, select Inner Glow from the left-hand side and apply the same settings as with the Background. Once the settings are entered, click OK.

To enhance the mask in both tone and reflection, create two new copies of the mask, and change the blending mode for both to Soft Light. Delete the applied styles for these two layers (see Figure 7.48).

The mask appears a bit grainy, but you don't really want to blur the primary Mask layer. Instead, a blur applied to the Soft Light layers will help clean up the graininess. Command/Control+click a Mask layer and run a Gaussian Blur on both Soft Light layers (see Figure 7.49).

Now open image `comedy.jpg` from this book's CD, which is the Comedy mask image (see Figure 7.50). Repeat the entire process done to the other mask, with the exception of the placement on the Background. Instead, angle this mask as seen in Figure 7.51; repeat all other processes done to the Tragedy mask to this mask also.

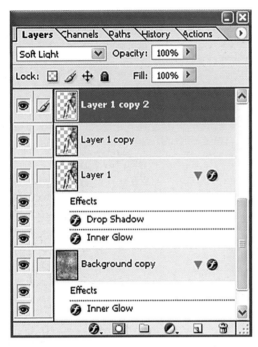

Figure 7.48: Soft Light layers enhance color.

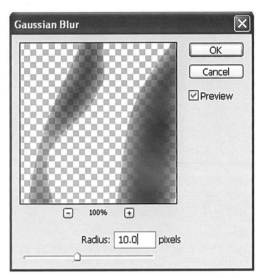

Figure 7.49: Blurring the grain

Figure 7.50: Comedy mask

Figure 7.51: New mask in place; effects reapplied

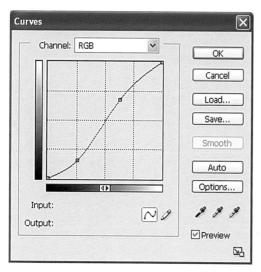

Figure 7.52: Curves adjustment

Figure 7.54: Comedy and Tragedy poster

Figure 7.53: Brightness/Contrast adjustment

To finalize the image, you really only need to darken the shadows a bit and lighten the highlights. A quick combination of two Adjustment layers will work in this case. First, create a Curves Adjustment layer; use the settings seen in Figure 7.52. Next, apply a Brightness/Contrast Adjustment layer, the settings of which are seen in Figure 7.53.

Figure 7.54 shows the final image. The process was painless and short, yet the result looks professional.

Enhanced Close-up: Macro Art

Concept Create an enhanced piece of macro art from a close-up object photo.

Visualize This project will bring out the richly patterned texture of rusty steel.

Realize In this project, you'll again use the High Pass filter trick (covered in Chapter 1). All you need is a photo of a rusty tool; you'll apply a couple of techniques already learned to create some high-definition macro art.

Macro art deals with high definition close-ups, showing us details that require extreme magnification to be revealed. Generally these shots require high-resolution equipment and a very steady hand. (The latter is something I've never had.) As you have seen in previous chapters, Photoshop has the tools to help generate high-definition images from pretty standard photographs. Open the image `wrench-3.jpg` (see Figure 7.55) found on this book's CD.

First, enhance the wrench with the High Pass filter trick from Chapter 1. Note that the actual hairs of the rust begin to appear as you adjust the slider. When you have a good contrast, click OK (see Figure 7.56).

I'm not going to play with this much, other than to add a couple of Adjustment layers. Add a Brightness Contrast Adjustment layer. Decrease the Brightness to −20, increase the Contrast to +12, and click OK.

A Gradient Map will take away a lot of the red in the image and restore a graying metal quality. Create a Gradient Map Adjustment layer. Create a gradient (see tutorial in Chapter 1) as seen in Figure 7.57 and click OK.

Apply one last Adjustment layer, this time selecting Hue/Saturation. Don't tweak the Hue, but rather increase the Saturation to +20 and decrease the Lightness to −10. Click OK.

Figure 7.58 shows the final image. This effect wasn't really about creating new art, but about enhancing an existing photo using elements that, for the most part, already resided in the original.

Figure 7.55:
Rusty wrench

Figure 7.56: Apply the High Pass filter trick from Chapter 1

Figure 7.57: Make a new gradient.

Figure 7.58: The final enhanced photo

eight

Going Beyond Canned Filters

Filters are one *of the first features that a new Photoshop user typically starts with. They draw people into the software, providing instant gratification with just a few clicks. You don't need to know the theory behind a filter in order to apply it to an image. The drawback to using filters is that no matter how cool an image may look after a particular filter is applied, other Photoshop users will notice it in an instant. Many is the time I've been asked to critique someone's "masterpiece," only to see that they applied one or two filters and sent it out to the digital world to stun the masses. The masses, especially those who use Photoshop, are usually left unstunned.*

The key to using filters is to know when and where to apply one (and which one to apply) to an image that incorporates other features and tools in the program. Filters are spices; they are not the meal. Use them sparingly. This chapter shows several ways to make your photos appear aged, drawn, painted, and vectorized, without using the Filters menu exclusively. I think you will find that the end results not only have a greater realism, but are far more satisfying.

Retro Photo: Aging

Concept Photoshop is not only a photo correction tool, but as you have seen in previous chapters, it is also a great program for manipulation. The concept for this section is to take a perfectly good photograph that could have been taken yesterday and age it sixty years, complete with damage to the paper.

Visualize At the end of this project, I see a photo that looks as though it has been sitting in a box on a shelf since before WWII.

Realize A combination of layers, filters, and Adjustment layers (with a layer style or two thrown in for good measure) will work to produce age.

Open the image `thoughtful.jpg` (see Figure 8.1) from this book's CD. This photo is clearly intended to look like a period capture; the clothing and hat are certainly not something you would expect to see in these so-called modern times. One can almost imagine that the woman was caught waiting at a train station decades ago, perhaps waiting for her sweetheart to return home from the war. Will he be on the train? Will he remember the one he left behind?

In the Layers palette, duplicate the Background layer. Rename the new layer **Aged**. Create a duplicate for this layer also, but shut off the layer. You will return to it soon, but a few things need be done to the Aged layer first. Shut off the Background layer. With the Aged layer selected, choose Image → Adjustments → Desaturate and remove all the color from the Aged layer (see Figure 8.2).

This layer will provide the foundation for the aging process. Create a Brightness/Contrast

Figure 8.1: Waiting for a lost love

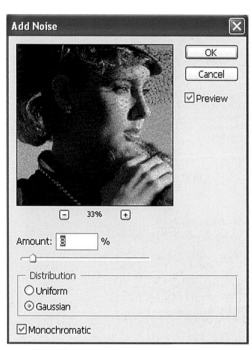

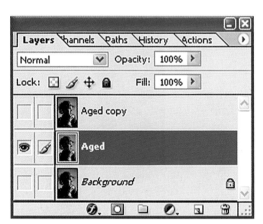

Figure 8.2: Setting up the Layers palette   *Figure 8.3: Add Noise filter in action*

Adjustment layer just above the Aged layer, but beneath the Aged Copy layer. Leave the Brightness slider alone, but increase the contrast to 25 and click OK.

One problem with a lot of old photographs is the quality of the camera or film available at the time. Graininess was a definite problem, so adding some will increase the aged look of this piece. Select the Aged layer and choose Filter → Noise → Add Noise. In the Add Noise dialog box, set the Amount to 8% and the Distribution to Gaussian, and select Monochromatic at the bottom (see Figure 8.3). Click OK.

If you apply the Add Noise filter with Monochromatic unchecked, the filter will actually change the color of some pixels. With Monochromatic checked, the filter affects only the tonal elements of the image or layer, leaving the colors alone.

Create a new Hue/Saturation Adjustment layer above the Brightness/Contrast Adjustment layer. This layer will give the black and white layer beneath it a sepia tone. Most aged photo techniques stop there, but this technique will allow some original color to be retained.

With the Hue/Saturation dialog box open, move the slider (or type in the settings manually) as follows:

Colorize (Lower Right Corner)	Checked
Hue	30
Saturation	20
Lightness	0

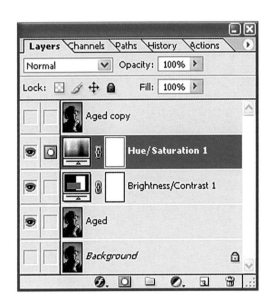

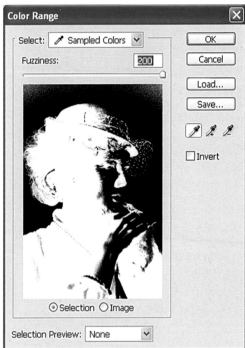

Figure 8.4: State of the Layers palette—progress check

Figure 8.5: Selecting the shadows

Click OK to apply the setting. The Layers palette at this point will look like Figure 8.4.

I mentioned that some of the original color will be retained, and the Aged Copy layer will be the medium used for that color. Some manipulation of the pixels needs to take place to combine the color of this layer with the sepia from the layers beneath. You may think that a simple blending mode change or opacity reduction will give the desired effect, but this technique is a bit more involved than that.

Select the Aged Copy layer. Change the blending mode to Overlay and reduce the opacity to 50%. Many old photos were originally black and white or sepia toned, and later colored by hand. You are going to use this layer to give the photo that hand-colored effect, while retaining the original sepia in other areas of the picture.

Choose Select → Color Range. The default selection (indicated by white in the viewer window) should grab the shadowed areas of the image. If not, use the eyedropper to sample the dark areas, and move the Fuzziness slider to 200 (see Figure 8.5). Click OK.

With the selection active, hit the Delete key. If you hold down the Alt/Option key and click the eye icon next to the layer, all other layers will become invisible and you can see the state of the current layer (see Figure 8.6). The dark areas have been wiped away, leaving only faint colored pixels in the areas of sky, skin, and clothing. Alt/Option+click the eye icon again to turn all the layers back on.

There still seems to be a bit too much color in the overall image, so choose Select → Color Range again. This time, select Midtones from the Select menu at the top of the Color Range dialog box and click OK. Again, hit the Delete key to wipe away the selected pixels

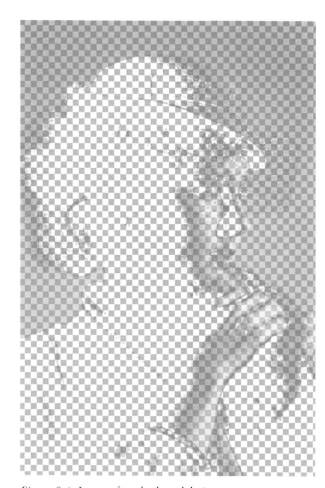

Figure 8.6: Layer after shadow deletion

from the layer. Figure 8.7 shows the image thus far. The overall tonal effect is sepia, with just a hint of color left in the sky and on the woman's face. Trust me, it is there. If you would like a bit more color, just increase the opacity of the layer.

With the image appropriately colored for age, you may now simulate damage to the photo produced by years in a box. Normal wear and tear produces scratching; moisture can bubble or blemish the photo as well as produce mold and age spots. Photoshop can do this too, or at least give the illusion of such.

Create a new layer above the Aged Copy layer; name the new layer **Clouds**. Press the D key to reset the swatches to Black (foreground) and White (background), then choose Filter → Render → Clouds. The new layer will be filled with a random pattern of blacks, whites, and grays merging in a cotton candy pattern of gradual fluffiness. OK, how else would you describe it? Name the new layer **Clouds** (see Figure 8.8).

Select Filter → Brush Strokes → Sprayed Strokes. Set the Stroke Length to 0, Spray Radius to 25, and Stroke Direction to Left Diagonal. Click OK. Now choose Image → Adjustments → Brightness/Contrast. Set the Brightness to 75 and the Contrast to 100. Click OK.

Change the blending mode of the Clouds layer to Linear Burn. You'll notice that the layer is now almost completely white with a few black spotted patterns. Changing the blending mode to Linear Burn hides the white, but retains the dark spots on the image (see Figure 8.9).

This layer can also be used to add color to the photo. Choose Image → Adjustments → Hue/Saturation and set the options as follows. When you're done, click OK.

Hue	25
Saturation	25
Lightness	−20

Duplicate the Clouds layer and change the blending mode to Screen, the opacity to 20%. This will lighten the image somewhat.

Figure 8.7: Remove a few more pixels.

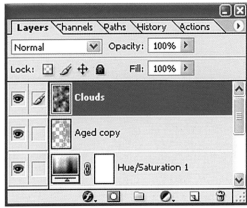

Figure 8.8: Clouds layer for creating blemishes

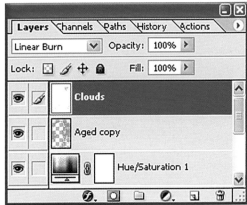

Figure 8.9: Age spots

At this point, it may be a good idea to save your work thus far. You can either save the image as a PSD file to retain the layers, or simply open the History palette and create a new snapshot. You can return to this state of the image at any time by selecting the snapshot in the History palette (see Figure 8.10).

I had you save a snapshot at this point because you're going to merge all the layers together with the exception of the original background. Link all the layers in the Layers palette (except the Background). Open the Layer menu, and near the bottom of the menu, select Merge Linked (Command/Control+E). Rename the new layer created by the merge **Aged–2** (see Figure 8.11).

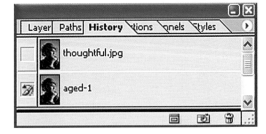

Figure 8.10: Snapshot

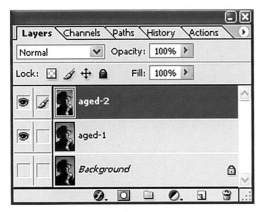

Figure 8.11: Merged new layer

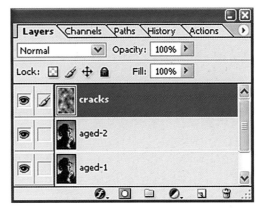

Figure 8.12: Working with clouds

A few more blemishes can be added in the form of cracking or peeling. To do this, create a new layer named **Cracks** and run the Clouds filter on this layer also (Filter → Render → Clouds) (see Figure 8.12).

The Clouds Filter

This filter generates patterns using soft variations between the foreground and background colors. To generate a more emphasized cloud pattern, hold down the Option key (Mac) or Alt key (Windows) as you choose Filter → Render → Clouds. When you apply the Clouds filter, the image data on the active layer is replaced. (Pixels are added on layers with no image data.)

Open the Filters menu again, this time selecting Texture → Craquelure. This filter reproduces the effect of cracks on a plaster surface. Apply the following settings in the Craquelure dialog box:

Crack Spacing	90
Crack Depth	8
Crack Brightness	8

Click OK. Choose Image → Adjustments → Brightness/Contrast and increase the Brightness of the layer to +75 and the Contrast to +100. Click OK.

The whites and blacks of this layer need to be swapped (the cracks will be darker than the photo), so press Command/Control+I to invert the colors. You will not need the white in the image, so choose Select → Color Range, and select the white portions of the layer with the eyedropper (see Figure 8.13). Click OK, and press the Delete key to wipe away the white pixels. Deselect.

The image is nearly done; a couple of quick styles will top it off nicely. Open the layer styles for this layer and select Bevel and Emboss. This setting will allow for depth in the cracks. Adjust the Bevel/Emboss settings as follows:

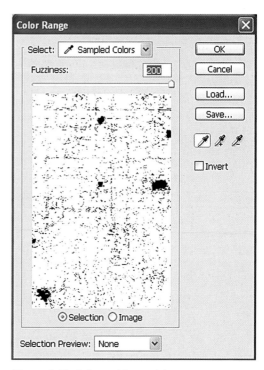

Style	Inner Bevel
Technique	Chisel Soft
Depth	1%
Direction	Down
Size	1 px
Soften	0 px
Use Global Light	Unchecked
Angle	120 degrees
Altitude	10 degrees
Gloss Contour	Default
Highlight Mode	Screen
Highlight Color	White
Highlight Opacity	28–30%
Shadow Mode	Multiply
Shadow Color	Black
Shadow Opacity	35–40%

Figure 8.13: Select white to delete.

Before closing the Layer Styles dialog box, select Color Overlay from the left-hand menu. Set the color to a tan-gray, the blending mode to Color Burn, and the opacity to 20% (see Figure 8.14). Click OK to accept the style.

Figure 8.14: Layer attributes changed

You aren't quite done with styles just yet. Select the Aged-2 layer. By manipulating an inner glow, you can add a studio-style shadow around the perimeter of the image. Open the layer styles for the Aged-2 layer and select Inner Glow. Tweak the settings for the style as follows:

Blend Mode	Multiply
Opacity	100%
Noise	0%
Color	Tan/Gray
Technique	Softer
Source	Edge
Choke	0%
Size	200%

The default settings will work for the remainder. Click OK. Figure 8.15 shows the final aged photograph.

Figure 8.15: Final shot—aged and scratched

Photo to Line Art: Sketching

This section is a bit complicated for me as a teacher. Not that creating drawings from photographs is difficult; quite the contrary. It is an easy process, no matter which approach you take. Therein lies my problem; there are so many ways to generate line art and pencil drawings, which do I demonstrate? The variations on lineart effects could take up a book or two themselves.

For this section I've selected just two methods to give you a general idea of how to approach your sketches. The first retains shading from the original to create pencil effects; the second converts edges into lines for the effect of a pen-and-ink sketch.

Pencil Drawings

Concept Create the effect of a shaded pencil sketch from a photograph, first in grayscale and then using color.

Visualize To see the versatility of this technique, you'll apply it to a car and then to a portrait of a child.

Realize This technique uses familiar tools: an inverted Background layer, the Color Dodge blending mode, and the Gaussian Blur filter.

Start the first technique by opening a photo of a car. The image used here is `musclecar.jpg` (see Figure 8.16), found on this book's CD.

First, convert the mode of the image to Grayscale (Image → Mode → Grayscale). Duplicate the Background layer and choose Image → Adjustments → Invert. Set the blending mode for the new layer to Color Dodge.

Figure 8.16: The best Ford ever made

Figure 8.17: The car is nearly invisible.

Figure 8.18: Lightly sketched

The image now appears nearly entirely white, with a few spots of gray. The car can barely be seen as a result of the Color Dodge layer and inversion of the same mingled with the opposing grays of the Background layer (see Figure 8.17).

Color Dodge

This blending mode samples the color information in each channel and brightens the base color to reflect the blend color. This is done by decreasing the contrast.

The trick for creating a drawing is only one step away. With the Background Copy layer selected, choose Filter → Blur → Gaussian Blur. Set the radius of the blur to 4 and take a look at the image (don't click OK just yet). The car now appears drawn, with thin pencil lines outlining the contours and edges of the car (see Figure 8.18).

Increase the Gaussian Blur to 8. The more you increase the blur, the more the layer beneath is revealed, making the lines in the drawing appear thicker and the shading more pronounced (see Figure 8.19).

Figure 8.19: Deeper lines

Figure 8.20: Time for a nap

Figure 8.21: Pencil art colorized

 Let's go through the process once more, only this time you will not convert the image to grayscale. Open the image younggirl.jpg (see Figure 8.20) from this book's CD. By running through the same steps as given previously, only without the grayscale conversion, you will get a colorized lineart drawing (see Figure 8.21). The amount of blur again dictates the amount of color and sketching revealed.

Pen-and-Ink Art

The second trick I want to show you for generating line art has a completely different approach, but is excellent if you want clearly defined lines.

> **Concept** Convert a photograph of a textured surface into a purely linear sketch.
>
> **Visualize** A human hand has not only a recognizable outline, but plenty of texture to work with.
>
> **Realize** The Smart Blur filter's Edge Only mode is the key to creating this type of line drawing.

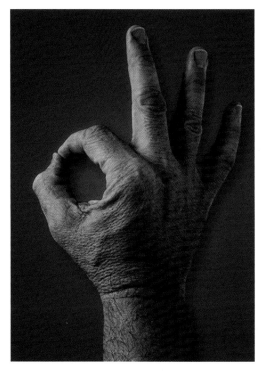

Figure 8.22: *O.K.!*

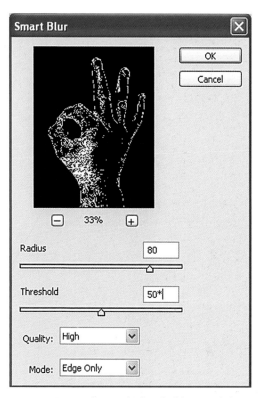

Figure 8.23: *Radius and Threshold control the intensity of the drawing.*

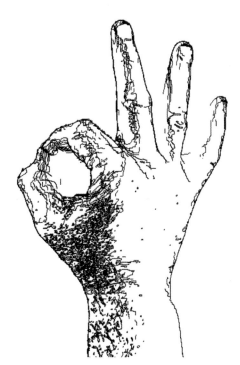

Figure 8.24: *Inverting black and white*

The image `OK.jpg` (see Figure 8.22) from this book's CD is well suited for this because it has plenty of contrast that we can turn into linear detail.

Duplicate the Background layer and choose Image → Adjustments → Desaturate. Press Command/Control+I to invert the colors of the gray layer. Now choose Filter → Blur → Smart Blur and select Edge Only from the Mode list at the bottom of the Smart Blur dialog box. Take a look at the viewer; the image appears to be made of white lines on a black background. When you move the Radius and Threshold sliders, more lines are added or more are removed, depending on the Radius and Threshold values (see Figure 8.23). Click OK. Press Command/Control+I again if you want to invert the black and white (see Figure 8.24).

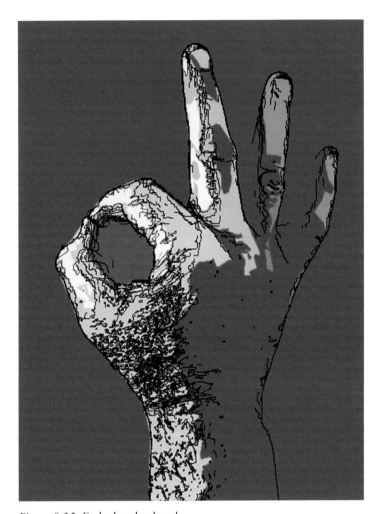

Figure 8.25: Etched and colored

For added effect, duplicate the Background layer again, placing the new layer just above the original background. Select Filter → Artistic → Cut Out. This filter is cool for making photos appear vectorized. Set the Levels to 4, Edge Simplicity to 4, and Edge Fidelity to 2. Click OK. Figure 8.25 shows the new image, combining vector-style color and lineart sketching.

Portrait to Painting: Artistic

There are simply dozens of ways to achieve paint effects in Photoshop, so as with sketch-style effects, deciding which paint effects to demonstrate is a tough choice. Many of the techniques forget one vital element: a realistic portrayal of what they are supposed to reflect. Realism is the focus of this project; the fine details will turn the photo into a realistic oil-on-canvas painting.

Concept The concept for this piece is to generate a painting from a photograph.

Visualize What I see for this piece is an oil-on-canvas painting. I want to take a photograph and have it appear to have been painted on a textured background sometime in the distant past.

Realize As I said, Photoshop CS has several tools to help us realize a painting. The trick is to know what else is required from the toolbox to make the thing work. Sometimes all a car needs to turn over is a spark plug and an oil change. You have the parts and the tools; the trick is getting the pieces under the hood in the right way, saving a bundle on a mechanic. You will achieve this with a combination of filters (Median, Paint Daubs, and so on) and blending modes. You will also use channels as a composite layer to achieve the final paint feel.

To begin, open the image `Oldportrait.jpg` (see Figure 8.26), found on this book's CD. I've chosen this photo due to its obvious age; I just think the effect will be best demonstrated as an old painting. Don't let that deter you from trying this on newer images!

Duplicate the Background layer twice. Name the first copy **Untouched**; this will remain as named (for the time being, anyway). Name the second layer **Paint-1**; this is where you will start applying the effects. Set the blending mode for the Paint-1 layer to Overlay (see Figure 8.27).

The first layer of paint is actually application of the Median filter to the Paint-1 layer. Choose Filter → Noise → Median, set the Radius to 8 pixels (see Figure 8.28), and click OK.

That softened the layer somewhat; now you can add some defining lines within which the paint will fall. This process is nearly a reverse of the actual painting process, but the results will be almost the same as the real thing.

Choose Filter → Stylize → Find Edges.

Figure 8.26: Portrait of great-great-grandpa as a young man

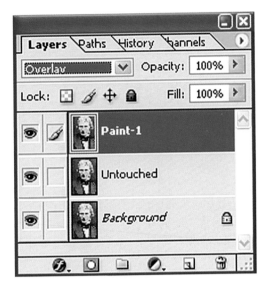

Figure 8.27: Setting up the layers/canvas

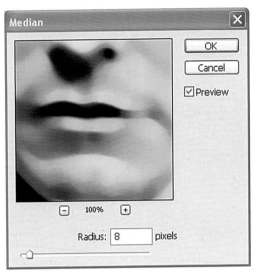

Figure 8.28: Median Noise filter acts almost like a blur.

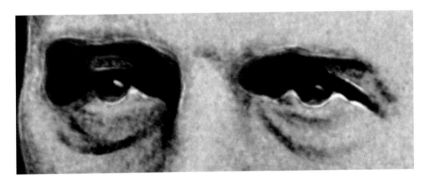

Figure 8.29: Some paint-like qualities appear.

Now invert the layer (Command/Control+I). See how the image (see Figure 8.29) is taking on a painted quality?

Now duplicate the Paint-1 layer; rename the new layer **Paint-2**. Set the blending mode for the layer to Soft Light and drop the opacity to 50%. This will lighten the painting back up a bit, counteracting some of the darkness imposed by the Paint-1 layer.

By adjusting the Hue/Saturation for this layer, you can tweak the base paint strokes to appear as if they were laid with the same color. Trust me, it works. Choose Image → Adjustments → Hue/Saturation, enter the following settings, and click OK.

Colorize	Checked
Hue	360
Saturation	25
Lightness	0

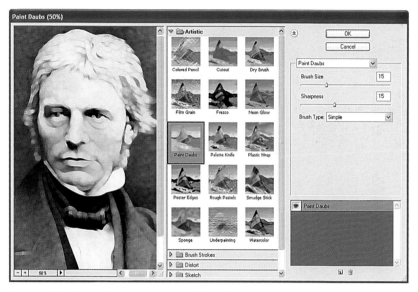

Figure 8.30: Paint Daubs in the new Filter dialog box

Create another instance of the Background layer, placing it at the top of the layer stack, and name it **Paint-3**. I couldn't go through a painting tutorial without actually using one of the paint filters, could I? Sure I could, but I'm not going to.

Set the blending mode for the new layer to Soft Light. Choose Filter → Artistic → Paint Daubs. Set both the Brush Size and Sharpness to 15, the Brush Type to Simple, and click OK (see Figure 8.30).

Duplicate the Untouched layer and set the opacity to 30%. Run the Paint Daubs filter once more on this layer. Rename the layer **Base Paint** (see Figure 8.31).

That's a pretty fair painting, but thus far the canvas being painted on has no characteristics. As I said, this is actually being painted nearly in reverse. The pixels needed to be in place prior to manipulating them into a canvas.

Select the Untouched layer. I just can't leave it untouched; something has to be done. This will actually provide the foundation for the canvas. Choose Select → Color

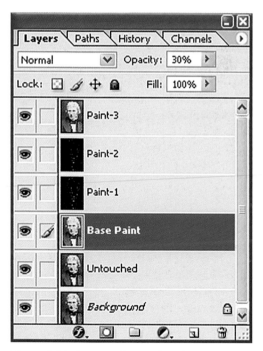

Figure 8.31: Rename the working layer to Base Paint.

Range. Select an area in the face (see Figure 8.32). Quite a bit will come up in the selection, but no worries. It needs to be that way (see Figure 8.33).

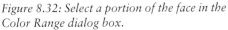

Figure 8.32: Select a portion of the face in the Color Range dialog box.

Figure 8.33: The active selection

With the selection active, go to the Channels palette and create a new Alpha channel. Select the RGB channel and run the Paint Daubs filter again, this time setting the Brush Size to 5 and Sharpness to 10. Stay with the Simple Brush and click OK.

Select the Alpha channel and choose Filter → Texture → Texturizer. Select Canvas for the texture, and set the Scaling to 100% and Relief to 5. Click OK.

Deselect, and click the RGB channel. Run the Texturizer one more time

Figure 8.34: Rough canvas surface applied to new painting

with the same settings as before. The image now appears to have a rough surface similar to those used in standard oil paintings (see Figure 8.34).

Figure 8.35: Good enough to frame

Figure 8.35 shows the effect complete with canvas extending beyond the border. It almost looks good enough to frame, don't you think?

Anime Woman: Vector Art

Concept Vector-based graphics tools such as Adobe Illustrator have made popular a cartoon-ish drawing style with big blocks of solid color. This project takes a photograph and converts it to the "vector art" style.

Visualize Sometimes a photo will lend itself to the imagination, stirring up ideas for art inspired by the image. In this case, I have a particular photograph that reminds me of a character in the anime-style cartoons that Japanese animators create so well. The model is already posed and dressed as such a character, so all we need to do is give her some anime-style characteristics.

Realize Along with some familiar techniques, you'll use Swatches to create a palette of only a few colors and Paths to define where the colors will be applied.

Open the image `hero.jpg` (see Figure 8.36), found on this book's CD.

Figure 8.36: Some images inspire the art.

This image seems ready-made for elaboration. The pose, the costume…this young lady has already made half the job easier. She is already made up as a caricature of someone we might see in a movie, on television, or in a comic book.

When converting an image to vector-style art, it is good to start with a realistic swatch palette containing the most important colors of the original photograph. First, open the Swatches palette. The first step in creating a custom color palette is to remove the colors that are already there. You will note that, if you open the Swatches menu, there is no option for removing all of the colors at once.

Dragging and dropping each color to the trash bin is a tedious and time-consuming process, but there is a cool little shortcut to speed up the process. With the Eyedropper tool selected, hover the eyedropper over one of the colors in the palette. Hold down the Alt/Option key and the eyedropper cursor will change to a pair of scissors. Now click the left mouse button and the color will be deleted. Pretty cool, eh? When you're finished, the empty Swatches palette will look like Figure 8.37.

To create a new palette for the image, select colors representing different primary areas: the skin, the lips, hair, and so on (see Figure 8.38).

After taking the samples of the primary areas, the Swatches palette will look similar to Figure 8.39. I've also included this Swatch set (`Hero-vector.ACO`) on this book's CD; you can find it in the `Color Swatches` folder.

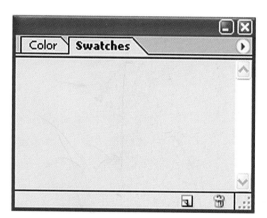

Figure 8.37: Empty the Swatches palette.

Figure 8.38: Sample colors from the primary areas.

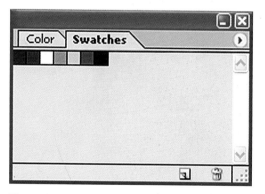

Figure 8.39: New Swatches sampled from the photo

Figure 8.40: Extracting

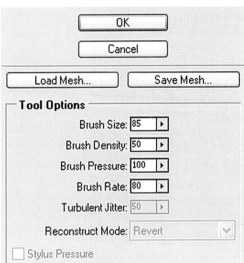

Figure 8.41: Bloat tool settings

Duplicate the Background layer and rename it **Working Layer**.

To enhance the end effect, the image may look better on a black background. Extract the woman from the white background. Figure 8.40 shows the Extract tool in action once again.

Create a new layer between the Background and Working layers and fill it with black.

There are a few features that distinguish anime characters from standard Americanized cartoons, and the Liquify tool helps immensely to create these attributes on regular photos. For instance, anime eyes tend to be large and watery with wide pupils and bright reflective areas, and the lips, chin, and nose tend to be extremely small. Using combinations of the Forward Warp, Pucker, and Bloat tools and varying brush sizes for each, the eyes can be reshaped and the other features shrunk to provide the effect.

Figure 8.41 shows the Bloat tool settings. Set the brush size to something a bit larger than one of the eyes and with the cursor centered over the pupil (or where the pupil should be), bloat the eyes steadily until the size of each is increased without distorting the areas around the eyes (see Figure 8.42).

Although we may not need this for the final effect (the eyes are the primary feature that will show in the final result), try reducing the size of the nose (see Figure 8.43) and lips (see Figure 8.44) with the Pucker tool. Again, a smaller brush is better for this tool, because you do not want to distort large portions of the face.

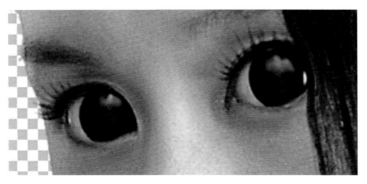

Figure 8.42: Exaggerating the eyes

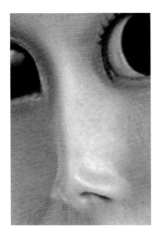

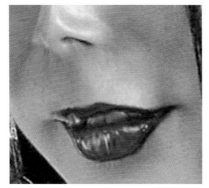

Figure 8.44: Lip/mouth alteration

Figure 8.43: Reducing the nose

Reduce the size of the cheeks and chin until the chin is nearly to a point. Take a look at Figure 8.45 and use it as a guide for your Liquify transformation. Once you have a reasonable duplicate, click OK to accept the changes.

As mentioned in the beginning of this project, paths will be utilized to help generate the character. Each portion of the image will now be converted to a path—or a better way to put it is that a path will be created to represent each portion/feature in the image.

Select the Polygonal Lasso tool and set the options as follows:

Selection Type	Add To Selection
Feather	0 px
Anti-aliased	Checked

To make our model into an anime character, we also need to work on her skin tone. In addition to enormous eyes and a tiny mouth and nose, these characters typically have a uniform skin color, with little or none of the shading seen in photographs or more realistic cartoon animation. We'll fix that next.

Figure 8.45: The woman takes on anime characteristics.

Figure 8.46: The active selection

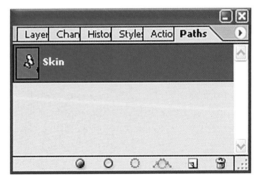

Figure 8.47: Create and name a path called Skin.

Figure 8.48: Fill the path with her skin tone.

Select all the areas of skin in the photo, being sure to omit the hair, eyes, and costume from the selection (see Figure 8.46).

At the bottom of the Paths palette, click the icon that says Make A Work Path From Selection. Rename the new path **Skin** in the Paths palette (see Figure 8.47). Once the path has been generated and renamed, go to the Swatches palette and change the foreground color to the hue of her predominant skin tone. Right-click the Skin path in the Paths palette and select Fill Path from the menu that opens. Fill the path with the foreground color. The image will now look like Figure 8.48.

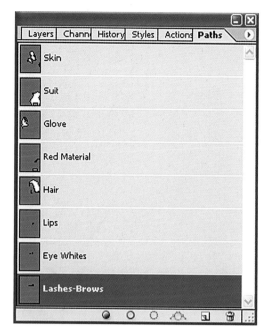

Figure 8.49: A path for each area of the image

Figure 8.50: The character coming to life

Create paths for all the major areas and rename the new paths accordingly in the Paths palette (see Figure 8.49). As you work, fill each with its corresponding color from the Swatches palette. Separate the pupils and whites of the eyes into their own paths.

Once a path has been created for each area and the paths filled with their corresponding hues, your image will look like Figure 8.50. It may appear a little rough around the edges as this example does, but that is OK. You will see it begin to come together shortly.

Note the areas behind the paths where the image is still visible along the edges. These areas need to be deleted, and to do this, you need to select all the paths, invert the selection, and then delete. After the selection has been inverted, press the Delete key to wipe away those offending areas. To create selections on the paths, right-click a path (start with the Skin path at the top of the Paths palette). Select Make Selection from the menu that opens. The first time you do this, only New Selection will be available. Ensure that the Feather radius is set to 0 and that Anti-Aliased is checked, and click OK. A selection of the Skin areas is now active.

Repeat the previous step on all the other paths. When you open the Make Selection dialog box with a selection already active, the option Add To Selection becomes available (see Figure 8.51). Select this for each path until a selection has been made of the entire woman.

Choose Select → Inverse and with the Working layer selected in the Layers palette, press the Delete key. This will trim away all the excess left over by the photo (see Figure 8.52).

Duplicate the Background layer again and place the new copy above the layer filled with black. This layer will be used as a guide for the addition of the new mouth and nose to

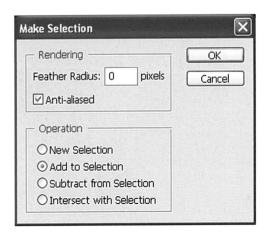

Figure 8.51: *Generating selection from paths*

Figure 8.52: *Excess photo trimmed away from art*

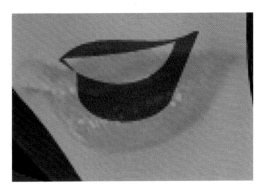

Figure 8.53: *Duplicate the background to use as a guide for creating the lips.*

Figure 8.54: *Freehand a new set of lips with the Lasso tools and fill with her lip tone.*

the art. You will now have your drawing chops tested, because the new mouth will be selected and filled by hand.

Select the Working layer in the Layers palette and reduce the opacity of the layer to about 80%, so that the Background Copy layer can be seen beneath. Using the Lasso tools, create a smaller version of the lips and fill the selection with the lip color from the Swatches palette. Make your new lips about half the size of the originals seen in the layer beneath (see Figure 8.53).

When you have the lips created and filled, select the Background Copy layer. Set the foreground color to her skin tone and with the Paintbrush tool, paint over the mouth so that it can no longer be seen though the layer (see Figure 8.54). What I'm trying to do here, and what I want you to do also, is utilize some of the reflections from this layer in the final image, but with the new face that we are in the process of generating.

Select the Working layer and press Command/Control+E to merge it with the Background Copy layer. Rename the newly merged layer **Anime-Art** (see Figure 8.55).

Now create a duplicate of the Anime-Art layer and set the blending mode to Overlay. We can use the existing layers with a bit of filter application to make the new cartoon take

Figure 8.56: Material reflections take on airbrushed qualities.

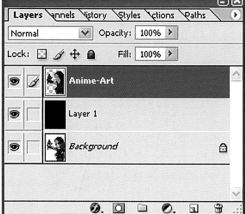

Figure 8.55: Merge the layers and rename the new layer.

on an airbrushed appearance. Choose Filter → Blur → Gaussian Blur and set the radius of the blur to 4. Click OK.

Take a look at Figure 8.56. Your image should have similar features as this image: The face appears airbrushed a bit, with reflections off the material showing up through the filled path areas on the costume.

Now you can begin working on a very prominent feature found in most Japanese animation: the distinctive watery eyes found on most of their female characters.

Create a new layer above the Anime-Art Copy layer, and rename the new layer **Extra Paint-Eyes**. Zoom in close to the eyes and change the foreground color to black. Using the Paintbrush tool and a hard-edged brush, round out the irises (see Figure 8.57).

With the Magic Wand tool, select the black areas. The selection may be a bit distorted, but that's fine (see Figure 8.58).

Figure 8.57: Round out the irises

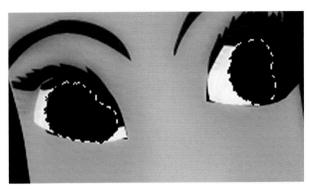

Figure 8.58: Selection for fill color

Figure 8.59: Blurring for airbrushed irises

Figure 8.60: Pupil creation

Set the foreground color to bright green. Create a new layer and rename it **Eye-Fill**. Fill the selection with the foreground color, then run a Gaussian Blur so that the edges of the fill allow some of the black beneath to show through (see Figure 8.59).

Select the Elliptical Marquee tool with no feather and create large selections over the green areas that will serve as the pupils. Fill these areas with black (see Figure 8.60).

Select the Polygonal Lasso again. Now that the pupils are in place, the reflections can be created by making rough rectangular selections around the center of the pupils radiating out from the center point and filling the selections with white (see Figure 8.61).

The image still retains a bit too much of the original photo, but with a Brightness/Contrast Adjustment layer (see Figure 8.62), the characteristics of the original leather top can be reduced to give it a painted impression (see Figure 8.63).

If you are a fan, or are at least aware of anime, then you know that the animators use some pretty strange, stark hair colors on many of their characters. This is particularly true of female characters. To alter the hair tone, simply create a new layer beneath the Adjustment layer and name it **Hair Tone**. Create a selection of the Hair path again and fill the selection with a bright color, in this case red. Use the Gaussian Blur filter again to allow the edges to appear airbrushed, and you will have a vector-style anime character as seen in Figure 8.64.

Figure 8.61: Reflections on the eyes

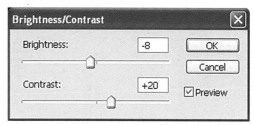

Figure 8.62: Brightness/Contrast Adjustment layer

Figure 8.63: Our anime heroine

Figure 8.64: Anime heroine revisited

Industrial Art: Photo, Paint, and Texture Merge

Concept Create an artistic rendering using elements of a photo, paint/line art, and texture.

Visualize The idea behind this project is to meld elements covered in this and other chapters, creating something that combines a photo with drawn or painted outlines, and then adds texture by combining the image with another photograph. In my mind, I see an image that emulates metal, rust, and nature.

Realize With a couple of photographs and some lineart techniques, this should be a snap. You will use line art combined with blending modes and the application of a texture.

Start with a photo that has elements of both nature and an oxidizing car. Open the image `old_car.jpg` (see Figure 8.65), found on this book's CD.

Set up the Layers palette by duplicating the Background layer twice. Shut off the top layer and select the one just above the Background (see Figure 8.66).

To add drawn edges (or at least give the appearance of such), the Find Edges filter will work just fine. Choose Filter → Stylize → Find Edges. Set the blending mode of the layer to Overlay.

Select the topmost layer (it will activate once again) and rename it **Desaturated**. Change the blending mode to Soft Light and choose Image → Adjustments → Desaturate to

Figure 8.65: A forgotten classic

wipe away the color. Choose Filter → Stylize → Find Edges again on this layer. If you were to turn off the layers beneath the Desaturated layer, the Automobile layer should appear as seen in Figure 8.67.

The lines on the edges of the old car can be more clearly defined by choosing Image → Adjustments → Threshold. Take a look at Figure 8.68. Moving the Threshold slider to the right (a value of 132 in this case) darkens the edges of the car and rusted areas, but lightens the whiter portions of the layer. Click OK.

You don't need all that white on this layer, because only the edges of the car need darkening, and not the rest of the image lightened. Choose Select → Color Range and click the eyedropper in the white areas of the layer. Click OK and delete the selection (see Figure 8.69).

Now you can apply another image to the photo for texture. Open the image car-texture.jpg (see Figure 8.70) from this book's CD. Select the entire image and copy it, then paste it into a new layer in the car document. Set the blending mode for the new layer to—what else—Overlay.

Let's give the color saturation a good tweaking. Create a Hue/Saturation Adjustment layer and reduce the saturation to –65. Click OK to accept the adjustment. Take a look at the image: It should be fairly close to the example seen in Figure 8.71. I love how this technique outlines not only the car, but the minute spots of rust on the hood and the chrome bumper of the car, almost like an intricate watercolor painting mingled with airbrushing, perhaps?

Create another copy of the Background layer just above the Background. Choose Filter → Brush Strokes → Paint Daubs. Using a Simple Brush type, set the Brush Size to 28 and the Sharpness to 24. Click OK.

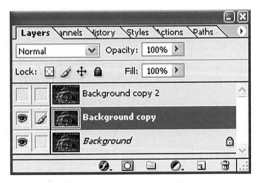

Figure 8.66: Set up the layers.

Figure 8.67: Desaturated Lines layer

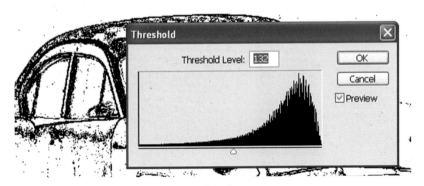

Figure 8.68: Increasing the intensity of the lines

Figure 8.69: Delete the white from the lined layer.

Apply a Gaussian Blur to this layer also, with a Radius setting of 20 pixels. The final image (see Figure 8.72) shows the combined effects: paint, photo, and texture. Sweet!

Figure 8.70: Texture photo

Figure 8.71: Texture merged with the car photo

Figure 8.72: A new art form?

People are like stained glass windows: they sparkle and shine when the sun's out, but when the darkness sets in, their true beauty is revealed only if there is light within.
—Elisabeth Kubler-Ross

nine

CHAPTER

People as Art—Digital Manipulation

Photoshop is a tool *that releases the inner artist in those who, like me, have brains that are creative to a fault but lose it when attempting to recreate the visions with a pencil or paintbrush. Photoshop has given digital artists new media in which to work—media that real-world artists would never think to use. Some artists use the human body as a canvas; a digital artist can use it as their clay. We can shape it, mold it, color it, add appendages or remove them, with no harm to the model.*

This chapter is specifically about using the human form as a medium for artistic molding and manipulation. You will color it, texture it, melt it, and mold it. Of all the chapters in this book, this is the one closest to my heart because the manipulations in this chapter are from my imagination working with the medium I love. In this chapter, you get to open my head and see the right side of my brain, and in the process I hope you will pick up some ideas on how to apply what you see to your own work.

Chex-Girl: Impressionist

I categorize this piece as impressionist, but I'm using the term loosely, because the art being formed varies from the original definition. Impressionism took shape in France in the 1870s. The focus was on capturing and communicating an initial visual impression, with the primary elements of the style being unmixed primary colors and small strokes that simulated reflected light.

This piece may better be categorized as digital impressionism. Stark primary colors come into play and lighting is of the essence, but the medium is photography. This technique demonstrates how these elements work together in a photo intended to generate instant reactions.

Concept Take a photo of a person and blend them into their background. The idea is not a true camouflage, but rather something you might expect from a chameleon.

Visualize What I see in my mind's eye is a woman whose body paint mimics the pattern on the wall behind her. In particular, to create an image that might be used to advertise automotive products, you'll take a sexy model and blend her into a NASCAR checkered flag.

Realize To realize this effect, only two images are needed: the subject and the background they will attempt to blend with. Photoshop and you will do the rest, using familiar techniques such as layers and displacement maps.

The subject for this technique is a young woman in a bikini on a white background, so open the image `Purple-Bikini.jpg` (see Figure 9.1) from this book's CD. I can read the minds of about half of you already: "Come on, Al, isn't this just an excuse to work on a woman in a bikini?" Actually there are practical uses for this effect: conforming a logo to a surface that is contoured; affixing a label, poster, or billboard and warping it to match the surface; and so on. I chose this image because a human form presents a contoured surface that allows me to demonstrate the effect. That's my story and I'm sticking to it.

You are probably familiar with blue screens, which are used in movies to add special effects to a scene. In this instance, the white background serves a similar capacity; the model can be easily pulled from this background and the secondary background inserted.

Duplicate the Background layer and following the extraction techniques presented in Chapter 1, remove the woman from the white background. Because the edges are crisp, the extraction should be pretty straightforward, but pay close attention to the hair and touch it up when you preview the extraction (see Figure 9.2). You may add back hair that was removed by selecting the Cleanup tool and while holding down the Alt/Option key, running the tool over the area to be recovered. Check the rest of your edges, and be sure to get the white that you may have missed between the fingers. Once satisfied that the edges are as clean as possible, click OK.

The image that will serve as both the new background and the body paint is `checker-tile.jpg` (see Figure 9.3). Open the image from this book's CD, select the entire thing, copy it, and paste it into a new layer just above the Background layer in the model photo (see Figure 9.4).

The idea is to have the entire background covered in checkers. First, use Command/Control+ (minus key) to reduce the view to a manageable size. Shrink it quite a bit so that the transform corners will appear in the next step. Choose Edit → Transform → Scale and increase the size of the background so that the squares stay in proportion, and so that the entire background is covered (see Figure 9.5). After accepting the transformation, zoom in again.

Now would be a good time to finish any cleanup work on the model layer before applying the paint. Rename the layer with the extracted woman **Model**. Select the Eraser tool and using a small, semi-hard round brush, wipe away any of the white that may have remained in and around the hair during the extraction (see Figure 9.6).

Figure 9.1: *Model in a sterile environment*

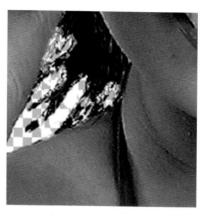

Figure 9.2: *Watch the hair during the extraction; clean up while previewing.*

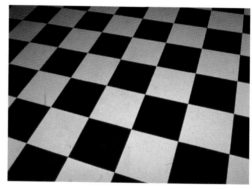

Figure 9.3: *Checkered pattern for background and body paint*

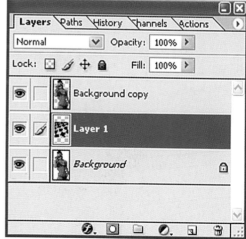

Figure 9.4: *Adding the pattern to the model photo*

Figure 9.5: Increase the size of the background pattern to cover the image, but keep the proportion.

Figure 9.6: Clean up the extra white pixels around the strands of hair.

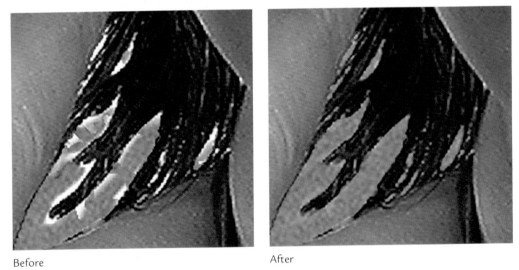

Before   After

It's time to call on Chapter 1 again. Create a displacement map of the Model layer to be used to conform the texture to the contours of the woman.

Be sure to render the checkered layer invisible before switching to the Channels palette to create the map. The map that I've created was created using the green channel and is seen in Figure 9.7. This is also available as `chex-map.psd` in the `Displacement Maps` folder on this book's CD. Once the map is saved to the hard drive, you can delete the green copy channel.

Figure 9.7: The displacement map for warping the checkered paint

Figure 9.8: Select the model's shape, but stay on the checkered layer.

Duplicate the checkered background and place the new checkered layer above the Model layer. Command/Control+click the Model layer to select her form (see Figure 9.8), but remain in the new checkered layer. Reduce the opacity of the layer to around 75...just enough so that you can see the form of the woman beneath. This will allow you to gauge how many times to run the Displace filter.

Speaking of the Displace filter...choose Filter → Distort → Displace. Enter 10 for both the Horizontal Scale and the Vertical Scale, and click OK. Find the displacement map just created and click Open to apply the map to the checkered pattern (see Figure 9.9). The primary reason for using a setting of only 10 is to not overdo it; you can always apply the filter again. Run Displace one more time with the same settings to increase the distortion; continue doing so until the pattern conforms to the body as you like, but one, two, or three times more should be plenty. Figure 9.10 shows the distortion after three applications of the filter.

The portions of the checkered layer that were not displaced can be removed now. Choose Select → Inverse and press the Delete key to erase the excess. Rename this layer **Checkered Paint**, increase the opacity to 100%, and change the blending mode to Overlay (see Figure 9.11). Deselect the shape. Figure 9.12 shows the effect thus far.

It looks as if she is covered in some sort of dye, but that isn't really what we're trying to achieve. The pattern should not be running through her hair or eyes, or over the bikini; also,

Figure 9.9: Apply the displacement map to the pattern.

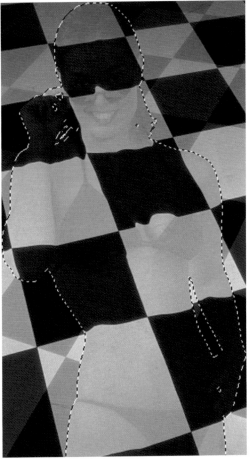

Figure 9.10: Displacement after three filter applications

the end result will be more black and white than brown and yellow, the result of the overlay applied to the skin tones beneath.

Start by removing the paint from the hair and eyes. This can be accomplished with a mask. Create a layer mask for the Checkered Paint layer and with a black, hard-edged round brush, paint over the areas of hair and the eyes to erase the caramel color away. Wipe away the pattern from the lenses of her glasses also, as well as her ears. If the pattern crossed over the bridge of her nose, then wipe away the color so that the curve appears natural. If your pattern has covered teeth, lips, or fingernails, mask these areas also (see Figure 9.13).

Go to the Model layer and select the Magic Wand tool with the Add to Selection button depressed in the Options Toolbar. Select the bikini top and bottom. When both areas or all instances of purple (including the straps) are selected, return to the mask in the Checkered Paint layer and fill the selections with black (see Figure 9.14).

I'll bet you are wondering when this gal is going to take on the color of her background, and not just the pattern. That will happen now. First, duplicate the Model layer; rename it **Model-2**.

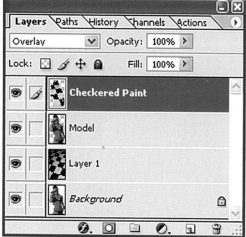

Figure 9.11: Set the attributes for the new Checkered Paint layer.

Figure 9.12: The body paint thus far

Select the Magic Wand with the same settings as before. Go to the Checkered Paint layer and select the white tiles. Expand the selection by two pixels and hit Delete. This will take some of the edges off the black tiles also, but that's fine. Her natural flesh tone is now seen where the white tiles were placed over her skin (see Figure 9.15). If some white still remains, expand the selection again by two pixels and delete. Repeat as needed to get rid of the excess white.

Choose Select → Inverse and click the Model-2 layer. Increase the size of the selection by eight pixels again. Create a Hue/Saturation Adjustment layer just above the Model-2 layer, decrease the saturation to –75, and click OK.

Select the bikini again on the Model-2 layer with the Magic Wand. The color needs to be restored, so select the mask attached to the Hue/Saturation Adjustment layer and fill the selection with 100% black. Now select the paintbrush and paint in the mask with black over those areas that you want to restore color to, for instance, the hair, ears, or wherever the saturation has been removed that needs to be restored (see Figure 9.16).

To give the rest of the model a coat of light gray or off-white paint, desaturate the Model-2 layer, reduce the opacity to 75%, and change the blending mode to Hue. Create a

Figure 9.13: Mask away the excess pattern.

Figure 9.14: Reveal the bikini's true colors.

Figure 9.15: Working with the tiles again

Figure 9.16: Restoring absent color

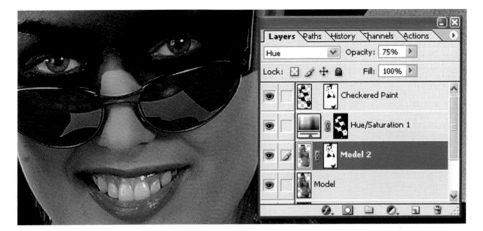

Figure 9.17: Add the white paint.

new mask nearly identical to the one used in the Checkered Paint layer, but this time paint over the lips and hair in the mask with black to reveal the natural colors beneath (see Figure 9.17).

This looks like it may serve well as an ad for a motor oil company, but the color is a bit washed out yet. To solve this, simply create a Brightness/Contrast Adjustment layer at the top of the layer stack and increase the contrast to +20 or so.

The final thing to do with this image, at least as far as this section is concerned, is to give emphasis to the light source by creating a drop shadow. Command/Control+click the Model layer to generate a selection. Create a new layer just above the checkered background and with the arrow keys, move the selection to the right a few clicks (right 20 clicks of the arrow, down 15 clicks: this should work well at this high resolution). Fill the selection with 70% black and deselect. Now just apply a Gaussian Blur of around 65%. Figure 9.18 shows the final model image,

Figure 9.18: A cheerleader at a NASCAR racetrack

freshly painted and ready for bright logos, miniature product pictures, and text selling high-performance motor oil. Where advertisers came up with the idea of selling automotive maintenance with sex I'll never know, but judging from the calendars hanging in nearly every auto body shop I've been in, it must work like a charm!

Zebra Woman: Adventures in Advertising

This technique is very similar to the previous. This time, however, the texture being applied is a pattern out of nature rather than geometric textiles created by man.

Concept Merge a pattern taken from nature and blend it with a human face. The convergence of two elements from the natural world will help to put forth the feeling of intelligence combined with a wild element. Both of those connotations are important here because the final image will be used in an advertisement for the fictitious company Savannah Running Gear, which has the slogans "Still Wild after All These Years" and "Outrunning the Competition Since 1927."

Visualize Unlike the last piece, this time I see a facial close-up, yet with only half exposed. The primary subject will have a smart yet feral appearance, and the background will add to the effect of the piece. I also see a lot of color in natural tones to help the end effect.

Realize Following the same idea (if not the same process) of applying a pattern to a human form using displacement maps and masks as in the Chex-girl tutorial, this will be a piece of cake to realize. One hopes, anyway!

To begin, open the image `half-face.jpg` (see Figure 9.19) from this book's CD. Although the edge where the hair joins the background is a bit blurry, the extraction should still be fairly clean. Duplicate the Background layer and follow the procedures for extracting the woman from her background as given in Chapter 1 (see Figure 9.20).

Figure 9.19: Photo of the primary subject

Figure 9.20: Extract the subject from the existing background.

Open the image `Zebra.jpg` (see Figure 9.21) from this book's CD. Using a pattern from a wild animal will assist in the feral quality of the final image. The zebra pattern is a bit smaller than the woman's photo, so use the Transform tools to resize the pattern to cover the entire image. Reduce the opacity of the zebra pattern layer to around 60% and position it so the eye of the zebra roughly matches that of the woman. The zebra's eye will not be visible in the final image, but note the black stripe that curves beneath the eye. I want to use that to curve along the contours of the woman's face (see Figure 9.22).

Shut off the zebra pattern layer for the creation of the displacement map. Although there is some curve to the fur pattern, it still needs to conform to the curves on the woman's face.

Although I'm not going to walk through the entire process of creating the map, I do want you to see the settings I'm using, and the channel on which I'm using them. Call it a spot check, if you will. For this particular image, I'm using a copy of the blue channel to create the map. Figure 9.23 shows the Brightness/Contrast adjustment that I'm applying to lighten and darken areas of the face. When you get to this point and have a good contrast between the lights and darks in the channel, click OK.

Next apply a Gaussian Blur to the channel. Figure 9.24 is a representation of my settings in this instance. Once you have a good blur but still have good contrast between the whites and darks, click OK and proceed with saving the map normally.

With the displacement map saved, Command/Control+click the face layer with the zebra stripes still selected. Run the Displace filter with a setting of 10 Vertical and 10 Horizontal; you may desire to run this twice if the distortion does not yet appear to conform to the contours in a realistic fashion (see Figure 9.25).

Figure 9.21: Zebra pattern

Figure 9.22: An opacity change to resize and position the pattern

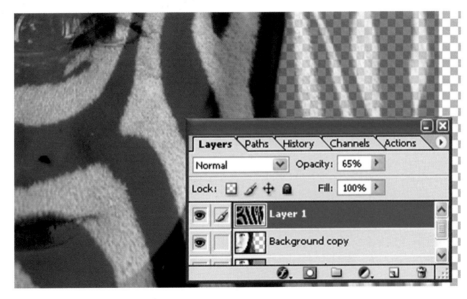

Figure 9.23: A spot check on channel manipulation for the displacement map

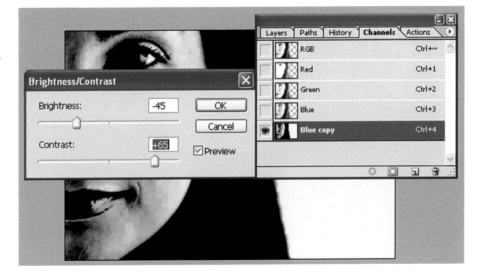

Figure 9.24: *The blur applied to the map channel*

Figure 9.25: *Distorted fur layer*

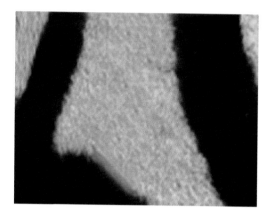

Figure 9.26: *Sample areas where the patterns are not distorted*

Figure 9.27: *Fur layer after displacement, healing, and deletion of excess pixels*

Displacements often produce stretching and smearing patterns, and this example is no exception. Apply these settings to the Healing Brush:

Brush size	100
Mode	Replace
Source	Sampled

Then take samples from undistorted areas of fur (see Figure 9.26) and heal the stretched areas.

The areas of fur that extend beyond the woman's hair to the right can be discarded, because the pattern will be applied only to her and not to the background. Command/Control+click the woman's layer, invert the selection on the zebra pattern layer, and hit Delete. Then deselect (see Figure 9.27).

You'll now apply the pattern to the woman's face. Set the blending mode for the fur layer to Overlay, and duplicate the layer twice (see Figure 9.28).

As with the previous technique, the color needs to be wiped away from the face to get rid of the caramel color. At present it looks as though the woman has been splashed with motor oil. Use the Magic Wand tool set to Add To Selection and select the black stripes on the topmost face layer (see Figure 9.29).

Select the Background Copy layer and open the Adjustment Layer menu. Create a new Hue/Saturation Adjustment layer. Move the Saturation slider to the left until the black is revealed as black once again, as it was in the original zebra pattern (see Figure 9.30).

You may want to deepen the tones of the overall piece, so a quick Levels Adjustment layer at the top of the layer stack will be a handy tool to accomplish this. Figure 9.31 shows the adjustment I've used to enrich the tones, but feel free to experiment.

Figure 9.28: Placing the pattern in the woman document

Figure 9.29: Select the black stripes on the fur pattern.

Figure 9.30: Desaturate the skin beneath the black stripes to bring out the animal.

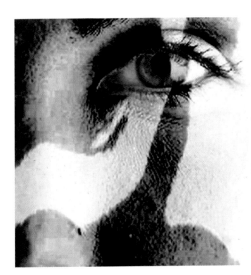

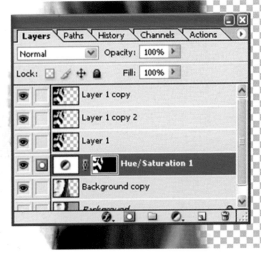

One thing about eyes: it is a very short trip when working with brown eyes to achieve red or orange, which adds to the unreal quality of the creation or the creature. In Figure 9.32, I've simply used the Dodge tool, as in Chapter 2, to lighten the browns of the iris to a blend of orange and yellows.

In the final image (see Figure 9.33), I've chosen a background of a sunset (`sunset3.jpg` on this book's CD) with a feral cat (`kitty.jpg` on this book's CD) overlay, and added the text for the company's name and slogans. It's now ready to present to the client for approval. This is a slightly simplified version of how ads are usually created in the real world—companies start with a slogan and have a logo and so forth before commissioning the advertising. If you go on to do any ad work on your own, your ability to dream up the perfect right-brain version of the company's idea for their product will be as important as your command of Photoshop.

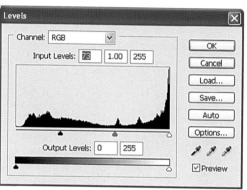

Figure 9.31: Deepen the color saturation with levels.

Figure 9.32: Eyes lightened with the Dodge tool

Figure 9.33: The final advertisement

Alien Boy: Digital Distortions

I had the pleasure earlier this year to spend two days teaching Photoshop to a group of digital photographers at the Rocky Mountain School of Photography (www.rmsp.com) in Missoula, Montana. I'd spent a lot of time getting together all the cool things I could teach them in the limited time allotted me. Because 90% of the students were film photographers making the leap to digital and had only limited experience with Photoshop, the range of things available to teach that had not been covered by the other authors and instructors was still vast.

I decided to just go for the coolest stuff I could find and teach them the right-brain way—envision the effect and then learn the tools along the way, rather than tackle tools and show what they could be used for. The people taking the course varied in age from mid-teens to mid-fifties, and each showed interest in different areas. You could almost see the light going on over their heads when they made the connection of how the technique being taught could apply to their own work.

The one tool that stood out over all the rest, that made nearly everyone immediately sit up straight and pay close attention, was the one tool that gets the least serious coverage by authors and art purists: the Liquify tool.

The Liquify Tool

This tool is extremely powerful, allowing you to manipulate the pixels in a layer in interesting ways. You can stretch them, twist them, compact and expand them, or simply push them around into new positions.

This technique approaches the Liquify filter as a serious, no-nonsense tool for some pretty astounding digital manipulations. The key is to work in micro steps (as opposed to macro): small changes gradually working toward the final image, rather than large changes that will often leave the subject, and the finished art, stretched and distorted.

Concept Take a photograph of a friend or family member, and change them into something from popular modern mythology.

Visualize I see a creature that has been getting a lot of publicity over the past thirty years or so, what is commonly referred to as a Gray alien. I'll leave the debate over whether or not they exist to people concerned with that sort of thing. For a right-brainer, they are excellent subject matter, whether they really crashed at Roswell or not.

Realize With the Liquify filter at your disposal, realizing this is actually a lot easier than it may seem at first glance. The effect you are looking for is certainly larger than life, but the best way to realize this is not with big sweeping alterations; small changes will better help produce the alteration. The small changes will add up to a whole, complete alien.

The photo for this piece is of my son, one of my favorite models because he works for very cheap. Open the image `seriousboy.jpg` (see Figure 9.34) from this book's CD.

Figure 9.34: Caught in deep thought

Aliens—if you are prone to believe in the critters (or perhaps believe you have suffered through an abduction yourself)—tend to show up at night, so eventually the background will be black. Another reason for the black is that the creepy image we are trying to produce has better effect on a dark canvas. Duplicate the Background layer. Create a new layer just above the Background layer and fill it with a dark color; gray or black will work just fine. Follow the extraction method from Chapter 1 and remove the boy from the Background, wiping away the wall. Some extra pixels may remain after the extraction (see Figure 9.35). If that is the case, use a hard-edged eraser and wipe these away. You can also use the eraser to

*Figure 9.35:
Some pixels may
be left behind
after the
extraction.*

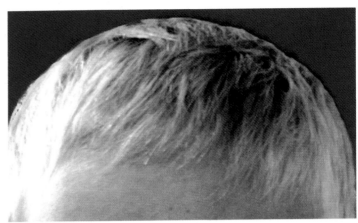

*Figure 9.36: Use the Eraser tool to round out the top of the head and
remove the unwanted pixels left by the extraction.*

*Figure 9.37: Run
through the High
Pass sharpening
trick.*

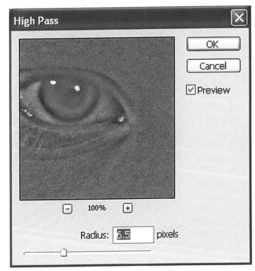

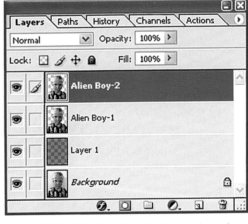

*Figure 9.38: Alien Boy-2 is the layer where the
alien will be born.*

round out the hair border a bit…stray hairs will not be required or desired, because gray
aliens (or so I'm told) are bald as a rule (see Figure 9.36).

You will be opening the Liquify tool in just a second, but before jumping in to actually
warp the photo, go ahead and run the High Pass sharpening trick from Chapter 1 (see
Figure 9.37).

Rename the extracted boy layer **Alien Boy-1**; duplicate the layer and rename the new
one **Alien Boy-2** (see Figure 9.38). As always, it is good to have a copy of the primary subject
that won't be altered…just in case.

Grays (the aliens, not the color) have very prominent almond-shaped eyes, large domed
heads, and pinched mouths and noses. All of this can be accomplished with the Liquify tool.

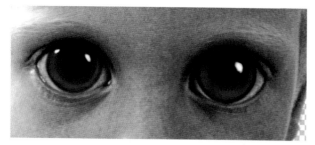

Figure 9.39: Increase the size of the eyes slightly.

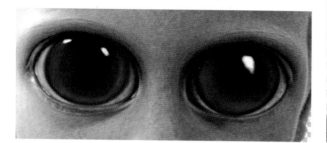

Figure 9.40: Increase the eyes some more.

Figure 9.41: Reduce the size of the mouth and nose with the Pucker tool.

Generally when working with aliens, I start with the eyes, getting the size and shape just right, and then work on the proportions for the rest of the face. Choose Filter → Liquify. Select the Bloat tool and set up these Bloat tool attributes:

Brush Size	300
Brush Density	35
Brush Pressure	40
Brush Rate	80

Center the brush over one of the pupils and gradually expand the eye to a larger, rounder shape with the Bloat tool. Repeat the process on the other eye, and work back and forth between the two until they are uniform, expanded nearly as far as the current Bloat tool settings will allow for a stationary alteration (see Figure 9.39). Do not move the brush once you start bloating!

Increase the size of the Bloat brush by 50 or so, and again work on the eyes in the same fashion. Note that, as you bloat with the brush centered on the pupil, the brows are pushed up into well-defined ridges. Continue to increase the size of the eyes until they are extremely large caricatures of their original selves, as seen in Figure 9.40.

When you have a good round pair of large, bulging eyes, switch to the Pucker tool. Set the Brush size to 200 or so and reduce the size of the nose and mouth (see Figure 9.41). In this case, you may want to move the brush around a bit while compressing the pixels, but strive to keep things in proportion.

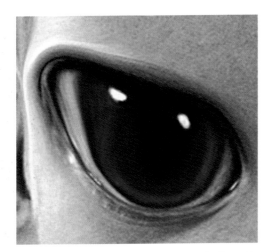

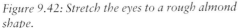

Figure 9.42: Stretch the eyes to a rough almond shape.

Figure 9.43: Both eyes with their new shape

The eyes aren't quite done yet; the almond shape still needs to be worked out. To do this, switch to the Forward Warp tool, found at the top of the Liquify toolbar on the left side of the Liquify dialog box. Reduce the size of the brush to 100 or so and gradually pull the corners of the eyes toward the temples. Reduce the size of the brush as needed to create rounded points (see Figure 9.42). This may take some patience, so stick with it and work slowly. When you are done with both eyes, the face should be really close to the one seen in Figure 9.43.

Once the eyes are huge and almond-shaped, you can use the Forward Warp tool to bring the ears in tight to the sides of the head, and then increase the size of the forehead and skull. Simply push the pixels into place, using Figure 9.44 as a guide. Aliens have large craniums, so push that hairline up and widen the head above the temples.

Next, work on the lower portion of the face. Using combinations of the Forward Warp tool and the Pucker tool, decrease the size of the cheeks so that the cheekbones become prominent. Reduce the nose size some more as well as the mouth; the distance between the nose and mouth should be increased. Also, shrink the chin. The key here is to work on one side of the face in a specific area (for example, a cheek) and then repeat the process on the other side to help maintain proportion. When you have a pretty fair alien shape, fill the gray layer beneath the Alien Boy-1 layer with 100% black (see Figure 9.45).

To get rid of the color in the eyes (both the whites and the blues), select the Burn tool and set the Brush Size to 30, the Range to Highlights, and the Exposure to 70%. Burn the white away in both eyes with the exception of the light reflecting off the surface (see Figure 9.46), then change the Burn tool settings to Midtones. Burn the blue away also (see Figure 9.47).

Figure 9.44: Push the forehead into a round dome.

Figure 9.45: The shape of things to come

You have probably already looked at the stretch marks on the forehead and said "EEWW! That looks ugly!" There's no way you want those in the final image. Select the Healing Brush and set these options:

Brush Size	175
Mode	Multiply
Source	Sampled

Sample areas on the lower portion of the forehead that were not stretched in the Liquify process and use them to heal the distorted areas. You can even take samples of the cheeks if you like; just remember to sample areas where the color and brightness are approximately the same as the area you want to cover.

I've yet to see a picture of a Gray alien with hair, so this one will be bald also. Duplicate the Alien Boy-2 layer (see Figure 9.48). Generate a selection around the head (Command/Control+click the layer). Continue sampling and healing the forehead right to the top. Don't work on the sides yet, just the large center portion (see Figure 9.49).

Select the Lasso tool. In the area where the Healing Brush was used to replace the stretches, draw a large round selection (see Figure 9.50) and copy it. Paste it into a new layer (see Figure 9.51).

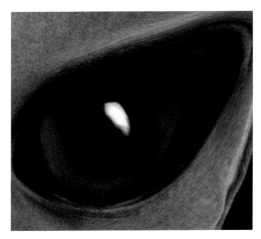

Figure 9.46: Darken the eyes, but retain the reflections.

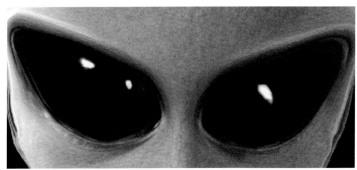

Figure 9.47: Remove the blue color with the Burn tool.

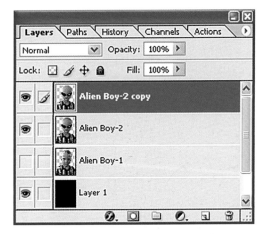

Figure 9.48: Duplicate the Alien Boy-2 layer.

Figure 9.49: Heal away the stretch marks and hair.

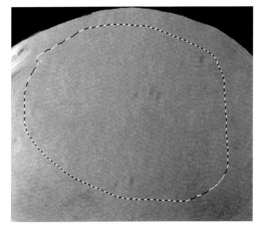

Figure 9.50: Select and copy a large chunk of the forehead.

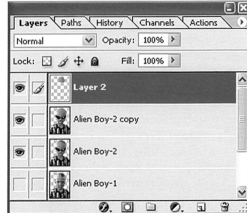

Figure 9.51: Paste the section into a new layer.

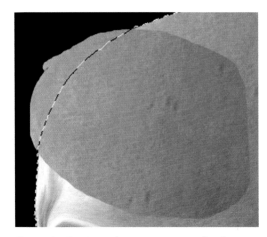

Figure 9.52: Move the section over other hair parts.

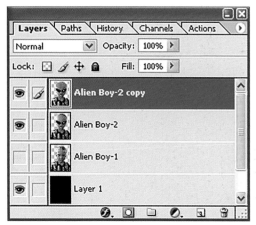

Figure 9.53: Merge the forehead section with the layer beneath.

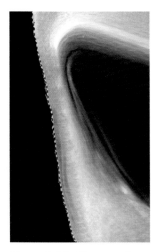

Figure 9.54: Clean up the skin around the eyes.

Figure 9.55: Creepy...

With the Move tool, place the forehead section over one of the sides where there is still hair. Generate a selection of the head again, select the inverse, and hit Delete (see Figure 9.52). This trims away the excess from the paste; now the section can be blended into the forehead. Press Command/Control+E to merge the piece into the Alien Boy-2 Copy layer (see Figure 9.53). Use the Healing Brush to finish blending the piece into the forehead. Create more pieces as needed to finish the forehead, repeating the process until all the hair is removed and the forehead is completely blended with no seams.

Grab the Healing Brush again, and sample/heal the areas around the eyes that still have hair. Also cover the ears so they are no longer visible. It is better to work within a selection so that no pixels stray outside the edge of the cranium, so select the head just before working around those edges (see Figure 9.54).

Repeat the process on the other side of the head, until your image looks like Figure 9.55.

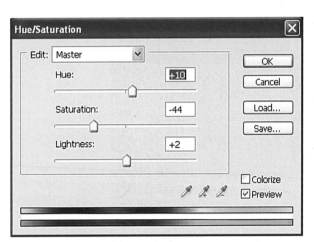

Figure 9.56: Adjust the hue and saturation.

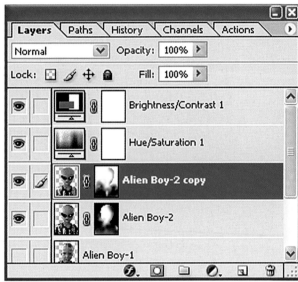

Figure 9.57: Use masks to hide him in the shadows.

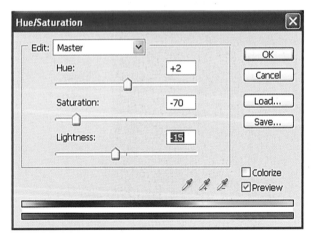

Figure 9.58: One more Hue/Saturation adjustment

This guy is looking kind of strange, but to the soon-to-be-abducted, nothing is more frightening than to see a pair of these huge eyes peering at them over the end of the bed in the deep, dark night. It's time to put them in their proper setting, and get rid of the coveralls at the same time.

To darken things up and alter the color to reflect the gray in the name of the creature, create two Adjustment layers in rapid succession. First, create a Hue/Saturation Adjustment layer. Set the Hue to +10 or so, and reduce the saturation to –40 or –45, somewhere in that range. The skin will take on a faint green tint, and with the saturation reduced, a sickly pallor (for a human, anyway) takes predominance (see Figure 9.56).

Create a second Adjustment layer; this time select Brightness/Contrast from the menu. Decrease the brightness to –45, and increase the contrast to +45. This deepens the shadows, increases the highlights, and enhances the effect of a night visit.

To complete the effect, first shut off the Alien Boy-1 layer in the Layers palette. Create a mask for Alien Skin-2, and paint in the mask with black (set the paintbrush to around 60% opacity) over the coveralls and shirt, as well as along the right side of the face and head. Repeat the process for the Alien Boy-2 Copy layer until the face is partially obscured in darkness (see Figure 9.57). You may want to tweak the Hue/Saturation again, decreasing the saturation even further and decreasing the lightness to –15 (see Figure 9.58).

For the final shots, I've supplied two images:the first is the full photo (see Figure 9.59) and the second is a close-up of the face (see Figure 9.60). How would you like to see that in your bedroom some night?

Figure 9.60: A nocturnal visitor from another galaxy?

Wicked Child: A Study in Dark Art

Dark Art uses the twisting of color and light for emphasis, using either extreme color and light or the alteration and removal of color and light. It is intriguing yet uncomfortable at the same time, because it bends the barriers of what is considered normal and safe.

Before we venture into the darker regions of design where nightmares and Photoshop collide in a twisted and eerie mix of art and terror, I must first offer a disclaimer for this next effect. As an author, I've had multiple opportunities (which I've capitalized on) to use my children for the various tutorials or effects I'm working on. Over the course of my books I've turned my son into a bat, an alien, and other creatures that make his mother wonder about the man she married. I've never been able to apply what I know to my daughter, however...other than to do nice, sweet images or color corrections. I could never warp my sweet little girl. Or could I?

This has been traumatizing to my little girl. When my last book was released, she combed every page to see what cool thing her daddy turned her into, only to go away heartbroken when the only image I used her in was for coloring her dress. Her brother had his face all twisted into some really disgusting creature, and she was making a fashion statement. Daddy, how could you???

So, against my paternal urge to keep my daughter from the laboratory, I submit this experiment. She has seen the final image, and I'm happy to note that it has met her five-year-old approval. I needn't have worried about warping her…I think someone beat me to it.

Concept Take a photo that is normal and sweet, and use light and color alterations to twist it into something sinister.

Visualize My sweet daughter complains that I never turn her into anything cool in my books; usually I reserve that for my son. She's called me to task this time, however, so the vision for this piece is easy. My daughter will become her evil twin. Think of the wicked little girl in the recent movie *The Ring*.

Realize The main conversion in this piece will take place in the realms of light and color, with a few grunge effects thrown in.

The first step in warping my little girl into a monster is to give her eyes a scary glow, and to do that you'll revisit the Channel Coloring trick from Chapter 1, where you applied color directly from the red, green, or blue channel for a deeply saturated effect. The Channel Coloring trick can easily be applied to portraits as well as inanimate objects, and can have some pretty incredible results, especially when working with eyes. The results may or may not be realistic, but realism is not the goal of this project.

First, open `SweetGirl.jpg` (see Figure 9.61) found on this book's CD. This is one of the rare photos where my little girl isn't hamming a pose.

I'll throw a curve ball at you now. This will be slightly different from the dice image in Chapter 1, in that you will be painting in the red channel to produce a rich turquoise/blue hue. To do this, type D to place black in the foreground. Select the Paintbrush tool and ensure that the blending mode is set to Overlay. Set the rest of the Paintbrush options as follows:

Brush Size/Type	Round, Feathered, 15
Mode	Overlay
Opacity	85%
Flow	40%
Airbrush	On

Select the red channel in the Channels palette. Paint over the irises in the photo, and watch as they become an incredible shade of turquoise (see Figure 9.62).

With the top layer selected in the Layers palette, click the Create New Fill Or Adjustment Layer icon at the bottom. Select Hue/Saturation from the menu. The colors present in the image now will have to be adjusted to something less than human. Set up the Hue/Saturation adjustments as follows, and click OK.

Hue	+140
Saturation	–75
Lightness	0

Figure 9.61: My favorite daughter

Figure 9.62: What beautiful (but unrealistic) peepers!

Figure 9.63 shows the resulting change with the Adjustment layer present.

The image is a bit bright. An Adjustment layer can be used to darken things also. Click the Create New Fill Or Adjustment Layer icon again, this time selecting Brightness/Contrast from the menu. Enter the following settings, and click OK.

Brightness	–55
Contrast	+35

Figure 9.63: Otherworldly hues

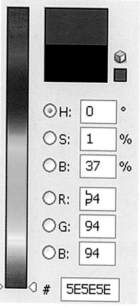

Figure 9.64: Change the foreground color to gray.

If the image appears too dark now, especially over the irises of the eyes, you may tone down the effect and let the eyes shine brighter by painting in the mask attached to the Adjustment layer. To do this, select the Brightness/Contrast Adjustment layer:

Select a gray for the foreground color (see Figure 9.64) and lightly paint over the iris area in the mask to allow the eyes beneath to be somewhat revealed.

Even though she is a bit off-color, I still see my precious little girl on-screen. It is time to turn up the proverbial heat a bit and see if we can't turn sweet to sinister.

Select the Burn tool. Set the options for the tool as follows:

Brush	Round, Feathered
Brush Size	25
Range	Midtones
Exposure	35%

The range is set to Midtones because the areas to be darkened first are not quite shadow, but not quite light (the lips, area around the eyes, and so on). Select the Background Copy 2 layer in the Layers palette. Run the Burn tool over the lips, being careful (for now) not to extend the brush beyond the lip edges (see Figure 9.65).

Once the lips have been darkened to the point where all but the reflection is nearly black, move the Burn tool around the eyes, darkening the skin below, and the lids and brows above. Don't extend too far down the cheeks, but just to the point where one might expect a three-day-old black eye to extend, as shown in Figure 9.66.

The eyes can be brightened now as well. Hold down the Alt key to switch to the Dodge tool without changing tools in the Toolbar. Run the Dodge tool over the irises in the same layer that the burn is being applied to and watch them lighten (see Figure 9.67).

OK, this is starting to creep me out a bit…this kid is going to be grounded for life, but for personal safety reasons, I'll let her mother tell her. See Figure 9.68 to check your progress.

I don't think she is quite as scary as she could be…not yet. Let's dig just a little deeper into the cobwebs and see what we can find.

Create a new Brightness/Contrast Adjustment layer, placed just above the Background Copy 2 layer. Use these settings:

Brightness	–75
Contrast	+45

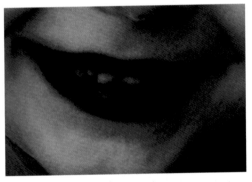

Figure 9.65: Darken the lips.

Figure 9.66: Burn the area around the eyes.

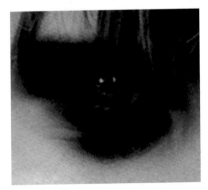

Figure 9.67: Lighten the eyes with the Dodge tool.

Figure 9.68: Children frighten me…

The result will render most of the face too dark to be seen, but that will be corrected now. Select the mask for the Brightness/Contrast Adjustment layer just created (see Figure 9.69). Set up a radial gradient with Mode set to Normal and Opacity to 100%. Starting somewhere around the girl's left eye, draw the gradient out toward the right side of the image (see Figure 9.70).

Figure 9.71 shows the new version, with the areas away from the face shrouded in darker tones while the face regains much of its visibility.

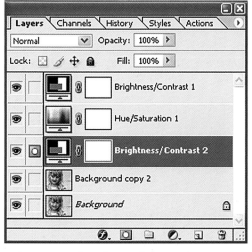

Figure 9.69: Select the Brightness/Contrast mask.

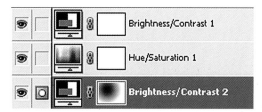

Figure 9.70: Draw the gradient across the mask.

Figure 9.71: Not so sweet-looking now, is she?

Figure 9.72: Lighten the hair strands with the Dodge tool.

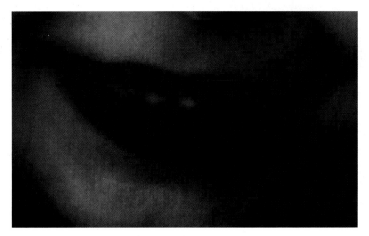

Figure 9.73: Add tone to the lip highlights.

To add some contrast to the image, strands of hair can be made to stand out with some dodging. A bit of color strategically applied to the image will help to round out the creepy feeling of the piece.

Return to the Background Copy 2 layer and select the Dodge tool. With a small brush set to Highlights, run the tool over a few lighter strands of grouped hair, as shown in Figure 9.72. Select a dark red foreground color. Create a new layer at the top of the layer stack and set the blending mode to Color.

With the Paintbrush tool, paint lightly over the reflection on the lips, even extending partially over the teeth if you like (see Figure 9.73).

Age and corruption can be added to the image simply by using a grunge-type brush. I have a set in the `Brush Sets` folder on this book's CD called `Right Brainer-Grunge 1.abr`. Because the Paintbrush tool should already be active, load this new set into the Brushes palette (see Figure 9.74).

Create a new layer at the top of the layer stack. Change the blending mode for the new layer to Overlay. With a dark gray/brown as the foreground color, select a grunge brush, increase the size, and paint lightly in the new layer. Select another brush and do the same in a different spot (see Figure 9.75). If it seems as if I'm glossing over this part, I apologize, but this will be covered later more in depth.

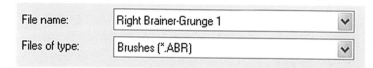

Figure 9.74: Loading grunge brushes

Figure 9.75: Adding grunge

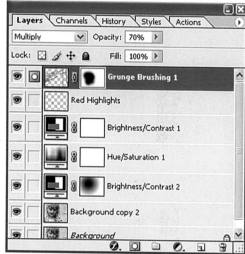

Figure 9.76: Masking grunge from the face

To erase any grunge from the face, simply create a layer mask and paint with black over the areas that you want to reveal (see Figure 9.76). I want to clean up the face a bit, so I've applied black to the mask in that area.

Select the Background Copy 2 layer. You may also use the grunge brush in conjunction with the Burn tool to darken portions of the Background Copy 2 layer a bit. Not much…just a couple of streaks in the face or on the borders.

In proposing a book concept to my editor, I mentioned that I'm a fan of Alice Cooper, which she indicated to be true of herself as well. As my homage to Alice, let's add just a bit more to this image before we go.

With the Burn tool selected, set up the options:

Brush	Round, Feathered
Brush Size	18–20
Range	Midtones
Exposure	35%

Burn streaks down from the corners of the mouth and a couple from around the eyes. Take a look at Figure 9.77. This cannot be my sweet little girl!

Figure 9.77: The world's youngest Alice Cooper fan

I think we have room for just one more adjustment. Let's see what the image looks like with a change in the overall tone and see if it is still creepy. Select the top layer and create a new Hue/Saturation Adjustment layer. Move the sliders to imitate these settings and click OK.

Hue	–165
Saturation	–25
Lightness	0

Figure 9.78 is the result of the adjustment on my computer.

I thought I'd leave you with a before/after photo (see Figure 9.79). Quite a change! I think I'd better get this kid some ice cream, or at least raise her allowance.

Figure 9.78: Ta-daa!

Figure 9.79: Parting shot—before and after

Flesh to Stone

Concept So far in the course of this book, we've merged stone to stone, wood to metal and glass, and even applied flesh of one type to flesh of another type. What we haven't done is merge living tissue with a natural yet inanimate element. The concept for this project merges the living world with the fundamental building block of our world: stone.

Visualize As my mind visualizes this piece, I see a gradual transition of flesh to marble. Recalling a bit of mythology as well as a few old movies, a vision of a Medusa turning her victims to stone with her gaze comes to mind. What if that Medusa had fallen in love with her victim? Realizing too late that his fate had been sealed by her adoring stare, she opts to share his fate, embracing his statuesque form and then casting her spell upon herself. Okay, this may seem like a scene from a bad romance novel, but it will serve well for this particular project.

Realize Merge two photos together, creating a gradual transition from flesh to stone. You will be using Layer masks and Apply Image to take the characteristics of one material (stone) and apply them to human skin. You will also use Extract in a unique way.

First, open the image `hug.jpg` (see Figure 9.80) found on this book's CD. This photo lends itself well to the effect I envision, because skin dominates the majority of the photo. Something that just came to mind is that the end result would be more effective if a portion of the "statue" were removed as though broken. A finger should work nicely.

Duplicate the Background layer and rename it **Couple**. Duplicate the Couple layer. Use Extract to highlight a portion of the index finger and fill it with the fill color. Make the selection at the breaking point of the jagged edge, as seen in Figure 9.81.

Click the Preview button prior to accepting the extraction and clean up the edges with the tools found on the left-hand side of the dialog box (see Chapter 1 for more on these tools). Accept the change to remove the finger from the surrounding skin (see Figure 9.82).

Command/Control+click the layer with the extracted finger to generate the selection, render that layer invisible in the Layers palette, and select the Couple layer (see Figure 9.83). With the selection active, press the Delete key. Deselect. As an aid to better see the area we are working on, create a new layer beneath the Couple layer and fill it with black. Return to the Couple layer. Choose Select → Reselect. Figure 9.84 shows what the image will look like.

Click the Clone tool and begin sampling and filling the empty area where the finger was with the skin from the man's back (see Figure 9.85). Be sure to clone over the shadow at an angle down to the other finger so that the lighting appears correct. Adjust the hardness setting of the brush (see Figure 9.86), increasing it as you move closer to the finger so that no soft edges will be seen at the breaking point (see Figure 9.87).

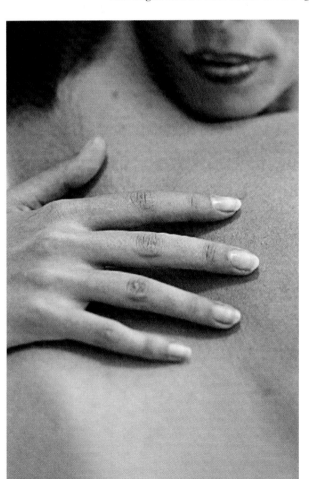

Figure 9.80: Her gentle hug

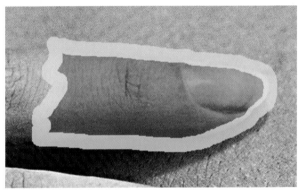

Figure 9.81: Extract the index finger.

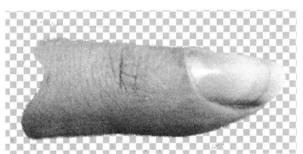

Figure 9.82: The extracted finger

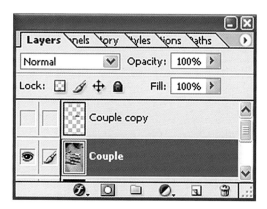

Figure 9.83: Working on the Couple layer

Figure 9.84: Remove the finger.

Figure 9.85: Clone over the removed finger area.

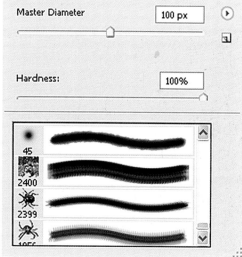

Figure 9.86: Increase the hardness of the brush.

Figure 9.87: The finger removed

Figure 9.88: Generate a selection at the finger breaking point.

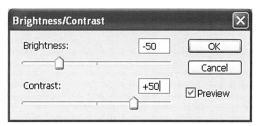

Figure 9.89: Adjustments in the Brightness/Contrast dialog box

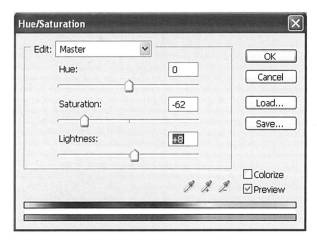
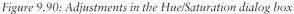

Figure 9.90: Adjustments in the Hue/Saturation dialog box

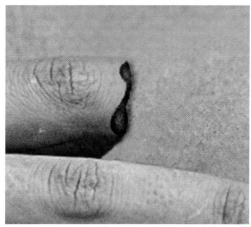

Figure 9.91: Broken finger

Take a look at Figure 9.88. Using the Lasso tool, make a similar selection, because we will make it appear as though excess stone can be seen at the breakaway point. To do this, choose Image → Adjustments → Brightness/Contrast and decrease the brightness and increase the contrast a few points as seen in Figure 9.89. Click OK to accept the adjustment.

As it stands, the breaking point appears to be burnt flesh. With an adjustment to the Hue/Saturation of the selection, the breaking point of the finger can be made to look a bit more like stone. Choose Image → Adjustments → Hue/Saturation and decrease the saturation to about –60. You may want to increase the lightness a bit also (see Figure 9.90).

Now select the Burn tool and with the range set to Highlights, burn along the edges of the selection with a small brush (see Figure 9.91).

Now open the image `veined_marble.jpg` (see Figure 9.92) from this book's CD. Because you will be using Apply Image to apply this image to the couple, both images need to be the same dimensions. Resize the marble image to match the exact dimensions of the couple, as seen in Figure 9.93.

Select the Couple layer (see Figure 9.94) and choose Image → Apply Image (see Figure 9.95). Note that you will need to select `veined_marble.jpg` as the source image. Set the rest of the Apply Image attributes as seen in the figure.

Figure 9.96 shows the result of applying the marble texture to the couple. I find this interesting because the veins in the stone maintain the same pattern on both individuals.

Now create a mask for the Couple layer. There should be a point in the image where the flesh appears to be gradually changing

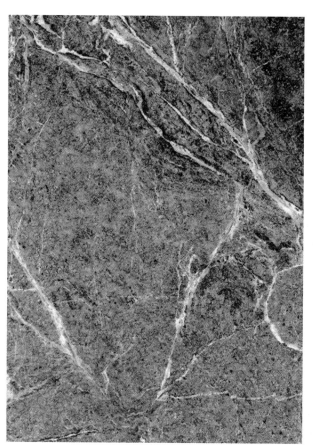

Figure 9.92: Marble photo

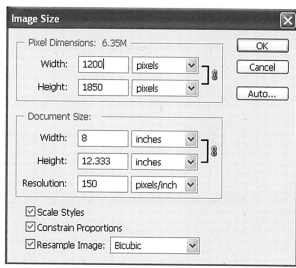

Figure 9.93: Resize the marble photo.

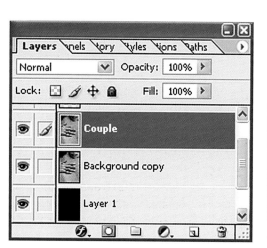

Figure 9.94: Get ready for the metamorphosis…

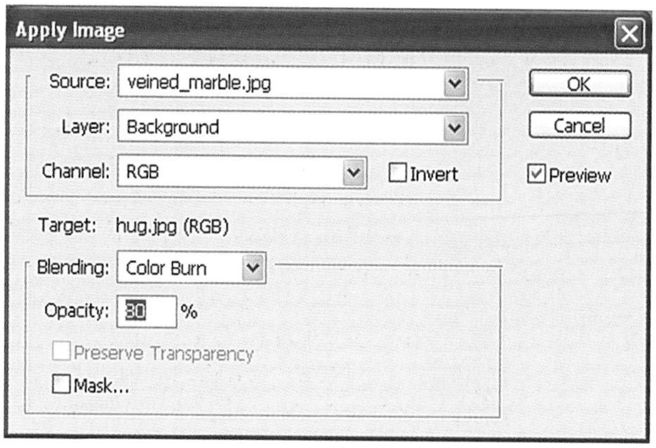

Figure 9.95: Apply Image settings

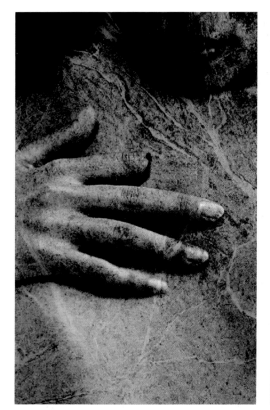

Figure 9.96: The couple in stone

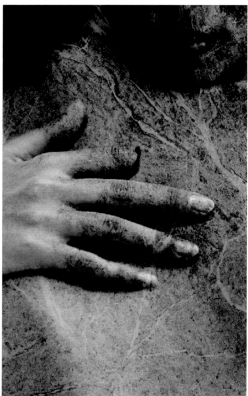

Figure 9.98: Transition from flesh to rock

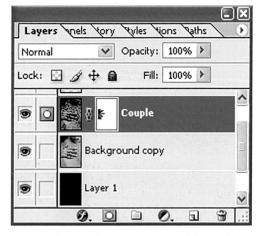

Figure 9.97: Masking away some of the rock

to stone to remain true to the original concept/vision. A mask will work great here, because another unedited version of the Couple layer already resides beneath the one merged with stone. With the mask selected, set your foreground color to black (see Figure 9.97) and paint over the back of the woman's hand, extending up the fingers a short way but not to the point where the finger is broken. The result should look like Figure 9.98.

Just a couple more finishing touches and you are all set. First, choose Image → Adjustments → Hue/Saturation and decrease the saturation of the Couple layer, as seen in Figure 9.99. You may also adjust the color

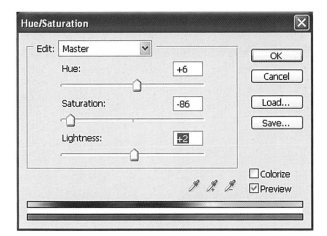

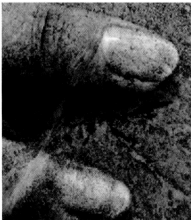

Figure 9.100: Deepen the cracks with the Burn tool.

Figure 9.99: Reduce the saturation.

of the rock at this point with the Hue adjustment slider, but try to reach a nice granite hue.

Next, you can burn in a few cracks into the stone with the Burn tool set to Shadows (with a Brush Size of 19 and the Exposure set to 50%) and applied to darker portions or veins in the marble (see Figure 9.100).

You may duplicate the Couple layer and change the blending mode to Overlay, tweaking the opacity to taste until you get a result you like, or similar to the one seen in Figure 9.101.

Figure 9.101: A sweet yet sorrowful goodbye

ten

Displaying Your Work

I hope you have *gleaned a few new tricks to use in your work in the previous chapters. This chapter isn't a chapter of artistic styles or effects as the preceding ones were. This chapter tackles Photoshop's tools for displaying your photos after the editing is done.*

Now that you have several masterpieces burning a hole on your hard drive (not a pretty sight), what are you going to do with them? The same software that allows for the creation of digital art also supplies several options for displaying your hard work. This chapter will take a look at some of these options, one by one: Web Photo Gallery, PDF Presentation, Contact Sheet, Picture Package, and Photomerge. The oddball in the mix is Photomerge. This one isn't so much about displaying pictures but rather about tying successive images together. Still, Adobe groups this function with the display group, so it will be covered in this section also.

Building a Web Photo Gallery

Photoshop's Web Photo Gallery (WPG) feature not only allows you to generate web page layouts for your photos but goes a step further. It allows you to generate functioning web pages complete with navigation, thumbnails, captions, image information, and any additional information about the photo or photographer that you care to display. The pages are generated automatically with minimal input from you. Adobe ships several templates to choose from, or if you're more web-savvy, you can create your own page in a WYSIWYG web-authoring program and import it into Photoshop. You need to know a bit about Cascading Style Sheets to generate one from scratch, but changing the images in an existing template and then saving it as a new template is relatively simple.

(2)5x7
(1)5x7 (2)2.5x3.5 (4)2x2.5
(1)5x7 (2)3.5x5
(1)5x7 (8)2x2.5
(1)5x7 (4)2.5x3.25 (2)1.5x2
(1)5x7 (4)2.5x3.5
(4)4x5
(2)4x5 (2)2.5x3.5 (4)2x2.5
(2)4x5 (8)2x2.5
(2)4x5 (4)2.5x3.5

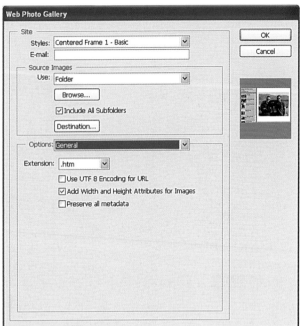

Figure 10.1: Finding the Web Photo Gallery option

Figure 10.2: The Web Photo Gallery dialog box

To access the Web Photo Gallery, choose File → Automate. You'll find Web Photo Gallery near the bottom of the listed menu that appears (see Figure 10.1).

Choose this option and you'll see the Web Photo Gallery dialog box shown in Figure 10.2. It doesn't look too daunting; there are only a few options, with a nifty little viewing window on the right-hand side. Let's take a walk through the process of creating a page.

To create a Web Photo Gallery, you must first have two things set up on your computer: a folder full of source photos that you want to display and a destination folder that resides outside of the folder that your source images are in. You cannot have the destination folder inside the folder where the source files reside or this function will not work. If you have not created a folder, you may do so while setting up the gallery.

The best way to demonstrate setting up and creating a gallery is to simply go through the process. Have a folder full of images ready for the gallery; any will do at this point. In Photoshop, open the File menu, then select Automate → Web Photo Gallery to open the Web Photo Gallery dialog box.

The first drop-down menu at the top of the page lists the styles in the Photoshop CS folder. Here you have 11 selections to choose from (as of this writing). The styles here have changed a bit from those included with Photoshop 7; actually, the CS WPG styles seem a bit simpler and quite frankly, don't look quite as hot as the ones in Photoshop 7. If you have Photoshop 7, however, you can add those Web Photo Gallery Styles to CS.

- Go into the Adobe Photoshop 7 folder on your hard drive and open the `Presets` folder.
- Open the folder called `WebContactSheet`. The folders here are the Web Contact Sheet styles.
- Select them all and copy them to the Clipboard.
- Go to the Photoshop CS Presets folder.

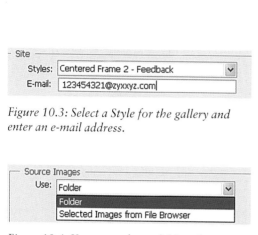

Figure 10.3: Select a Style for the gallery and enter an e-mail address.

Figure 10.4: You may select a folder of images or flagged images in the file browser.

Figure 10.5: Choose a folder of images.

- Open the folder called `Web Photo Gallery`.
- Paste the Photoshop 7 Web Photo Gallery style folders into Photoshop CS.

You will be asked if you want to overwrite the folder called `Simple`; I recommend you not do this—overwriting default templates is never a good thing, because they are gone for good (or until you reinstall the software) once that is done. Simply say no and the rest will find a new home in Photoshop CS. This gives you a broader choice when creating your gallery, and a broader range of choices is (almost) always a good thing.

For this demonstration, select Centered Frame 2—Feedback as the style for the page. You can see the example thumbnail layout on the right side of the dialog box. With a "feedback" style, you're inviting visitors to comment about your site, so enter the e-mail address you want to use for this in the E-mail field (see Figure 10.3).

The next section allows you to select the source images and a destination where the completed HTML pages will be deposited. In the Use area, you have two options: selecting a folder that contains all the images you want to use (the option to be used here) or using selected images flagged in the file browser (see Figure 10.4). The first option implies that you are organizing files by the way they will ultimately be used, but if you plan to include some of the same images in more than one gallery, duplicating those files may eat up too much disk space.

> When you use the Selected Images from File Browser option with no files selected in the browser, the WPG will use all of the images in the active folder to generate the web page. If you want just a few of the images to be used, then make sure these are highlighted prior to running the WPG.

The next item you will see is the Browse button, which is available only if Folder is chosen as the Source.

Clicking the Browse button sends you to another dialog box where you can choose the folder that contains the files you want to use in your gallery (see Figure 10.5).

Figure 10.6: Select or create the destination folder for the gallery.

Figure 10.7: Creating a new destination folder

Next, you are given the choice to include subfolders. In this instance I'll choose none so it is left unchecked, but if you had additional images to include in the gallery that were in subfolders, you could select the folder for inclusion here. The last option in the Source Images area is to select a destination folder where the WPG will be placed (see Figure 10.6).

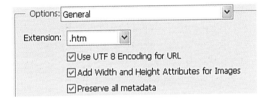

Figure 10.8: General options and settings

You can have a folder already created, or create one from the Browse For Folder dialog box by clicking the Make New Folder button. A hierarchy of folders will actually be created once the gallery has been processed that categorizes where the images, their HTML, and thumbnails will be kept (see Figure 10.7).

The Options area is where most of the customization for your Web Photo Gallery takes place. These options fall into six categories, available from the Options drop-down menu:

- General
- Banner
- Large Images
- Thumbnails
- Custom Colors
- Security

General options   With General selected in the Options drop-down menu, you are given the opportunity to set the extension of the pages created (.htm or .html). Either extension will work, but some web designers prefer one over the other. If you create many web pages, using the same extension consistently may help if troubleshooting becomes necessary. You are also given the choice to Use UTF 8 Encoding For URL, Add Width And Height Attributes For Images, and Preserve All Metadata (see Figure 10.8).

UTF 8 Encoding

What is UTF 8 encoding? A detailed answer would be more than the average photographer would ever want to know, but because the Web Gallery makes pages that are compatible with it, a brief explanation is warranted. At its most basic, UTF 8 is a system for implementing Unicode, the emerging standard "universal character set" that allows for virtually every alphabet to be represented as digital data so it can be displayed on a web page, in programming, and so forth. Because the author is not a programmer, this may be a bit simplistic. If you really want to know what UTF 8 entails (left-brainers may find this intriguing), then I suggest reading definitions online, such as the one found at **http://dict.die.net/utf-8/**.

So what's the bottom line for creating a Photoshop Web Gallery? If you are creating the gallery for a known audience—friends, relatives, colleagues—that uses a language in the Roman alphabet, there is no harm in using UTF 8, but there probably won't be any benefit. If your site may be translated into a language using another alphabet, there may be some benefit.

Adding Width and Height attributes for images is pretty self-explanatory, but Preserve All Metadata might need a bit of explanation. Metadata is any additional information attached to an image, such as copyright status, origin, history of documents, and contents. These can be added via the Metadata palette, and then can be viewed on the web page if you allow them to be (the options for allowing the metadata to be viewed are a series of check boxes accessed within the WPG dialog box, under the Large Image settings). When you allow a viewer to see the metadata, the information will appear in fields laid out by the selected WPG template. In the next project, you'll see how to add metadata, but for now, let's continue building a basic gallery site.

Banner options The second item in the Options drop-down menu is Banner. This allows you to set attributes for the banner of the page, such as Site Name, Photographer, Contact Info, and Date. Go ahead and enter the information for your images at this time (see Figure 10.9).

Large Image options Select Large Images from the menu. This area lets you customize how the large versions of your photos and art will be displayed on the web page. It is strongly recommended that you have Resize Images selected, or who knows how big the web page will be! This is especially true if you have many high-resolution shots. Photoshop will adjust their sizes and resolution for best viewing online, so the defaults should work well here (see Figure 10.10).

Thumbnail options Next on the list is Thumbnails. Again, the default settings should be just fine (see Figure 10.11).

Custom Colors options The next selection (Custom Colors) gives you the option of changing the color of various elements in the web page: Background, Banner, Text, and the links (see Figure 10.12). Some pages (including some default Photoshop templates) do not allow for the text and links to be altered.

Security options The last selection available in the Options menu is Security. This embeds a watermark on the images to be displayed so that they are not easily stolen online for use by viewers. When you set the attributes here, you are basically telling Photoshop what font to

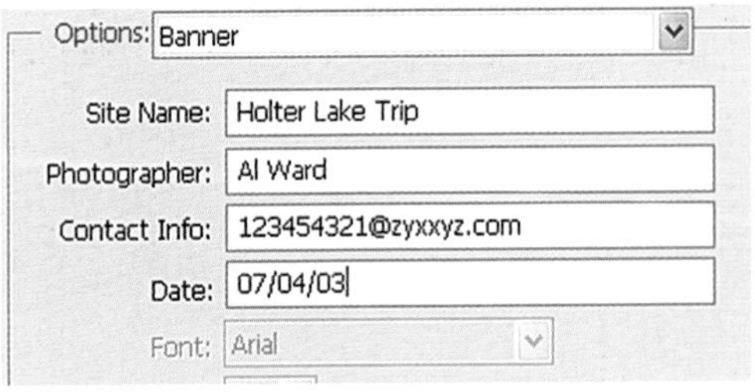

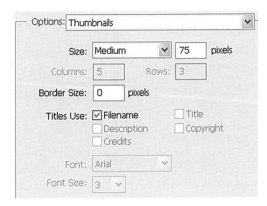

Figure 10.9: Banner options

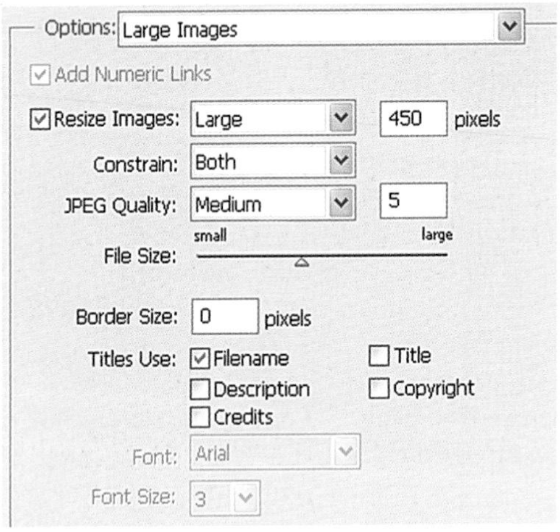

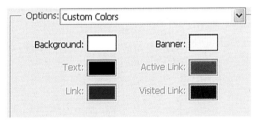

Figure 10.10: Options for large images

Figure 10.11: Thumbnail options

Figure 10.12: Custom Colors options

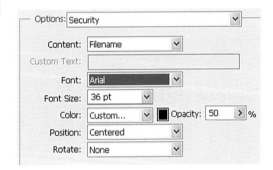

Figure 10.13: Security options

use, the attributes of the font (size, color), and where on the image the watermark will be placed (see Figure 10.13).

Once all of the Options have been set and changed according to your tastes, you can click OK. Photoshop will now create the HTML pages for your new Web Gallery. When the pages are complete, your web browser opens the website for your inspection. You may want to view the pages in more than one browser (Netscape, Internet Explorer, and so on) to ensure that your site works on a variety of browsers. Some browsers, especially older versions, read the HTML and coding data differently (see Figure 10.14).

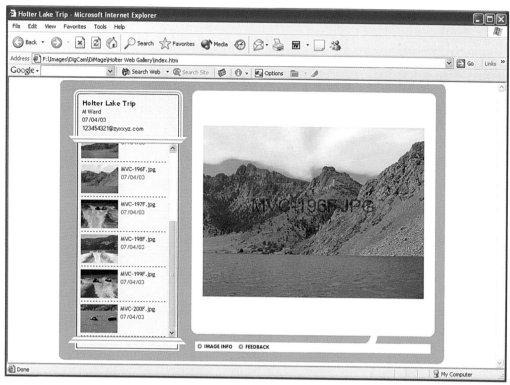

Figure 10.14: Completed Web Gallery seen in a browser

Saving Images for the Web

So now you know how to get your images on the Web, but there is one more issue to consider that is directly related to the subject—file size and optimization. You should reduce the size of your images for display online to make them small enough that your web page does not take forever to load on slower connections and sap a ton of bandwidth. You also need to do that without causing too severe a loss in quality. I can guarantee that if your images take too long to load, some people or potential customers will quickly become irritated and move on to another website. This could result in the loss of a sale, but Photoshop can help you out. To maintain color consistency between the original photo and the web version, it is good policy to first calibrate your monitor for a color-managed workflow using a visual calibrator such as Adobe Gamma (Windows) or Monitor Calibrator (Mac OS). It is also recommended that you set up color management (Edit → Color Settings in Windows, Photoshop → Color Settings on Mac OS). There you may choose to use a custom setting, the Web Graphics Defaults, or create your own using the sRGB profile so that more monitors will correctly display your image (see Figure 10.15). sRGB isn't more accurate, but it covers a larger gamut of colors.

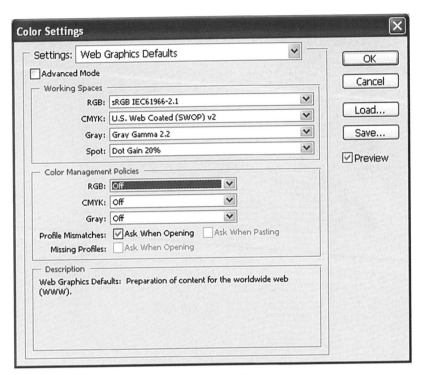

Figure 10.15: The Color Settings dialog box (Windows)

Like other areas of this vast piece of software, the Save For Web command can get pretty involved. Rather than tackle every nuance of the process, I'm going to show you what I do to get my images ready, and then allow you to experiment on your own.

Open the image Rose.jpg (see Figure 10.16) from this book's CD. To prepare this photo for the Web, first check the image size and resolution. Choose Image → Image Size to open the Image Size dialog box (see Figure 10.17). Note that the Document Size says that the photo is 5.73 inches wide by 8 inches in height. That is a pretty fair size—a bit large, but I'll leave that alone. What interests the photographer here is the resolution. Note this is set to 300 pixels per inch. That may work for photographic prints, but it is far too large for online display. As a general rule, monitors display only 72 pixels per inch. With Constrain Proportions checked, change this number to 72. Note that the pixel dimensions have been drastically reduced as a result of the change in resolution (see Figure 10.18). Click OK.

Next, open the Save For Web dialog box (File → Save For Web). As I stated before, I'm not going to cover this entire package of settings, but simply walk you through one way of doing it. First, click the 2-Up tab at the top. This will give you a window displaying your photo at the current resolution alongside a second view with a reduced resolution. The new resolution is controlled by the settings on the right-hand side of the dialog box (see Figure 10.19).

*Figure 10.16:
High-resolution
rose photo*

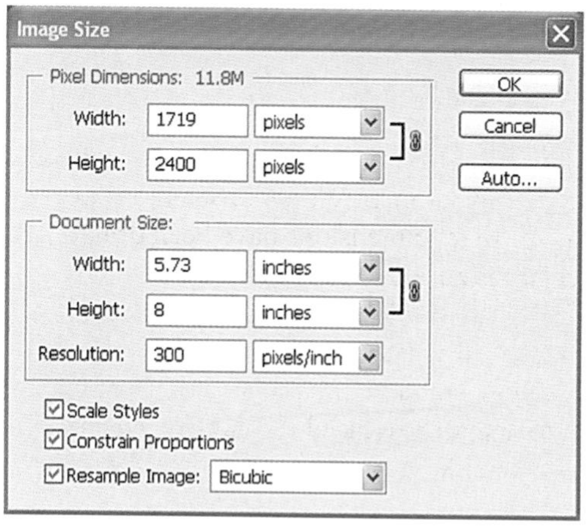

Figure 10.17: Image Size dialog box

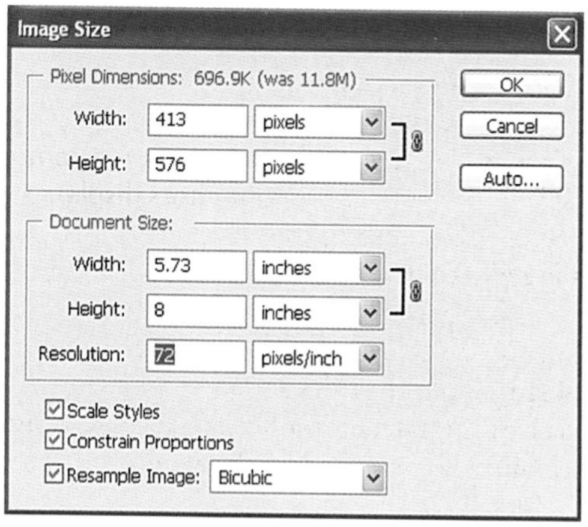

*Figure 10.18: Reduce the pixels per inch from
300 to 72.*

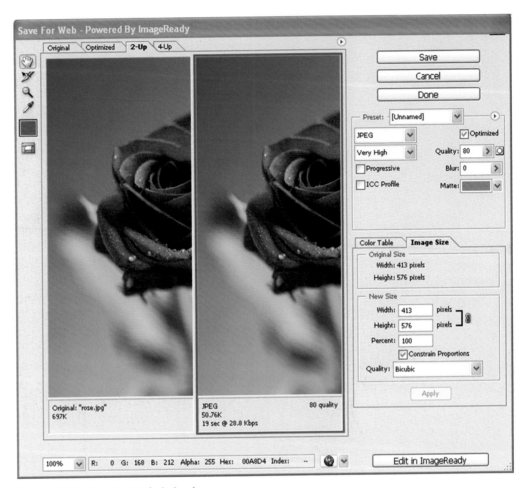

Figure 10.19: Save For Web dialog box

Take a look at the two instances of your photo, and the image sizes that are seen on the bottom of each example. The original Rose.jpg, even after it was resized to 72 pixels per inch, is still 697K. Slower connections (especially dialup) will take a long time to download files of this size. Compare it to the file size of the image with the Quality set to 80%. Just that slight change reduced the size of the file to 50.76K, with little or no noticeable change to the photo.

Reduce the quality of the second image even more by changing the Quality setting to 50% (see Figure 10.20). Now when you look at the two images, the alteration in quality still has little change visually, but the file size weighs in at a much slimmer 19.62K. That's quite a change from 697K, will save tons of download time and bandwidth, and make your online viewers much happier (see Figure 10.21).

On a personal note, I'd like to speak briefly to all of you who send photographs attached to e-mail. Please, please, PLEASE save those photos for the Web with the reduced image sizes prior to sending them! Mom, I hope you are paying attention…

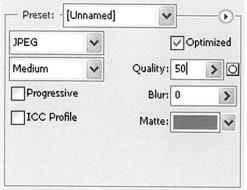

Figure 10.20: Reduce the Quality setting to 50.

Figure 10.21: There's little visible change, but the file size has been drastically reduced.

Adding Metadata to an Image

Photoshop has the fantastic ability to embed information into an image document, and these settings can be saved as a template to be applied to other images. Metadata can be attached to the following file types: PSD, PDF, PNG, GIF, JPEG, and TIFF. Metadata is attached using XMP (eXtensible Metadata Platform) to allow the exchange of metadata between Adobe applications, as well as publishing workflows. Metadata can be saved as a template and imported to other files. You may choose to allow visitors to see some of the data (filename, description, credits, title, and copyright) when creating a Web Photo Gallery by allowing it in the Options for the images.

To attach metadata to an image, open a photograph from the vast supply on your hard drive. (I've chosen the humorous portrait shown in Figure 10.22.) Select File Info from the

Figure 10.22: Open a photo to apply metadata to.

File menu, or use the shortcut keys (Control+Alt+I for Windows, Command+Option+I for Mac). This opens the Metadata dialog box. From here, you may enter descriptions, camera data, categories, history, origin, and advanced properties (see Figure 10.23).

Once you have all of your information entered, you can select the Advanced option from the left side of the dialog box and save the settings as an .xmp file, and apply these settings to other images (see Figure 10.24). To apply these settings to another image, open the photo, select Advanced, and select either Replace or Append from the buttons at the bottom of the dialog box. You may then select your saved settings and apply them to the new image.

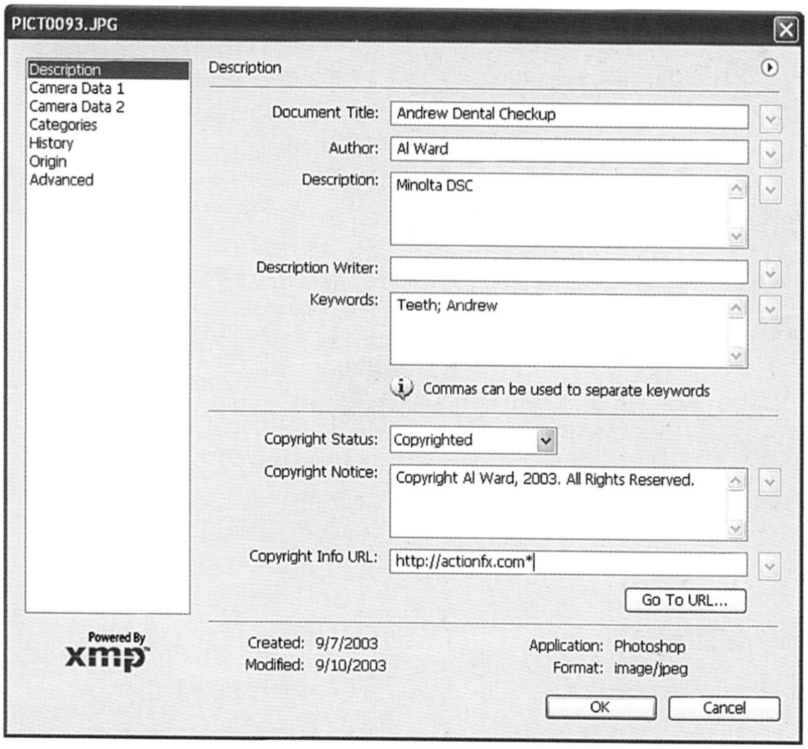

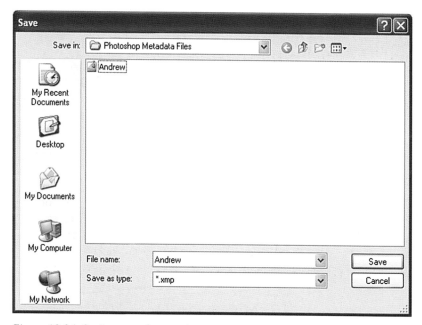

Figure 10.23: The metadata dialog box

Figure 10.24: Saving metadata settings

PDF Presentation

PDF, or Portable Document Format, has become a standard for file distribution across the Web and over networks. PDF stands out in that image and text data, search components, links, and navigation can all be embedded in the document and preserved, allowing someone with a PDF viewer such as Adobe Acrobat Reader to view documents the way they were intended by the person who generated the document. PDF allows for encryption and security measures, supports 16-bit-per-channel images, and allows for minor editing of the images in the documents.

Photoshop's PDF Presentation tool, new in Photoshop CS, allows you to create a multipage document or slideshow presentation in PDF format. You can specify the images to be used in the presentation, select transitions between the images, and save and distribute them quickly and easily.

The PDF Presentation option is found under File → Automate → PDF Presentation (see Figure 10.25). When you open the PDF Presentation dialog box (see Figure 10.26), it looks a bit sparse if you have no images open. If you have some open, then you are given the option of adding them to the presentation. In this instance, I have none open. To add files, simply click the Browse button, which gives you access to your hard drive. Track down the images that you would like in the presentation and add them to the list; they will appear in the dialog box in the order added (see Figure 10.27).

Below the Source Files area in the PDF Presentation dialog box, you will find Output Options. This area gives you two choices for outputting the PDF: either as a Multi-Page Document (similar to a standard series of text documents) or as a Presentation (operates

Figure 10.25: Selecting PDF Presentation

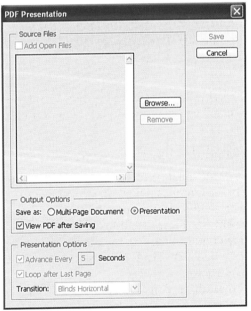

Figure 10.26: The PDF Presentation dialog box

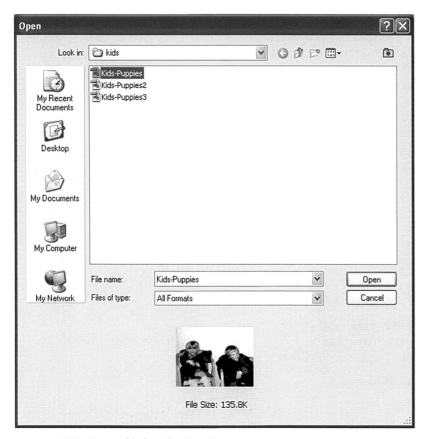

Figure 10.27: Items added to the PDF Presentation

much as a slideshow, displaying each image for a few seconds and then transitioning to the next). Here you'll try both options, beginning with Multi-Page Document.

Creating a Multi-Page Document

For the first run-through, add three images via the Browse menu and select Multi-Page Document in the Output Options area (see Figure 10.28). You will then be asked to save the document. Find a place on your hard drive, name the new file, and save it as a Multi-Page Document (see Figure 10.29).

You aren't quite done yet, because Photoshop is going to ask you to fill in a few options for the new PDF file. In this instance, simply select JPEG for your encoding, Quality 10 (see Figure 10.30).

For this example, don't worry about the Image Interpolation and Downgrade Color Profile check boxes. Just so you don't feel you have missed anything, Image Interpolation is a

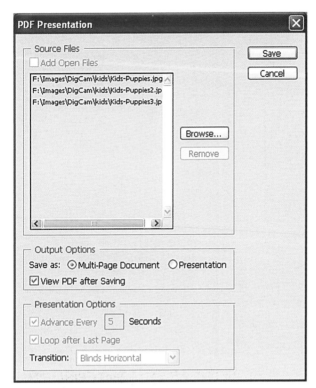

Figure 10.28: Multi-Page Document option

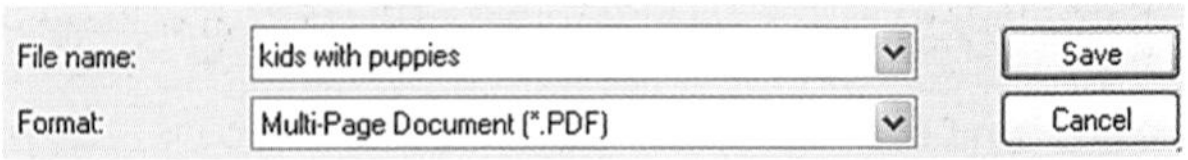

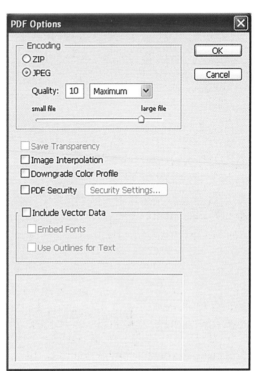

Figure 10.29: Save the new PDF document.

Figure 10.30: Additional PDF options

method of resampling that assigns color values to any new pixels generated by Photoshop. These values are based on color information already in the image. The point to Image Interpolation is to try and preserve the original quality of the photo during the resampling. Turning it on should give you a sharper-looking image.

Downgrade Color Profile need not be selected unless you intend to open the image in an application that does not support version 4 profiles. If you do intend to open the image in one of these other applications, Downgrade Color Profile will change the profile to version 2, allowing the image to be viewed by the other software.

Let's talk briefly about PDF security. When you check this box, another dialog box opens that allows you to set passwords for viewers of the document and passwords for editors of the document, as well as establishing what versions of Acrobat the document is compatible with. The compatibility addresses the level of security attached to the document. 40-bit RC4 (Acrobat 3.*x*, 4.*x*) specifies a low encryption level. 128-bit RC4 (Acrobat 5)

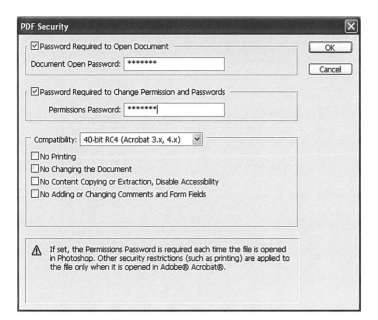

Figure 10.31: Restrictions and passwords

specifies a high encryption level, and the file cannot be opened by users of Acrobat 3.*x* or 4.*x*. 128-bit RC4 (Acrobat 6) sets a high encryption level, and these files cannot be viewed by users of previous versions of Acrobat. Choosing Acrobat 6 allows you to enable plain-text metadata and thumbnails, a feature unavailable in earlier versions of the Acrobat software.

You may also set restrictions on printing, changes, content copying, or changes to comment and form fields (see Figure 10.31). For sensitive file transfers that are, say, to appear in an upcoming show-and-tell-all book, securities may be added so that only those in the know have access to the files. If you just want to send a cool slideshow to Grandma, then you can probably bypass this feature.

If you chose to view the file once it was created, then you will get one more dialog box, Adobe Tasks, when it opens in Adobe Reader. This simply tells the viewer about ways they can work with the document, such as printing it or exporting it to another application (see Figure 10.32).

Figure 10.32: Acrobat Reader Special Features dialog box

Creating a Presentation

Back in the PDF Presentation dialog box, the other Output option available is Presentation. When you select this option, you are given control of how the presentation will be displayed in the Presentation options. You can set the length of time an image will be displayed before transitioning to the next, you can tell the document to continue looping the images or stop after one pass, and you can select a variety of transitions like cool little shutters, screen swipes, dissolves, and so forth (see Figure 10.33). Or, you may simply return to Acrobat in normal mode and view the images by selecting their thumbnails under the Pages tab (see Figure 10.34).

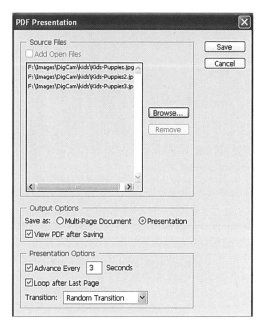

Figure 10.33: Presentation options

Figure 10.34: New PDF document viewed in Acrobat Reader

Creating a Contact Sheet

Contact sheets can be invaluable to photographers and artists alike, in that they allow you to create pages of thumbnail-sized images that can be printed and placed in a binder for cataloging, review, and easy locating of specific files. Generally they are created on a standard 8.5 × 11 inch page, complete with the file name beneath each thumbnail. You can create a contact sheet via the File menu (see Figure 10.35), or from files in the File Browser.

When you open the Contact Sheet II dialog box, you choose the location of your source images at the top of the box, set the document size in the center, choose thumbnail attributes and layout toward the bottom third of the box, and allow (or not) for the use of the filename as a caption for the thumbnails. You also have a couple of selections for fonts and font size. The display on the right side of the dialog box shows how the layout for the images you have selected will be displayed, the number of pages required, and total number of images to be thumbnailed (see Figure 10.36).

Click the Browse button to select some files. Again, I'm not going to supply images for this little exercise. Simply find a folder on your hard drive with photos; any will do (see Figure 10.37).

When you click OK, Photoshop CS will take every image in the folder (or those flagged in the File Browser) and generate thumbnails of each. If you selected the naming option, then the title of each image will appear below the image (see Figure 10.38).

Figure 10.35: Choosing Contact Sheet II from the File menu

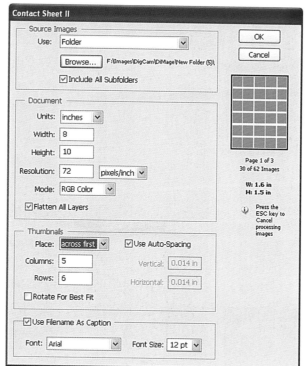

Figure 10.36: The Contact Sheet II dialog box

Figure 10.37:
Choose a folder
of images.

Figure 10.38:
Newly generated
contact sheet

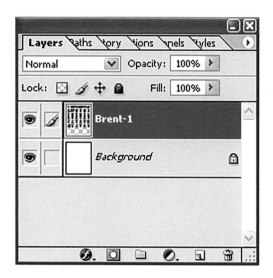

Figure 10.39:
Contact sheet
saved as layered
.psd file

Although there isn't much that needs to be said about this feature, there is one extremely cool thing besides the ability to quickly categorize and print sheets of examples. This may be of particular interest to web designers. Photoshop places the images in a layered .psd document named for the first image in the series (see Figure 10.39). What makes that so cool? Simply put, it generates tons of thumbnails for you, with very little loss of resolution. You can then put them on your website as buttons, icons, examples, and so forth, which is very useful if you plan to create web pages for photographs without using the Web Photo Gallery option.

Creating a Picture Package

Back when I was a kid in grade school, there was one day of the year that was dreaded more than any other: picture day. All the kids were required (who required it, I've yet to uncover) to dress up in their best clothes and sit for excruciating seconds while some evil photographer laughed gleefully behind his soul-capturing machine, snapping shot after shot of children on the verge of tears. That's how it seemed to me anyway, as each year we were all herded down the hall toward the auditorium.

Weeks would pass, until a day nearly as dreaded as the first finally arrived. You guessed it: the day the pictures returned and you had to show them to your parents! The shame! The outrage! A million little 2×3 images of you either blinking at the wrong time, looking in the wrong direction, displaying a stray glob of hair sticking straight up from your scalp…My mother's reaction still gives me chills. Grandma always thought they were precious, though.

Picture Package II is similar to the sheets those images used to come on, or that you may get when having photos done from a studio. You select the images that you want to

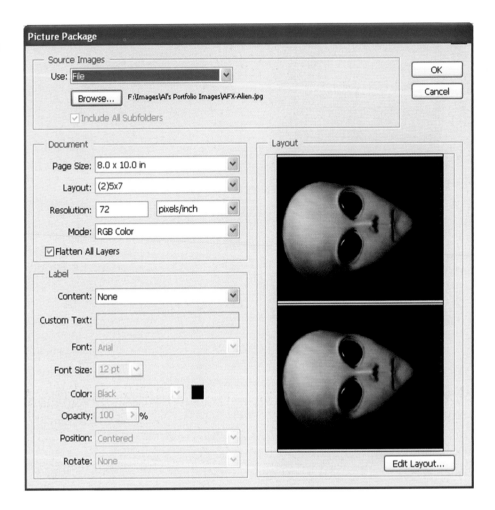

have printed, as well as their sizes and how they will appear on the sheet, and then generate a document that has your photos ready for printing. You can create a package that contains multiple versions of the same image, perhaps in different sizes, or one that contains multiple images.

Figure 10.40 shows a basic Picture Package II dialog box with a single photo selected. In the Document area, the page size is set to 8 inches × 10 inches; this allows for margins of 0.5 and 1 inch on the sides and top, respectively. By selecting (2)5×7 for the layout, the viewer shows that two photos will be placed on the resulting page sideways. Opening the Layout menu shows a vast assortment of possible sheet styles (see Figure 10.41).

You can set your other page attributes from this box, including custom text to be placed on each image, font, position, and so forth (see Figure 10.42). If you are unhappy with the layouts provided by Photoshop, you may create your own by clicking Edit Layout and creating your own dimensions for the images and how many times an image is repeated (see Figure 10.43).

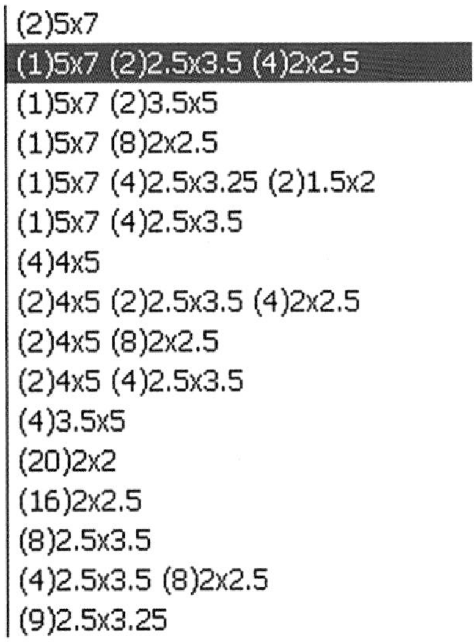

```
(2)5x7
(1)5x7 (2)2.5x3.5 (4)2x2.5
(1)5x7 (2)3.5x5
(1)5x7 (8)2x2.5
(1)5x7 (4)2.5x3.25 (2)1.5x2
(1)5x7 (4)2.5x3.5
(4)4x5
(2)4x5 (2)2.5x3.5 (4)2x2.5
(2)4x5 (8)2x2.5
(2)4x5 (4)2.5x3.5
(4)3.5x5
(20)2x2
(16)2x2.5
(8)2.5x3.5
(4)2.5x3.5 (8)2x2.5
(9)2.5x3.25
```

Figure 10.41: Multiple layouts to choose from

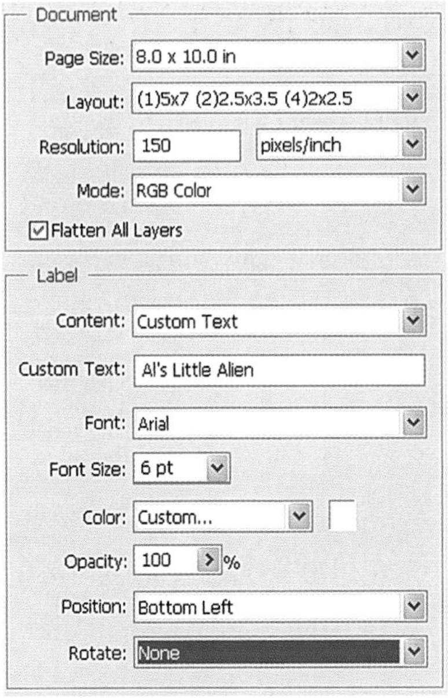

Figure 10.42: Descriptive text can be added to your photos.

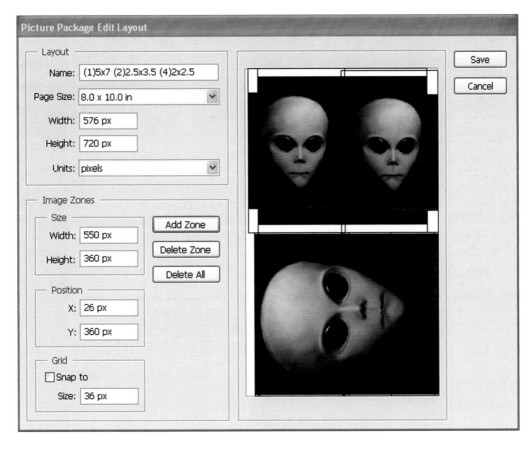

Figure 10.43: Create layouts that best suit your requirements.

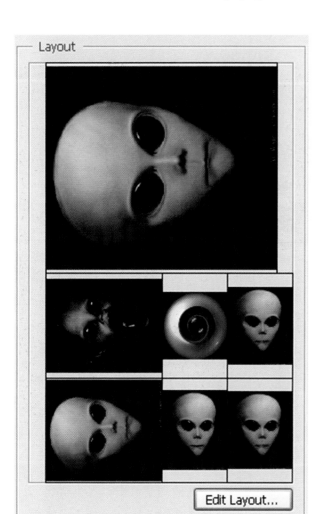

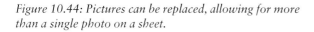

Figure 10.44: Pictures can be replaced, allowing for more than a single photo on a sheet.

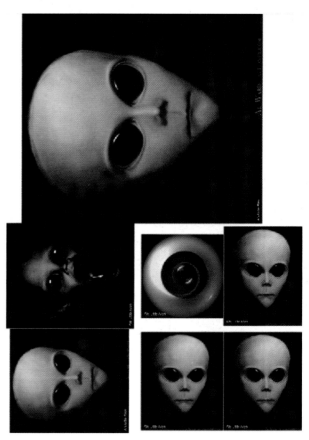

Figure 10.45: Photo sheet after Picture Package II processing

Another cool thing about Picture Package II: You need not have only one image printed, but can swap any of the photos on the sheet with others by simply double-clicking the photo in the viewer and finding the new one on your hard drive (see Figure 10.44). Once all your images are in place, click OK and the picture package is created for you (see Figure 10.45).

One thing to note about swapping in new images: If you added text to your images, the text you originally entered may not apply to the new image. As an example, I added the text "Al's Little Alien" to those in my package, but then changed one of the photos to my Bat Boy image (see Figure 10.46), and the caption is now incorrect. To fix it at this point, I would need to generate a new package without any text. That is just one of those things you'll want to be aware of, and will save you some backtracking later, because you may not edit text on individual images.

Figure 10.47 shows one of the images from the completed sheet as it was originally intended.

Al's Little Alien

Al's Little Alien

Figure 10.46: Oops! Make sure your descriptive text matches all the images on the sheet.

Figure 10.47: One of the final photos as it was originally intended

Photomerge

Living in western Montana, my family and I are deluged daily with beauty that is difficult to describe. Many have tried, and only a few authors and painters have been successful at scratching the surface. Charles M. Russell drove cattle on the plains where I grew up long before he gained fame trying to capture the land and sky on canvas. Teddy Roosevelt spent much time in the valley where I now live as a respite from the duties of the Presidency. During the writing of this book, my family moved into a home that is several miles from anything that resembles a city. Lewis and Clark wintered just north of here, and though the valley has changed—filled with homes and small ranches—the wilderness surrounding us has remained largely unchanged since their famous trek. Lewis and Clark were sent with the charge to catalog and describe in detail what they encountered; their task would have been much easier with a digital camera and Photoshop at their disposal.

Photomerge works, or is intended to work, just like it sounds. It allows you to take sequential photographs spanning an area and seamlessly merge them into one panoramic image. This was tricky and difficult in prior versions of the software, and still may take a bit of work on your part to pull off with successful results. The thing to note is that it can work with excellent results with a bit of forethought and some additional adjustments.

When shooting photos for a panorama, it is best to use a level tripod for the shots. Take one photo, and then swivel the camera so that the next photo will overlap the first by about one-third. Repeat this process until all the shots are taken, then attempt the merge in Photoshop.

 The Photomerge function is accessed, as are all the functions in this chapter, by choosing File → Automate (see Figure 10.48). For this technique, I've provided two images of the western view from my deck. Open the images `A1-View1.tif` and `A1-View2.tif` from this book's CD (see Figure 10.49).

In previous chapters you have used Match Color in a variety of situations, but this is actually one of those instances where it is used as intended by the Adobe programmers. You may find that, even with shots taken immediately after one another, variations in lighting and tone occur between your images. Even slight variations can hinder the merge, so running Match Color before attempting the merge could save a lot of frustration.

Select `A1-View2.tif` in Photoshop CS. Open the Match Color dialog box (Image → Adjustments → Match Color) and take a look at Figure 10.50. Because of the close proximity in which these photos were taken, the variation between the two images is faint at best, so the default settings need not be changed. Just change the Source at the bottom of the dialog box to `A1-View1.tif` and click OK.

Batch...
PDF Presentation...
Create Droplet...

Conditional Mode Change...
Contact Sheet II...
Crop and Straighten Photos
Fit Image...
Multi-Page PDF to PSD...
Picture Package...
Web Photo Gallery...

Photomerge...

Figure 10.48: Photomerge resides with the Automate functions.

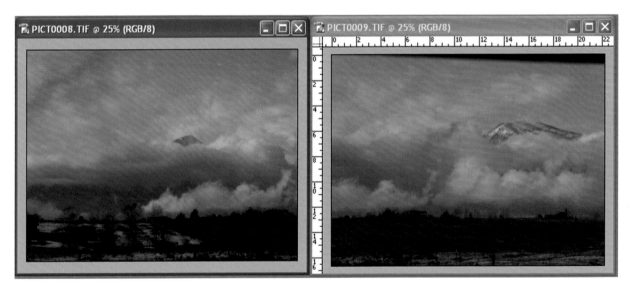

Figure 10.49: Two photos taken from the author's front deck

The color cast and lightness between the two images should be extremely close at this point, so you may attempt the merge. Choose File → Automate → Photomerge. Set the Use option to Open Files, and make sure that both images are listed in the viewer window (see Figure 10.51). Click OK.

Photoshop is going to take a look at the scenes and try to find where the two should be linked together. When you ran the merge, your image may have turned out to look something like the one in Figure 10.52. The merge is close, but not perfect, because elements such as the deck's overhang on the right-side photo have caused the merge to be a bit off. Also, changes in the clouds, perspective between the photos, and so forth have caused a faint diagonal seam to appear where the photos

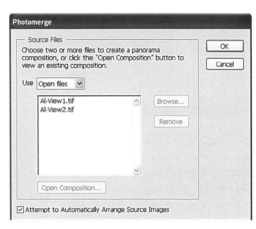

Figure 10.50: Match Color prior to the merge   *Figure 10.51: Selecting files to link together*

Figure 10.52: Two photos imperfectly joined

Figure 10.53: Clouds are a difficult merge.

Figure 10.55: You can line up the landmarks from within the Photomerge dialog box.

Figure 10.54: The land in the foreground is askew also.

come together. This can be fixed within the Photomerge dialog box, so don't close it just yet.

Zoom in and take a closer look. When you get in close, you can really tell where the two images did not merge correctly. The land is a bit off also, and there is definite variation in the clouds. That is one problem with clouds; they change so quickly that it is hard to create a quality merge right out of the shoot, even if the photos were taken moments apart (see Figures 10.53 and 10.54).

In the Photomerge dialog box, you have the freedom to select and reposition the photos. Select the Move tool at the top left, and click directly on the image to the right. The opacity of the photo is lowered to reveal the other photo beneath, and you can then move the photo on the right so that the landmarks (tree, house, ridgeline) match between the two photographs (see Figure 10.55). When you are done matching the landmarks, the two photographs (in this case, at least) will be even more askew as far as placement, but you will trim that later in the project (see Figure 10.56).

Once the landmarks in the images are straightened out and match properly, you can click out of the Photomerge dialog box. Photomerge is rarely, if ever, a cure-all function; you will still need to do a bit of standard image correction after the merge.

Take, for example, the seam in the clouds, which is still very apparent. You've had a lot of practice over the course of these pages in using the Healing Brush, and it will serve well here. Select the Healing Brush and in the Options Toolbar, select

Figure 10.56: The land is joined, but the photos are farther off center.

a round feathered brush between 100 and 150 in size. Set the Mode to Normal and the Source to Sampled.

Now simply sample clouds on one side of the seam (as close to the seam as possible without the feather of the brush interfering) and heal the disjointed areas in the sky. You may want to take a few samples, reduce the brush size, and so forth, but the cleanup should not take too long (see Figure 10.57). Repeat the process where the land in the foreground appears to have a seam (see Figure 10.58).

When the seams are sufficiently hidden, select the Crop tool and trim away the edges of the image so that it no longer appears to be two photos overlaying one another, but rather one panoramic shot (see Figure 10.59).

Ah, the problem with digital shots. This image, though seamlessly joined, still requires some simple image correction. It is far too dark and too blue to properly show what I see from my front yard. First, duplicate the merge photo layer (the Background layer). Then run through the standard practice of adjusting the levels, one channel at a time. The blue channel Levels adjustment is seen in Figure 10.60.

The photo should now appear brighter and with more contrast, but an additional Curves adjustment can help bring out the details in the midrange even more. Open the Curves dialog box and set an anchor point on the dark side halfway through the first square and an anchor point on the light end at the inner corner of the top-right grid square. This allows you to make adjustments between the two points without adjusting the very light or very dark areas. Add another point and increase the brightness of the midtones slightly, as seen in Figure 10.61.

In the photo that I'm working on, the mountains peeking through the clouds are extremely bright, to the point where the trees are not well defined. Create a Brightness/Contrast Adjustment layer, decrease the Brightness to −30 to −35, and increase the Contrast to the +45 to +50 range (see Figure 10.62).

The Brightness and Contrast do not need to be adjusted for the entire image, just the peaks. With all you have learned about masks, the solution to this should be an easy one: Select

Figure 10.57: Healing the clouds

Figure 10.58: Removing the seams in the field

Figure 10.59: Crop away the edges of the merged photos.

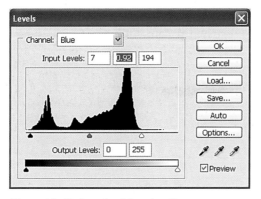

Figure 10.60: Standard Levels adjustments

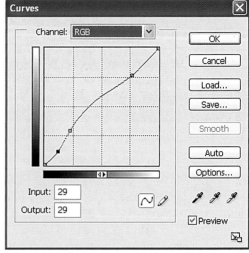

Figure 10.61: Use Curves to lighten the midtones.

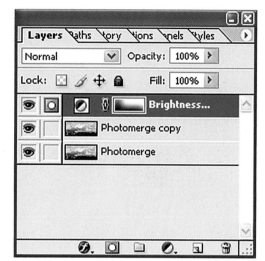

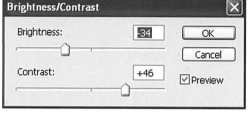

Figure 10.62: Brightness/Contrast Adjustment Layer to bring out definition in the mountains above the clouds

Figure 10.63: Paint in the mask to hide areas that did not require adjusting.

Figure 10.64: Montana truly is the Last Best Place.

the Paintbrush tool, set black as the foreground color, and paint in the Brightness/Contrast's layer mask to hide the areas (the lower portion of the image, areas of the clouds, and so on) to remove the adjustment from all the areas that didn't require altering (see Figure 10.63).

When all is said and done, you should have an excellent view of the Bitterroot Mountain Range, something I'm blessed to wake up to every day. If I can do my job anywhere in the world, scenes like this right outside the front door make me ponder: Why would I want to do this anywhere else (see Figure 10.64)?

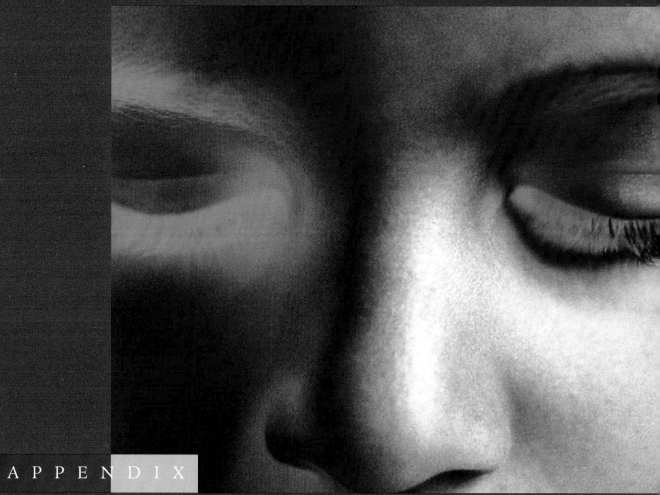

APPENDIX

Appendix: Where Do You Go from Here?

It's been said *that no matter how much you know about Photoshop, you never stop learning more. To help guide your further explorations of the software, here are some of the most valuable online resources.*

The Manufacturer's Site

Adobe Online (http://www.adobe.com)**:** For all the latest in Adobe's software releases and technology, check out the source of it all.

Information and Discussion Sites

Action Fx Photoshop Resources (http://actionfx.com)**:** The author's website. A vast resource for Photoshop training and custom add-ons for the software, including actions, layer styles, brushes, and so on. A large Free area and a huge Members area give access to literally thousands of custom-made Photoshop goodies.

Photoshop Café (http://www.photoshopcafe.com)**:** A website run by award-winning author and trainer Colin Smith. Tutorials, reviews, and more. Also one of the best Photoshop forums online. Stop in and say hello…I'll be lurking somewhere.

PS6.com (http://www.ps6.com, also accessible via www.photoshopcs.com or www.photoshopx.com)**:** Fellow Sybex author Richard Lynch's excellent website. Not only is Richard a qualified expert in Photoshop, but his talents have helped to unlock incredible features for Elements users also.

Digital Mastery (http://www.digitalmastery.com)**:** If I had to recommend one person on this planet above all the other Photoshop gurus out there for in-depth training and understanding of the program, Ben Willmore would instantly come to mind. Ben is one of the most sought-after teachers in the field, and I highly recommend checking out his website and getting on his mailing list. You definitely will not regret it. 'Nuf said. Note that this site does not offer free services.

Photoshop Groups and Organizations

National Association of Photoshop Professionals (NAPP) (http://www.photoshopuser.com): The premier organization for Photoshop users around the globe, founded by Scott Kelby, renowned author and editor-in-chief of *Photoshop User* and *Mac Design* magazines. Although NAPP charges an annual membership fee, it is well worth the price for any serious Photoshop professional. I write for the website, so drop me a line when you visit.

Planet Photoshop (http://www.planetphotoshop.com): Also operated by the team at NAPP, Planet Photoshop is a free resource for Photoshop users everywhere. Tutorials (many by yours truly), discounts, and resources abound; come check it out!

Adobe Photoshop Tutorials Online

Photoshop Workshop (http://psworkshop.net): When people ask me how to do a specific effect or where they may find tutorials on a technique, this is the website I recommend. As of this writing, there are nearly 800 tutorials linked to this site—definitely one for the books.

Team Photoshop (http://www.teamphotoshop.com): Tutorials, forum, actions, resources galore…by people who love what they do and do what they love. Thanks for an excellent website!

Sue Chastain's About.com Photoshop Pages (http://graphicssoft.about.com/cs/photoshop): Sue Chastain has been helping people master Adobe Photoshop for years, and her section at About.com is one of the best "how to" places that I know of online. Tell her I said howdy.

Designs By Mark (http://www.designsbymark.com): You like effects? This guy knows effects! Mark Monciardini has been around longer than I have in this biz, and he remains at the top of his game in the Photoshop world. His website is ultra cool, and be sure to check out his new training videos. Mark is a designer's designer, is innovative in his tutorials, and has the unique ability to teach others and make learning fun as well as informative.

Stock Images

Stock photography websites, while not free, are great resources for designers who are seeking to increase the professional level of their work. Many of these resources offer complete access to low, medium, and high resolution version of their photos, taken by professional photographers.

Some of those websites listed here allow members to download the images online, others offer their photos on CD, and a couple give you both options. If you have a high-speed Internet connection, membership is probably more appealing because you do not have to wait for your photos; those of you with slow Internet connections may want to save on download time and opt for the CDs.

So why pay for a service when there are so many free resources online for photographs? When you pay for a service, chances are you can get the resolution and professionalism that will make your work shine. Free resources, while they have their place, simply don't hold up to the quality that the paid sites offer. Free resources are generally operated by people who, while they have a passion for the photography, are not generating income for their website and must keep the image files small to save on bandwidth. Paid sites are set up so that bandwidth is not usually a concern, and they offer great service for those who choose their products.

Photos.com (http://www.photos.com): Photos.com is one of many excellent resources operated by ArtToday. They have a vast amount of stock photography available for download to their members. Most of the images in this book are from this great resource.

Photo Spin (http://www.photospin.com): This website offers to members over 80,000 images to download at the time of this writing. Another excellent online repository for high-quality photography.

Clipart.com (http://www.clipart.com): Also run by ArtToday, this website offers over 2.6 million downloadable images (clip art, photography, animations, and so on) to subscribers.

Getty Images (http://www.gettyimages.com): A vast resource for professional photographs, including Time-Life Pictures and National Geographic. Categories include creative, editorial, film, custom imaging, and media management.

Comstock (http://www.comstock.com): Specializes in commercial stock photography for advertising, graphic design, corporate marketing, publishing/desktop publishing, and web design. Offers royalty-free images that may be purchased individually or grouped on a CD.

PictureQuest (http://www.picturequest.com): Offers hundreds of thousands of images, free low-resolution comps, and high-resolution downloads. As of this writing, PictureQuest has nearly 500,000 images available.

Digital Vision (http://www.digitalvision.com): World-class royalty-free photography, music, digital art, animated imagery, and type.

Wetzel and Company (http://www.wetzelandcompany.com): Offers background, pattern, and photographic texture images on CD.

Able Stock (http://www.ablestock.com): Over 36,000 royalty-free digital images in three file sizes available to members for download.

iStockPhoto (http://www.istockphoto.com): Offers over 83,000 royalty-free files for members.

Index

A

Able Stock site, 325
About.com Photoshop Pages site, 324
access.jpg file, 137–143, *138–143*
acne removal, **57–59**, *58–60*
Action Fx Photoshop Resources site, 323
Add Layer Mask icon
    for background color, 12
    for eye color, 43
    for tattoos, 95
Add Layer Style icon, 93
Add Noise dialog box, 217, *217*
Add to Selection option
    for anime woman, 217, 239
    for Chex-Girl, 254
    for face swapping, 79
    for smile, 158
    for zebra woman, 262
Add Width and Height Attributes for Images
    option, 294
Adobe Gamma calibrator, 297
Adobe Online site, 323
Adobe Reader, 307–308, *307–308*
advertising, 187
    digital woman, **196–201**, *196–201*
    reverse, **202–206**, *202–206*
    zebra woman, **258–263**, *258–263*
aging, filters for, **216–223**, *216–224*
AI-View1.tif file, 316
AI-View2.tif file, 316
alcohol advertisements, 202
alien boy, **264–272**, *265–274*
Alpha channels, 232
angles in face-swapping, 78
animals, **157**
    comical critters, **157–163**, *158–163*

crossbreeding species, **180–184**, *180–185*
grizzly bear in clouds, **128–132**, *129–132*
snake collage, **175–178**, *175–179*
website for, **164–174**, *164–174*
anime woman, **234–242**, *234–244*
Anti-Aliased option
    for anime woman, 239
    for eye color, 47
Apply Image dialog box
    for crossbreeding species, 184, *184*
    for flesh to stone transition, 286–287, *287*
    for snake collage, 178, *178*
art
    clip art, 92–93, *92*
    common images in, **207–211**, *207–211*
    greeting card, **157–163**, *158–163*
    impressionist, **249–257**, *251–257*
    industrial, **245–247**, *245–247*
    line
        pen-and-ink art, **226–228**, *227–228*
        pencil drawings, **224–226**, *224–226*
    vector, **234–242**, *234–244*
artistic effects, **97**
    adding color to black-and-white images, **97**
        color cast for, **98–100**, *98–100*
        hand-tinted look, **101–104**, *101–105*
    gradients, **113–116**, *114–116*
    lightening, darkening, and coloring,
        117–119, *117–119*
    portrait to painting, **228–232**, *229–232*
    textures
        displacement maps for, **105–109**,
        106–109
        duplicate layers for, **109–112**, *110–113*

B

baby.jpg file, 46–49, *47–49*
background color, **11–12**, *11–13*
Background Copy layer, 22, *23*
Background Eraser tool, 26
background for mood, **148–154**, *148–155*

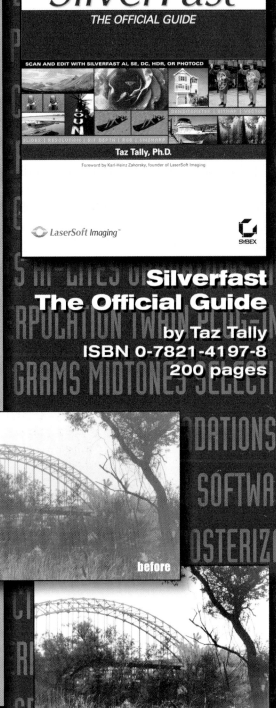

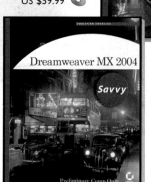

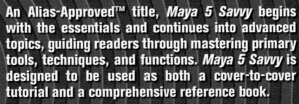

What's On the CD

The CD-ROM that accompanies *Photoshop for Right-Brainers* contains all the files you need to try out the book's lessons and projects for yourself—every source photograph you'll manipulate, along with software tools (curves, gradients, and displacement maps) that Photoshop actions guru Al Ward has created to streamline many of these exercises.

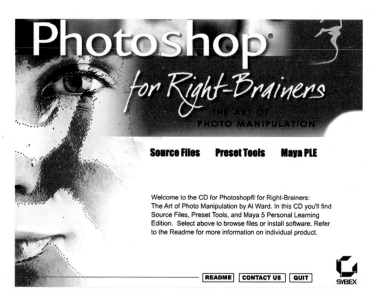

At each point where you need to use a file from the CD in order to work through an exercise, you'll see a symbol in the margin like the one shown here, and the text will refer to the specific filename. That way, you'll work on the same images that Al used while creating the projects, and you can compare your results to the book illustrations. (Of course, you aren't limited to following the book's instructions; in fact, you're encouraged to manipulate the images further, pursuing whatever ideas the projects inspire.)

Please note that the majority of these images are provided courtesy of Photos.com (www.photos.com). They are included here for your personal use with this book only; they are not in the public domain and you may not sell them, incorporate them in any commercial product, or distribute them in any way.

The CD also includes your own copy of Maya Personal Learning Edition, a noncommercial version of the award-winning Maya 5 software that we're providing so you can begin to explore 3D graphics and animation.